MW01009366

The New Creation

The New Creation

Church History Made Accessible, Relevant, and Personal

Robert P. Vande Kappelle

WIPF & STOCK · Eugene, Oregon

THE NEW CREATION
Church History Made Accessible, Relevant, and Personal

Copyright © 2018 Robert P. Vande Kappelle. All rights reserved. Except for brief quotations in critical publications or reviews, no part of this book may be reproduced in any manner without prior written permission from the publisher. Write: Permissions, Wipf and Stock Publishers, 199 W. 8th Ave., Suite 3, Eugene, OR 97401.

Wipf & Stock
An Imprint of Wipf and Stock Publishers
199 W. 8th Ave., Suite 3
Eugene, OR 97401

www.wipfandstock.com

PAPERBACK ISBN: 978-1-5326-6260-7
HARDCOVER ISBN: 978-1-5326-6261-4
EBOOK ISBN: 978-1-5326-6262-1

Manufactured in the U.S.A.   08/16/18

Unless otherwise noted, Bible quotations are from the *New Revised Standard Version of the Bible*, copyright © 1989 by the Division of Christian Education of the National Council of the Churches of Christ in the United States of America. Used by permission.

Contents

Preface

When Christians hear the phrase "the new creation," they tend to think of Isaiah's prophecies or of Revelation's vision of "a new heaven and a new earth" (Isa. 65:17; Rev. 21:1). Others think of unbelievers converted to Christianity or of believers transformed by the Holy Spirit.

The first Christians acknowledged individual transformation, but they would have viewed it corporately rather than in isolation. When God gave individuals a vision or called individuals to service, it was for the larger good. When Jesus spoke of the good shepherd leaving the fold for the sake of one lost sheep, he had the flock in mind. When Paul spoke of believers, he had the church, the "body of Christ," in mind. Though individuals are deeply beloved of God, they are members of a larger entity. Likewise, when Jesus tells his followers that they will do the works he does and even "greater works than these" (John 14:12), he had in mind not the deeds of individual disciples but the corporate endeavors of his followers.

Their origin as a "little flock," ongoing and expanding throughout history, would proliferate to a global religion of staggering size and pervasive presence whose faith, resulting in deeds of kindness and compassion, would literally "move" social and economic mountains (see Mark 11:23). Despite these accomplishments, Jesus reminds his disciples that they are to abide in him, the true vine, for individually and apart from him, they can do nothing (John 15:1–8). Only by following his example, propelled by his vision and empowered by his Spirit, would they fulfill their God-given destiny.

The letter to the Ephesians, written by a devoted admirer of Paul during the last two decades of the first century, is influenced by a dominant concern, namely, the unity of the church under the headship of Christ. The church at this time had become predominantly Gentile and was in danger of losing its sense of continuity with Israel. The author of Ephesians, desiring to underscore the larger history and tradition that defined Christianity, as well as the mystical unity of believers in Christ, portrays that oneness in three predominant images: the church is (1) the body of Christ (1:22–23), (2) the building or temple of God (2:20–22), and (3) the bride of Christ (5:23–32). The church's solidarity, Paul makes clear in Galatians 3:28, has social implications, namely, challenging racial, social, and sexual barriers. Because Christ is one, church members are united. Because Christ is one, church members are equal. Because Christ is one, church members are free to serve one another.

Why Study Church History?

As loss of memory in an individual is a psychiatric defect calling for medical treatment, so too any community that has no social memory is suffering from illness. While historians have the crucial task of helping each generation find its bearings, the recording of history tells the story of the human family.

Christianity is essentially a historical religion. It cannot be understood simply through a set of dogmas, a moral code, or a view of the universe. For through the stories of Israel, Jesus, and the developing church, Christianity acknowledges the revelation of God in action. As an institution, the church has an identity and a mission, and as an organism, it necessarily develops from infancy to maturity, undergoing the growing pains of adolescence, young adulthood, and midlife as well as periodic transformation due to changing cultural needs and challenges.

It is important to remember that when anyone—politician, social activist, or church reformer—calls for a radical new start, a complete break with the past, he or she is shooting at the moon, for no clean break with the past is possible. Every generation, just as every individual, is the result of the subtle yet dominant influences of the past. The philosopher Bertrand Russell claimed that one of the great faults of the twentieth century was that it limited itself to a "parochialism in time," viewing the old as antiquated and irrelevant and only the new as pertinent. Lord Acton made the same point: "history must be our deliverer not only from the undue influence of other times, but from the undue influence of our own."

History, then, has to do with the study of the "otherness" of the past. It involves trying to allow that "otherness" to speak to us. If we are to be liberated from the tyranny of the present, we must try to see life with the eyes of centuries other than our own. In that way we embrace the past in the present. We must allow individuals of the past to pose their own questions rather than imposing upon them our own fascinations, hopes, and neuroses. Only in this way will the study of the past open up to us a larger present.

Another benefit from the study of church history is that study of the past can be useful in shaping proper attitudes toward scripture. While Christians value the Bible, they do not always agree on its message. Studying the history of Christianity provides perspective on the interpretation of scripture, for it acquaints us with vast differences in how the Bible has been used and understood. Because its members and leaders are human, the church is not perfect, as its history makes abundantly clear. For that reason, the study of church history should increase our humility about who we are and what we believe. In addition, historical study helps us distinguish between biblical chaff and wheat, preserving our deepest commitment only to those aspects of Christian faith that deserve such commitment, while enabling us to act with even greater toleration in a cultural climate becoming increasingly diverse.

While many Christians value the study of church history, some disparage it as unnecessary and irrelevant to their spiritual wellbeing. Unlike traditional Roman Catholic or Eastern Orthodox Christians, who value tradition, evangelical Christians typically go directly to scripture for guidance or inspiration, neglecting the value of tradition for faith and practice. They often appeal to Martin Luther and other Protestant Reformers, who argued for the primacy of scripture above all other authorities.

When Protestant thinkers such as Martin Luther coined the phrase *sola scriptura*, establishing the Bible as the source and sole authority of their faith, they were protesting the role of tradition—particularly the medieval accretions that defined Latin Christianity—as equally binding. Their methodology, encapsulated in the phrase *ad fontes* (back to the sources), defined their strategy. They believed the scriptures, practically and clearly interpreted, to be adequate and sufficient for faith and practice. In addition, they argued, the church stood in need of purification from excessive reliance upon secular medieval institutions and practices such as state, culture, philosophy, and reason. Rejecting the synthesis mentality of the thousand-year-old Holy Roman Empire, which valued equally scripture and tradition, the Protestant Reformers attempted to return to an undiluted biblical way of thinking, without realizing that the scriptures upon which they were relying also included a synthesis mentality, as yet undetected. Unfortunately, the Reformers' search for purity resulted in the further fragmentation of Christendom, first into four sectarian bodies (Lutheran, Reformed, Anglican, and Anabaptist), and eventually into hundreds of denominations and thousands of sects.

While Protestants and non-denominational Christians remain influenced by biblical ideals, some reject the suspicion and anxiety produced by schisms of the past. As Christians of all denominations, cultures, and races are discovering, unity is better than discord, and cooperation more beneficial than isolation. Learning from history, modern Christians are setting aside ecclesiastical and sociological differences, affirming the trajectories that provide forward momentum to the faith.

A fragmented world awaits this unified church, its members working together for the healing of the nations. This cannot take place unless believers join hands, informed by their varied traditions and beliefs and empowered by the larger Christian narrative. What transpired during the canonical process—one Bible representing multiple voices and perspectives—needs to occur yet again, one church representing many voices, cultures, and traditions. Such unity in mission and service does not occur automatically, but only through an informed appreciation of a mutual heritage, a common scripture, and a shared story. Twenty-first-century Christians can no longer ignore church history. Aside from keeping Christians provincial and divided, such ignorance prevents them from fulfilling their destiny as the body of Christ.

The Church: Four Definitions

In my days as a seminarian and then as a young professor, I heard people speak of the church as central not only to the New Testament but also to the Old Testament. This idea perplexed me, for it appeared ignorant. After all, the birth of the church is recorded in the book of Acts. Could the church preexist its own birth? Over time, I became less literal in my understanding of biblical concepts, and I now find the idea of the church in the Old Testament attractive and even accurate, particularly if by "church" we mean something mystical and invisible rather than institutional. The Christian church did come into existence on the Christian Pentecost, but the prototype goes back to "Father Abraham," the founding member of God's church.

The New Creation defines the church as "the people of God," a reality traceable to God's covenant with Abraham. It is that concept we address in this study, related but not equivalent to Israel or to the institutional church. Paul speaks of this church as God's "remnant people" (Rom. 9:27–29; 11:5), an entity known to God but not discernible organizationally. Using Pauline language, the New Testament church is a "wild olive shoot" grafted into the olive tree (true Israel), and the "branch" of Gentile Christians is supported by the roots that reach deeply into God's choice of Israel and God's faithful dealings with this people (Rom. 11:17–24). This study assumes that from the beginning God had in mind what we term the church, a people chosen from every race and nation to enact the divine will and plan, and that this church is present in every generation.

In this text, we distinguish between four uses of the term "church," maintaining consistency in the meaning and use of the term when possible. The general practice is to capitalize the term when it refers to a specific ecclesiastical organization, such as the Greek Orthodox Church, the Roman Catholic Church, or the Lutheran Church. However, when speaking of Christianity or the Christian church in general, we do not capitalize the term. If we are speaking of a local church or group of churches in a region such as Jerusalem, Alexandria, Constantinople, or Rome, lower-case usage is appropriate, but when by the Roman Church we mean Roman Catholicism, or the papacy, upper-case usage is appropriate.

This study introduces another subtlety, the possibility of a mystical body of believers, whether in the pre-Christian period or throughout the Christian era, embedded in particular ecclesiastical organizations yet not confined or defined by such membership. This notion of God's people as an invisible church is biblical and yet was generally unknown throughout church history until it became widely acknowledged in the Reformation and post-Reformation periods. For this understanding of "church" we may use the term "*kirk*," based on the Greek adjective *kuriakē*, "belonging to the Lord." This term, found in several northern European languages, is often associated with the Scottish Church.

Though the tension between these perspectives of the church runs throughout Christian history, the New Testament writers did not distinguish between them. After all, the ecclesiastical structure was in its infancy, and the biblical writers assumed that "card-carrying" Christians, while worshipping in a local congregation, also belonged to the larger "body of Christ." Like an iceberg, the church was strategically visible yet largely invisible.

When we speak of the church, then, we envision four overlapping entities:

1. Christianity in general, in which case the term "church" is not capitalized.

2. A visible ecclesiastical organization such as the Catholic, the Anglican, or the Lutheran Church, in which case the term "church" is capitalized.

3. A local congregation of believers, in which case the term "church" is not capitalized.

4. The invisible church (*kirk*) throughout the ages, an entity on earth sometimes called "the church militant" (as contrasted with "the church triumphant," a reference to departed brethren). While the term "militant" suggests antagonism between the church and the world, used ecclesiastically the word refers to the church on earth working to overcome defective dimensions of human existence.

Augustine, the great medieval theologian, had this church in mind when he wrote his epic *The City of God*. According to Augustine, human society is composed of two cities, distinguished by two loves: the heavenly city (the City of God, characterized by the love of God) and the earthly city (the City of Man, characterized by the love of Self). He envisioned these "cities" or "loves," operative throughout human history, as abstract in nature, and cautioned that they should not be identified strictly with the visible church or state. Augustine viewed these cities as universal in scope, meaning that all human beings fall within one of these jurisdictions. Thinking imaginatively, Augustine noted that these societies had their origin after the expulsion of Adam and Eve from the Garden of Eden, in the ensuing offerings (lifestyles) of Cain and Abel, descendants of the earliest humans (the story is recorded in Genesis 4). God refuses Cain's offering, presumably because it results from impure motives, but accepts Abel's sacrifice. The result—the first fratricide—proves disastrous for family and social life. Both "cities," anticipating human history, progress along separate paths toward radically different ends. Unlike Abel, the members of God's city nevertheless remain in the world, their function a leavening or renewing force. While modern people might dismiss Augustine's portrayal of history as simplistic, his perspective nevertheless raises questions about the church's nature, its role in society, and whether the church has lived up to its nature and destiny as God's new creation. These are our concerns as well.

The Church and the Kingdom of God

A central feature in the Bible, equally important to Judaism and Christianity, is the kingdom of God. While the expression "kingdom of God" is not found in the Old Testament, the idea is everywhere present, related to God's election of the people of Israel. Over time it came to be associated with the rule of the house of David and, after its demise, with messianic hope. In the New Testament, the concept is one of the most distinctive aspects of the preaching of Jesus.

At the center of Matthew's Sermon on the Mount (found in chapters 5–7) we find the Lord's Prayer (6:9–13). These words, recited by Christians around the world, are arguably the most beloved of all the teachings of Jesus. But what is the prayer about? The clue appears in the first petition: "thy kingdom come." This prayer is about the kingdom of God, a petition for its realization in human history. When the prayer speaks of "heaven," this refers not primarily to a place in space but to the limitlessness of God. God's kingdom is therefore the experience of God's presence on earth. Thus the kingdom is realized whenever the reality of God becomes visible in a person or in a historical event. The prayer's next petition expresses the human yearning to be sustained in moments when the kingdom seems absent. That is what it means to pray, "Give us this day our daily bread." The petition, "Lead us not into temptation," more accurately translated "do not bring us to the test," requests readiness to greet moments of God's presence and not to miss them in our blindness.

Shortly after the passage on the Lord's Prayer we find these words: "But strive first for the kingdom of God and his righteousness" (Matt. 6:33). Here the disciples learn that the kingdom is to be their first and main concern. It was certainly so for Jesus, who gave up everything for the sake of the kingdom. The kingdom of God, we discover, is about "righteousness," a biblical term that has to do with right relationships, between human beings and between humans and God. For the ancient Jews, "righteousness" was a synonym for God's kingdom. To hunger for righteousness (Matt.

5:6) is to hunger for the coming of the kingdom. That connection between righteousness and the coming of the kingdom of God is one with which Matthew's Jewish readers would have been familiar. The prophet Isaiah referred to Israel as "God's vineyard," where righteousness—that is, God's kingdom—is to be established (Isa. 5:7)

Following the sermon, Matthew presents a second teaching section in chapter 10. The context is clear: Jesus calls his disciples in order to instruct them on the work of the kingdom of God and their place in it. In this section, Jesus wishes to convey to his disciples the authority that will be required to carry out the work of that kingdom. As ambassadors of the kingdom, their message is quite simple: "The kingdom of heaven is at hand" (see 10:7).[1] In the mind of Matthew, the kingdom of God is present and becomes visible when God's righteousness (God's will) is lived out in human history, when God's life is experienced as present in human life. Significantly, Matthew waits until this point to name the twelve disciples (10:2–4). The old Israel had twelve tribes; the new Israel has twelve apostles. In the Bible, Israel—and by extension the church, God's new Israel—is another name for the kingdom of God.

The New Creation: An Overview

While scholars date the birth of the church to the celebration of Pentecost on or about the year 30 of the Common Era, this book takes a more nuanced approach. The church—God's people—has not one but rather two biblical foundations:

- The Great Command (Gen. 12:1–3), when God said GO!, and

- The Great Commission (Matt. 28:18–20), when God said GROW!

The story of the church begins with Abraham in the second millennium BCE, long before Jesus or the birth of Christianity, and it proceeds through three epochs:

1. Formation (c. 1850–4 BCE)

2. Transformation (4 BCE–1500 CE), and

---

1. Despite Matthew's preference for the expression "kingdom of heaven," it is clear that the concept, as Jesus used it, refers to the destiny of God's people on a new, improved earth. It has nothing to do with the souls of dead people ascending to heaven.

3. Reformation (1500–present).

To understand the biblical concept of community one must begin with Abraham. God started with one family, declaring a promise so wondrous as to engender laughter, creating something in Sarah's womb when she was unable to conceive: "Is anything too wonderful for the Lord?" (Gen. 18:14). From Isaac came Jacoh, and from him the twelve tribes of Israel. They took his name, his personality, his style of life, and the covenant he had with God. They would call themselves "*bene* Israel," sons of Israel. The doctrine of election was not arbitrary. Rather it reminded them that they were beloved, God's new creation. They were not one nation *out of* many, but one nation *for* many. In such unity there is resolve, resilience, and strength.

The first Christians lived in a Greek world, dominated by alien values and beliefs. As Jews, they drew on Hebraic customs and beliefs, themselves shaped by alien cultural influences: Sumerian, Amorite, Egyptian, Hittite, Phoenician, Aramean, Assyrian, Babylonian, and Greek. Over time, these and other ancient neighbors in the eastern Mediterranean world had supplied beliefs and practices that resulted in views of God grouped variously under the rubric called ethical monotheism. Like their forebears, the first Christians tried to reconcile diverse visions of deity, and the results, far from uniform, elicited unstable answers to unending questions.

Affirming the action of God throughout the entirety of human history, this study envisions primeval, pagan, and patriarchal origins as preparatory to the Israelite period (first millennium BCE), and the latter as preparatory to the apostolic period (first century CE). An apt metaphor is the hourglass, the sands of time flowing from the upper globe through a narrow opening to the lower globe, or, as biblically conceived, from creation, through Christ, to consummation.

This book examines the church as God's mechanism to inspire and enable select individuals (such as patriarchs, prophets, apostles, priests, martyrs, monks, and laypeople), groups (such as the Israelite nation and later the Christian church), and reforming movements throughout history, to be the salt and light of the world. Their purpose is to live consistently, powerfully, lovingly, and faithfully, thereby challenging families, neighbors, clans, nations, and people around the globe to actualize their God-given potential. It is our contention that this movement did not appear as an afterthought, but that it was initiated and shaped by God from the beginning of recorded history.

The New Creation provides a clear and concise survey of the Christian church, God's instrument for the providential care of the earth and its human family. It divides church history into nine units, each discussed as a phase in the church's organic growth and development. In addition to the narrative, each chapter includes three features for that epoch of church history: (1) significant event, (2) turning point (decisive moment), and (3) study questions.

Acknowledgments

Have you ever read a book on a subject and thought how much you now know about that topic, only to read a second and possibly a third book on that topic and realize how little you know? If so, you have something in common with Einstein, who acknowledged, "The more I learn, the more I realize how much I don't know."

Upon graduating from college, I spent a "gap year" before attending graduate school. During that year, while performing administrative duties at my college, I audited a course on church history taught by Kenneth Scott Latourette, then the preeminent authority in that field. After reading his monumental 1516-page *A History of Christianity*, I became a "know-it-all." Over the years, after doing some additional reading and teaching classes on "Christian Theology" and on "Global Christianity," I conclude that Einstein was right.

A biblical scholar by training, I recognize my inadequacy in writing a survey of church history. I write not out of expertise but in reliance upon a few trusted sources. In addition to consulting such renowned scholars as Latourette, Williston Walker, Diarmaid MacCulloch, John McManners, Adrian Hastings, Dale Irvin, Scott Sunquist, Mark Noll, and Justo Gonzalez, I found one text indispensable for its focus, insight, and clarity, Bruce Shelley's *Church History in Plain Language*. Of the works consulted, this is the one I would like to have written. Also helpful was Mark Noll's *Turning Points*, particularly since the concept of "turning points" in church history is a feature I incorporate into this project.

ACKNOWLEDGMENTS

Because I write for a general audience—for readers who seek a reliable overview from a theologically moderate to progressive stance—I intentionally keep scholarly citations to a minimum, using footnotes primarily for clarification. In writing this book, I am grateful for four things: (1) an office provided by Washington & Jefferson College, where I have emeritus status and can secure resources, conduct research, and write undisturbed; (2) a laboratory such as Chautauqua Institution, a community where I spend my summers listening, learning, and interacting with peers; (3) an audience in the form of workshops arranged by Georgia Metsger and her colleagues; and (4) a home, shared with my wife Susan, who understands my need to read and write, and who creates an environment where these can flourish.

Part 1

Formation

(c. 1850–4 BCE)

Chapter 1

Phase 1: Beginnings (1850–1200 BCE)

Myths, Sagas, and Epics

Significant Event: Jacob's encounter with God, which resulted in his election as Israel, father of the twelve tribes.

Turning Point: Abraham's migration to Canaan and his subsequent call to covenant faithfulness.

The prologue to the Fourth Gospel begins memorably with a declaration of cosmic and historical import: "In the beginning was the Word (*Logos*), and the Word was with God, and the Word was God. He was in the beginning with God. All things came into being through him, and without him not one thing came into being. What has come into being in him was life, and the life was the light of all people. The light shines in the darkness, and the darkness did not overcome it" (John 1:1–5).

Scholars disagree over the meaning and interpretation of this passage, particularly its use of the term *logos*, for the term is practically untranslatable. "Word" is one way to translate the original Greek term *logos*, though it is certainly not the only possible translation. Other meanings, in addition to personified Wisdom, include concepts such as "conversation," "discourse," "telling a story," and even "a rationale for a way of living."

The first three words of John's prologue are the same words that open the book of Genesis. John makes this connection intentionally, for it suits his purpose and creates a bridge for his audience. Notice the parallels: in

Genesis God creates by speaking; in the Gospel God creates through the Word. In Genesis God's first creative act results in the emergence of light from the darkness; in the Gospel the Word is associated with light that shines in the darkness. In both cases the light is distinguished from darkness. In this regard, John's prologue clearly functions as a commentary on the creation account in Genesis 1. John, like Genesis, takes readers back to the beginning of time, to the relation between time and eternity. By making this connection with Genesis, John begins church history where Genesis begins: In the beginning.

From the beginning, the writer of John makes clear that the words of Jesus are meaningless apart from their relation to their essential underlying meaning in the Word, much as the apostles are insignificant apart from their relation to Jesus, and that Jesus profits little unless he be the incarnate Word of God. However, this Word is not an abstraction; it must be understood in relationship to this world, for it is incarnated in flesh—infinity to time, eternity to history. The world is where the Word of God is recognized, believed, and known. Because this Word is beyond time and space, it is timeless and spaceless and hence belongs to every epoch in time and to every race on earth. It is this *logos*, like the Priestly writer's (the author of Genesis1) "wind from God" sweeping over the primordial waters of history (Gen. 1:2), that drives not only church history but world history as well.

As we address the origins of the church in the pre-Israelite period, the following concepts, epochs, and events helped shape the Israelite identity:

1. God, time, and history

2. The formation of an Israelite epic

3. The primeval period (Genesis 1–11)

4. The patriarchal period (Genesis 12–50)

5. The election (the "call") of Abraham

6. The covenant with Abraham

7. The testing of faith

God, Time, and History

Ancient people viewed time as circular, or cyclical. Their reality was nature, to which everything was related. Even their gods, related to nature as personifications of natural forces or human ideals, were enmeshed in this cyclical series of events. Like a dog chasing its tail, history was going nowhere. Belief that human life was destined only to repeat itself and never to achieve any unique meaning or purpose led to a sense of futility. The early Greeks, like many of their predecessors and contemporaries, had a pessimistic view of history. Because they viewed nature as governed by the seasons, caught in repetitive patterns, they also viewed nature and time as eternal. For that reason, they had little concerns with origins or destiny. Greek philosophers such as Parmenides and Plato saw reality in the timeless and abstract ideals of beauty, goodness, and truth. Aristotle regarded the passing of time as destructive. Truth lay in unchanging universal ideas, not in unique and particular events in history.

The ancient Hebrews were the first to produce a comprehensive and accurate historical narrative. The modern conception of history, which views history as linear and historical events as unique, has its roots in the biblical writers, who viewed history as the arena of God's activity. Because God controls all events, history has a religious significance, and because God is guiding history toward a consummation, history has unity and meaning. It is in history, rather than in natural phenomena, that clues to God's nature are found. The Bible presents events such as Israel's exodus from Egypt, the Assyrian destruction of Israel, and the Babylonian captivity of the Jews as unique events that reveal something of the divine plan. They are not mere cyclical recurrences.

While concerned with history, the Hebrew scriptures provide more than a national history of Israel. They show God as the Lord of all peoples, involved in their victories and triumphs but also in their pain and suffering. It is in time and history that God enacts the global plan of salvation through dramatic confrontations.

If Christianity is a historical religion, it follows that all history is God's history. The succession of the years is not merely a tangle of events without general meaning. History witnesses to a divine purpose and is moving toward a divine goal, what Charles Kingsley called "the strategy of God." Because of the Hebraic concept of time, Christians have a reference point by which to judge the particulars of history.

In tracing God's continued activity in history, however, we must take care to avoid naïve arguments about power and its relation to goodness and truth, as if the great national and imperialistic victories by Christian armies somehow "prove" the righteousness of their cause or the truth of Christianity.

The Formation of an Israelite Epic

Those who read the Bible canonically, beginning with Genesis (Creation) and ending with Revelation (Consummation), do so to gain literary and theological perspective. They are not, however, reading the Bible chronologically, for the sources and books that comprise the Bible were not written in that order.

Biblical scholars customarily date Israel's first national epic as the product of a literary awakening that occurred during the reigns of David and Solomon, a period known as the United Kingdom. In this view, an unknown author in Judea known as "the Yahwist" (or Jahwist) composed a masterful prose epic using preliterary units of tradition to create Israel's first written source. This source, called J, was written about 950–900. He (or she) was interested in personal biography and in ethical and theological reflection. E, the second source, was composed between 850–750 BCE in the Northern Kingdom of Israel by an unknown author identified as the Elohist. This source is more objective than J, being less interested in theological reflection. About 715 BCE an unknown editor combined J and E into what is known as the Old Epic or JE.

While the period from Abraham to Moses to David was one of oral tradition, this does not mean that beginning with David (1000 BC) oral tradition was superseded by literary records, or that before David there were no written records. What it means is that the Yahwist was the first to record the all-Israelite epic, a core story that up to that time had survived orally through stories, poems, songs, and other "memory units." Some units of oral tradition were non-Israelite in origin and were later taken over by the Israelites. For example, the stories of Abraham's sacrifice of Isaac (Gen. 22) and Jacob's dream at Bethel (Gen. 28) could have been Canaanite cult legends whose original cultural meaning is now lost to us. These independent units of tradition were not simply borrowed but rather were appropriated by Israel and given new meaning.

The compositional approach used by the Yahwist is fascinating. Rather than starting chronologically with creation, adding accounts of the patriarchs, the exodus, the conquest, the tribal confederacy, and finally, the monarchy, the J writer worked backward, "viewing earlier stories through the prism of the crucial historical experiences that created the community of Israel."[1] Starting with the Mosaic tradition (the material that extends

---

1. Anderson, *Understanding the Old Testament*, 145.

from the oppression in Egypt to the entrance into Canaan), the Yahwist linked it with the Patriarchal tradition (the pre-Mosaic material found in Genesis 12–50), and finally with the Primeval tradition (the early material in Genesis that extends from the Creation, through the Flood, to the new beginning after the Flood).

The all-Israelite epic, read chronologically through its three movements or "acts," begins universally (with fundamental human experiences), continues with Israel's ancestors, and culminates in the Mosaic tradition. The Yahwist, it appears, was the first author to link the Mosaic tradition to a universal and cosmic context. It is to that broader context we turn.

The Primeval Period (Genesis 1–11)

The Primeval History belonged to Israel's basic narrative even in the period of oral tradition. The motifs of Creation, Paradise, the Flood, and the deliverance of humanity (Noah and his family) from total destruction are common in ancient Near Eastern legends and myths. An ancient Sumerian list of rulers makes a sharp distinction between the period "before the flood" and the period "after the flood" (see Gen. 10:1). Furthermore, Israelite narrators probably appropriated the ancient view of a "Golden Age" at the beginning of history, while inserting the notion of violence (sin) emerging on the earth.

The story of Adam and Eve in the Garden of Eden (Gen. 2:4b—3:24) is filled with images found in ancient folklore, such as the Tree of Life and the cunning serpent. This story once circulated as an etiology, the storyteller's explanation to social and sexual conventions such as the attraction of males and females to one another, the fear of snakes, the wearing of clothes, the pain of childbirth, the misery of hard work, the experience of guilt, the fear of divine retribution, and the presence of evil. While neither the later writings of the Old Testament nor Jewish tradition placed great emphasis on the expulsion account in Genesis 2–3, that story has been read by Christians for centuries as the paradigmatic story of a fall from grace, a Paradise Lost that accounts for the origin of sin, human estrangement from God, and death for all humanity. As indicated in Genesis 3:14–19, the primeval revolt against God is an act of violence that disrupts all relationships—with God, human beings, and the earth. In Genesis 3:15 the early church found a messianic prophecy, namely, the final victory of woman's seed (the Messiah) over evil.

Banishment from the Garden of Eden begins a period of history highlighted by two genealogical traditions, one godly (through Seth, Noah, Shem, Terah, Abraham, and his descendants), and the other ungodly (through Cain, Lamech, and his descendants). The godly line, characterized by the love of God (see Gen. 4:26b), leads to promise, hope, and salvation, while the ungodly line, characterized by violence and corruption, leads to futility, punishment, and desolation (see Gen. 6:11–13).

The story of Cain and Abel (Gen. 4:1–16), which reflects the animosity between farmer and shepherd and leads to murder, contains a hopeful note. Marked by divine protection, Cain marries and then builds the first city. Cain's role as city planner raises questions about prospects for urban culture, though the story is not blind to progress in technology and the arts. Cultural advance, however, is accompanied by violence, lust, and unbridled passion, a deteriorating chain reaction.

The archaic story of the Flood, which on its own defies understanding, functions as a second start for humanity. God, described as "grieved to his heart" (Gen. 6:6) about human failure, nevertheless resolves to make a new beginning. The story concludes with the statement that despite the inclination of the human heart to evil, God will never again curse the earth with such a calamity (Gen. 8:21). The new beginning is based not on human potential, but on divine grace. Henceforth the regularities of nature will continue uninterrupted as signs of God's covenant faithfulness (Gen. 8:22).

The narrative tells us that after the Flood, the earth was settled by descendants of Noah's three sons, Shem, Ham, and Japheth, regarded as the ancestors of ancient nations and social groupings. The Primeval History ends with the account of the Tower of Babel, a story that circulated independently as an explanation of the origin of diverse peoples and languages before being appropriated into the all-Israelite epic.

Several ancient texts have similarities to the Genesis account, such as the *Enuma Elish*—an ancient creation account work that describes how the god Marduk became the king of the gods and the chief god of Babylon—and the *Gilgamesh Epic*, which contains a striking parallel to the biblical flood story. These stories, dated to the First Dynasty of Babylon (1830–1330 BCE), show formal similarities to the biblical accounts, and were clearly known to the authors of Genesis. Furthermore, the prototype of the biblical "Tower of Babel" (Gen. 11:1–9) is the ziggurat (tiered temple-tower) of the city of Babylon, one of the famed wonders of ancient Babylon.

While historical investigation or archaeology cannot corroborate the literary episodes of the Primeval History, the biblical accounts are "historical" in the sense that they portray the conflicting realities of human existence and in the sense that they interpret human history as the drama of God's dealings with humanity as a whole. The ancient Israelite narrators and their original audience undoubtedly saw dramatic continuity in the progression from Genesis 11 to Genesis 12. The Primeval History, like the Patriarchal History, provides the dramatic prologue to the central theme of the all-Israelite epic, the particular identity and special vocation of Israel in God's world-embracing purpose.

The Patriarchal Period (Genesis 12–50)

The Pentateuch, sometimes called the Torah or the "Five Books of Moses," is the first section of the Hebrew Bible, the segment regarded as most authoritative by Jewish tradition. While some of the material may go back to Moses, the Pentateuch is the result of a long and dynamic process, from the time the Israelite story was shaped orally to the time it was given literary form in various circles during the monarchy. These literary strands were eventually unified by priestly writers and redacted into a consistent whole by the Jewish scribe Ezra around 400 BCE, a process of some eight hundred years.

The Pentateuch begins with an extended prologue to the exodus story, consisting of two units: the account of primeval beginnings (Gen. 1–11) and the stories of the Israelite ancestors (Gen. 12–50). Like the Primeval History, the Patriarchal History is in the form of a saga. There is an important difference, however. The sagas of the patriarchal period are clearly related to what was going on in the Fertile Crescent[2] at the time. This period may be dated to the first third of the second millennium (2000–1700 BCE), for the culture and customs reflected in the biblical story appear to match that epoch in ancient Near Eastern history.

Abraham, Isaac, Jacob, and Joseph stand at the center of the patriarchal narratives in Genesis. Despite the traditional term "patriarch," the

2. This term encompasses an area of fertile land shaped like an ark or crescent, reaching from the Persian Gulf up through Mesopotamia, the alluvial plain of the Tigris and Euphrates rivers, curving through Syria and Palestine, and continuing toward the Nile River in Egypt. This cradle of civilization, also known as the eastern Mediterranean or the Near East, has been a scene of human activity for centuries before the appearance of the Hebrews, who became the ancestors of Israel.

spouses of the patriarchs, particularly Sarah, Rebekah, and Rachel, also play significant roles in the Genesis narratives. For that reason the inclusive term "ancestors" seems more accurate than "patriarchs." While we can be reasonably confident that these ancestors were historical individuals, their family relationship is probably a construction of those who gathered the traditions for the purpose of fostering national unity. To be remembered so long, each must have been an outstanding leader among the nomadic ancestors of Israel, and it seems likely that each was a religious leader. In addition to seminomadic existence, another primary characteristic of the patriarchs was the theophanies they experienced at sanctuaries such as Shechem (Gen. 12:6), Bethel (Gen. 28:19, 35), and Penuel (Gen. 32:23–33). While scholars ponder the historical value of the patriarchal traditions, it is faith, not history, on which rests the belief that at each stage God had communicated with the patriarchs and maintained a unique ongoing relationship with them and their ancestors.

The family history of Israel's ancestors concentrates mainly on Abraham, Jacob, and Joseph. Isaac is relegated to a minor role, serving chiefly as a link between Abraham and Jacob, while Joseph is the main figure in the story of Jacob's twelve sons, said to be the ancestors of the twelve tribes.

The general them of the patriarchal narratives, featured in the Abraham story, is the promise of descendants and land. Abraham's migration from Mesopotamia initiated a new kind of history: the history of God's promises to Israel and to other peoples as well. From the Primeval History to the Patriarchal History the scope narrows until it concentrates upon the solitary figure of Abraham, the ancestor of the people of faith, chosen for a special task in God's historical purpose. Coming after the stories of the Expulsion from the Garden, of Cain, the Flood, and the Tower of Babel, which present a dark picture of human rebellion and ambition, the story of the call of Abraham is like a burst of light that illumines the whole landscape. These are stories in contrast: While the builders at Babel fail in their ambition to make a name for themselves, God promises to make Abraham's name great (Gen. 12:2; compare 11:4). Israel's greatness, we are told, and by implication the church's destiny, will lie not in its ambitions or achievements, but in its witness to the God who acts in history to overcome the confusion, disharmony, and violence of the Primeval History.

The theme of promise, central not only to the patriarchs and Israel, but also to the first Christians and the developing church, involves three subheadings: (1) election, (2) the covenant with Abraham, and (3) the testing of faith (the delay of the promise).

The Election (the "Call") of Abraham

Election, the idea of being "called" or chosen by God, is an essential biblical motif, indispensable to Israel's identity and later to Christian self-understanding. As we discover throughout the Bible, God takes the initiative in establishing a covenant relationship, with individuals such as Abraham, with nations such as Israel, and with all people of faith. Abraham does not first choose God; Israel does not first choose God; Christians do not first choose God, but rather all are chosen by God.

The notion of election raises profound theological questions, about whether God is racist, favoring some people over others. The Bible answers these questions with a resounding "No." The covenant God establishes with Israel should not be regarded as an expression of divine preference for Jews over others, or as divine commission for one group to rule others, or as reward for good conduct on Israel's part. As the history of Israel demonstrates, the establishment of the covenant is not followed by good conduct. Moreover, the Bible portrays the covenant people as sinful, stiff-necked, stubborn, and singularly inept at learning from their experiences. In fact, in the Bible the Israelites are punished repeatedly, and more severely than others are. Nevertheless, God does not nullify the contract or make it void.

Scholars emphasize that the underlying significance of the patriarchal stories in Genesis is not so much the stories of the patriarchs but the story of Israel's self-understanding. At the time this material was put into writing, the main question was not, "Who are Abraham, Isaac, Jacob, and Joseph?" but "Who is Israel?" Israel was grappling with her identity, her self-understanding as a people called by God. The theological answer was found in the doctrine of election.

What does election mean? The biblical answer is given in the portrayal of Abraham, Isaac, and Jacob, patriarchs whose lives were characterized by the following traits:

1. They *lived by faith in God*. In Abraham, Israel understands something about herself, that she has been called into existence by God himself, that she has been created by God's initiative and preserved by God's

grace. The story of Abraham becomes the prototypical model for the journey of faith.

2. They were *called to be a servant people*. Election does not mean that one people is chosen because they are better than others, but rather that they are called to spread God's grace. God's purpose is seen in Genesis 12:3 ("in you all the families of the earth shall be blessed"); it is a universal purpose, one that moves from particulars to universals, from individuals to communities and nations. In Abraham, God brings one person of faith into existence in order that God's blessing might be extended to all humanity. This is the Bible's stress on election, that when God calls a people, they are called to service, and the rest of the Old Testament, and then the Gospels and Epistles, show what it means to be a servant people. The Bible makes it clear that Israel's calling is part of God's healing intention (the biblical word for healing, health, wholeness, and goodness is "salvation," similar in meaning to the Hebrew word *shalom*). In the Bible, the election of a people becomes the basis for good news, what the New Testament calls "gospel."

3. They were *called to pilgrimage*, namely, to a life of mobility, movement, and change. Biblical faith is a calling faith, a calling to go forth, to be on the way, to be moving in God's direction, to be pioneers of faith. Abraham was told to break his ties with his land and his former security, a way of life that up to that point had been deeply rooted to the land. Like Abraham, God's people are called to a nomadic consciousness. As we see in Abraham, faith is not so much consent or agreement as something dynamic, manifested in movement. So Abraham is the ancestor of a pilgrim people, and his story highlights the themes of mobility and change, meaning that when faith becomes lifeless, stagnant, or frozen, whether in institutions with superiority complexes or in self-serving lifestyles, God breaks them down and forces his people into radical recommitment. The story of Abraham and the patriarchs is the story of God on the move with his people.

The Covenant with Abraham

The divine address in Genesis 12:1–3 provides the theological foundation for interpreting the ancestral tradition. Here God singles out one individual and opens an expansive horizon before him. The passage consists of three elements:

- *The command* (12:1): with the word "Go," God initiates the relationship. This corresponds to the beginning of Israel's national history in Exodus 1.

- *The promise* (12:1–2): under the promise of land and posterity God guides the patriarchs and Israel into the future. The promise is repeated to each patriarch, reinforcing the element of hope.

- *The blessing* (12:2–3): the promise of blessing unfolds in three stages, from those close at hand to all the races of the world.

To possess a land, to become a great nation, to be a blessing to the peoples of the earth—this threefold divine promise punctuates the patriarchal narrative.

The Testing of Faith (Delay of the Promise)

In Israel's ancestral period, a blessing or curse was believed to have immediate effect. The patriarchal narratives, however, institutes a major change. The blessing is postponed to the future, beyond the lifetime of the original recipients. Hence the blessing becomes a promise. Postponement of the promise means that the whole ancestral period becomes an interim between promise and fulfillment, with the resulting tensions and anxieties of faith. This is a lesson not only for the patriarchs or for Israel, but for all people of faith. When the interim seems unbearably extended, people raise cries of lament, as in Psalm 13:1 ("How long, O Lord? Will you forget me forever?") and Psalm 22:1 ("My God, why have you forsaken me?").

An initial answer appears in Genesis 15:6: "And [Abraham] believed the Lord, and the Lord reckoned it to him as righteousness." The root of the Hebrew word "believe" is "amen," meaning that Abraham trusted in God's faithfulness. While the word "faith" is sometimes taken to mean "belief in certain doctrines as true," that is not the connotation here. Unlike belief, which can be abstract, trust is relational. Whereas other nations lived in fear and uncertainty, Israel was to rely upon God's faithfulness. The concept of promise, coming from a trustworthy God, is hopeful, as we are reminded by an unknown poet encouraging exiled Jews in Babylon: "those who wait for the Lord shall renew their strength, they shall mount up with wings like eagles, they shall run and not be weary, they shall walk and not faint" (Isa. 40:31).

As we know from the biblical narrative, Abraham did not always respond to his circumstances with trust and hope. As all biblical personalities, indeed as people of faith in general, Abraham is a flawed individual with a steep learning curve. He encounters the tension in God's promise almost immediately, beginning in Egypt, where he attempts to deceive the pharaoh in order to keep the promise alive (see Gen. 12:10–20). Deceit is followed by distrust in chapter 16, where he tries to force God's hand by cohabiting with Sarah's servant Hagar. Once again God intervenes, for Ishmael, the child born of Hagar, is not to be the child of promise. When Abraham is ninety-nine years old, God repeats the promise that Sarah will conceive, and Abraham responds with laughter (17:17); the promise has become absurd. Later, after Isaac's birth, Abraham's faith is taken to the limit.

The moving account of Abraham's testing in Genesis 22 brings to a climax the history of God's promise to the patriarchs. Here we are told that Abraham is commanded by God to sacrifice his only son, whom he dearly loved. Isaac was the child of the promise, and God now asks Abraham to sacrifice the only means by which the promise can be fulfilled. Abraham undergoes the supreme trial as he prepares to slay Isaac, thereby sacrificing the future of Israel on the altar. Only when the knife is upraised does God intervene. In that critical moment Abraham spies a ram caught in a thicket, which he offers in place of Isaac. Once again the promise is renewed (see Gen. 22:16–18).

On almost every level, this story is disturbing. It raises questions that border on the absurd. How could Abraham agree to such a command? How did he know the command was from God? And if he could be sure, how could God make such immoral demands of Abraham? Is God's word to be obeyed even when obedience is contradicted by reason? Is faith the triumph of obedience over conscience? If so, what is the role of conscience in religion?

Verse 8, which seems to be structurally central to the narrative, merits special attention. There, in a statement of utter trust and confidence, we are told that God will provide. The statement, of course, is open-ended, for we are not told all that we want to know. Abraham cannot tell Isaac all he wants to know because Abraham himself does not know. He does not know if Isaac is God's act of provision or whether God will provide a rescue for Isaac. Abraham does not know, but he trusts God unreservedly. The narrative leads to a new disclosure of God. At the beginning, God is the tester (Gen. 22:1); at the end, God is the provider (Gen. 22:14). The fundamental issue at stake here, as in all scripture, is the faithfulness of God.

Søren Kierkegaard, the noted Danish Christian existentialist, made an important contribution to the religious journey in his formulation of three levels of existence or stages through which humans go in their ascent toward God. On the first level, which he labeled the *aesthetic stage*, individuals are ruled by their senses, in which case they can be called "sensual aesthetes." Such persons live solely for the present, and particularly for self-gratification. Aesthetes, characterized by the absence of either moral standards or religious faith, remain detached and uncommitted. Kierkegaard extends this attitude to include the "intellectual aesthete," the contemplative person who tries to stand outside of life and behold it as a spectator.

The second level, the *ethical stage*, requires that one abandon attitudes of selfishness and embrace universal standards, making commitments to others. Here moral standards and obligations are adopted as dictated by reason. The third and final stage, which Kierkegaard called the *religious stage*, entails a life of faith. This is final because it recognizes the existence of God and the need to relate oneself wholly to God.

In each stage, Kierkegaard selected a figure from literature or history as an example. For the model of the religious stage of life, the highest level through which humans go in their ascent toward God, he selected Abraham, whose trust of God and unwavering obedience led him to choose to sacrifice his only son Isaac, even in the face of absurdity, for to question God would be to place reason over faith. In selecting this example, Kierkegaard was not denying the validity of ethics. He stated that the individual who is called to break with the ethical must first be ethical, that is, must first have subordinated to universal morality. The break, when one is called to make it, is made in "fear and trembling" and not arrogantly or proudly. In this final stage, the ethical is not abolished but dethroned by a higher purpose or end, a phenomenon he described as the "teleological suspension of the ethical." The key to this final stage is not the commendable humanistic goal of universal duty to others, but the unqualified giving of oneself to God. For Kierkegaard, if one doesn't go beyond the ethical realm, beyond moral obligation, one cannot properly say that one is related to God, or obedient to God. Ethical duty, Kierkegaard believed, must ultimately lead to God, but since it usually leads to humanity (i.e. to humanism), then this stage must be transcended. An absolute relationship to an absolute (God) requires a relative relationship to relative ends. And for Kierkegaard, everything other than God is relative.

Like Sarah, Rebekah was barren, and would not have presented Isaac with a son if God had not intervened. The result is a new complication that almost abolishes the promise. Rebekah conceives two sons: Esau, the father of the Edomites, and Jacob, the ancestor of Israel. Even in the womb they struggled together, as these nations did in real life. Esau was born first, and therefore had a right to be his father's heir (Gen. 25:21–26). But Jacob shrewdly tricks his twin brother out of his birthright, and with the help of his mother, receives Isaac's final blessing. Though Jacob's behavior qualifies him as a "trickster," the biblical emphasis highlights the theme of election, in Jacob's case, even of unworthy persons, though he is later vindicated by his persistence in wrestling with a divine assailant, presumably God (Gen. 32:22–32). At this point he is renamed "Israel," a name meaning "one who wrestles with God." Earlier, in the Bethel story (Gen. 28:10–19), God appears to the despairing Jacob in a dream and renews the threefold promise given to Abraham: to give Israel the land; to make Israel a great and numerous people; and through Israel, to bestow blessings upon all the families of the earth (Gen. 28:13–15).

The patriarchal narratives trace the history of Israel as a nation to Jacob (renamed Israel), and his twelve sons. Jacob had two wives, who were sisters. One of these sisters, named Leah, was the mother of Judah, whose descendants grew to become the dominant tribe in the Southern Kingdom, and the other, named Rachel, was the mother of Joseph, whose descendants grew to become the dominant tribe in the Southern Kingdom. After the reigns of David and Solomon, the northern tribes, dominated by the descendants of Joseph (Ephraim and Manasseh), successfully established their independence from the southern tribe of Judah. Out of Judah came the royal family that produced David and Solomon, and the house of David reigned over the nation of Judah for about four hundred years, with Jerusalem as its capital.

The Joseph story (Gen. 37–50), a biblical masterpiece, is marked by the motif of providence. Betrayed by his brothers and sold to Midianite traders, Joseph is taken to Egypt, where he overcomes great odds to rise in power in the Egyptian court. Eventually, during a time of famine, Joseph reunites with his father and brothers, who migrate to Egypt. Joseph's magnanimous words to his brothers at the end of the story highlight God's providential role and care: "Even though you intended to do harm to me,

God intended it for good, in order to preserve a numerous people, as he is doing today" (Gen. 50:20). Human affairs are not governed by evil designs or by economic distress, but by the overruling providence of God, who works for good in all things.

According to the book of Exodus, after Joseph's death the family of Jacob lost favor in Egypt, owing to a change of administration: "Now a new king arose over Egypt, who did not know Joseph" (Exod. 1:8). As a result, the Hebrews were reduced to the status of slaves—430 years of enslavement, according to Exodus 12:40. Hence, the patriarchal narratives end in paradox, for the descendants of Abraham are not in their homeland but in Egypt, their future precarious. Nevertheless, the ancestral stories provide a dramatic prologue to a central theme of the Bible: the particular identity and special vocation of God's elect people (Israel; the church) in God's history-long and world-embracing purpose. The promise made to the ancestors—that through Israel the nations would bless themselves—was moving toward fulfillment.

Study Questions

1. In your estimation, who is the primary protagonist in the epoch of "Beginnings"? Support your answer.

2. Do you agree with the author's choice that the election of Abraham is this epoch's turning point? Why or why not? Is there another event you consider more significant? If so, what is it? Support your choice.

3. In this epoch, does "the church" live up to its nature and destiny as God's new creation? Why or why not?

4. In your estimation, which statement makes a more compelling announcement of biblical origins: "In the beginning was the Word," or "In the beginning God created the heavens and the earth"? Support your answer.

5. What do scholars mean when they speak of the all-Israelite epic? Explain the process that led to the formation of Israel's first national epic.

6. What are the principal motifs of the Primeval History? How are these topics similar and dissimilar from motifs in ancient Near Eastern mythology and folklore?

7. What significance did Abraham's story have for ancient Israel? What significance does it have for modern Christians?

8. Explain the significance of the concept of election (a) for Jewish self-understanding and (b) for Christian self-understanding.

9. Evaluate Kierkegaard's "religious stage" of existence. What merit do you find with his three-stage model for the religious journey?

10. If you were to write a history of the church, would you begin with the story of the birth of the church recorded in the book of Acts, with Jesus, with Israelite history, or where the author begins, with the ancestral period? Explain your answer.

Chapter 2

Phase 2: Israel (1200–4 BCE)

Prophets, Priests, and Kings

Significant Event: While numerous events shaped Israel's self-understanding as the people of God—consider the role of the exodus, the conquest of Canaan, the institution of the monarchy, the temple, and the process that culminated in the Hebrew Bible—the most significant is the role of Moses in establishing the legal covenant with Israel at Sinai. Believing they had received the law of God, known as the Torah, at Sinai the Israelites received their moral, legal, and religious identity.

Turning Point: Two events vie equally as turning points during the Israelite period: the selection of David as ruler over a unified nation and the Babylonian exile. David's rule, idealized as Israel's Golden Age and interpreted through the lens of royal theology, led to hopes for the Messiah and the kingdom of God, aspects central to Jesus and the early church. The Babylonian exile, more than any other event, provided Israel a global lens to rethink its understanding of God's purpose and identity as well as its own vocation. This change in perspective formed Judaism into a world religion and led to the emergence of Christianity.

In a remarkable passage, recorded near the end of the letter to the Galatians, Paul addresses local church members—and by inference the church universal—as "the Israel of God" (Gal. 6:16). Such allusion might strike modern believers as odd, since they do not consider themselves Jewish, but for believers in the first century, this designation was natural. The membership of the first church was predominantly Jewish, and even those Gentiles who joined in increasing numbers came to consider themselves descendants of Abraham and heirs of his promise (see Gal. 3:7, 9 14, 29). Thus, in our study of church history, we turn to the history of Israel. Our task, covering that history in one chapter, is daunting. For that reason, we will be selective regarding subject matter (identifying seven historical and sociological themes) and deliberate in perspective (focusing on Israel as the people of promise). The following concepts, movements, and events helped shape the Jewish conception of faith, governance, and vocation:

1. The exodus story

2. The covenant at Sinai

3. The prophetic task

4. The Deuteronomistic History

5. The Babylonian exile

6. The postexilic restoration

7. The birth of the apocalyptic mindset

The Exodus Story

The earliest civilizations, whether Asian, Indian, or Middle Eastern, were religious, and their religions preceded and gave rise to their cultures. This principle particularly exemplified the Egyptians and the ancient Semitic empires of the Middle East. From the first, these cultures conceived of the problem of life on earth as dependent on the larger reality of the cosmos and the transcendent. We know of no time when humans in this region were conscious of themselves but not yet of the divine. As early as the fourteenth century BCE there was an Egyptian monarch (Akhenaton; also known as Amenhotep IV) who conceived of a god who was the creator of the world and of all humankind.

About a century later, an Israelite named Moses led a captive people out of slavery toward a new land of settlement. This event, known as the exodus, was marked by a wilderness encounter with deity that resulted in a new self-understanding and identity for the people. Moses and his Israelite followers defined their religion in terms of that experience. Their God was the one "who brought them out of the land of Egypt, out of the house of bondage" (see Exod. 20:2). It was the first statement of belief in the Judeo-Christian tradition; like all those that followed, it was an affirmation that something significant had happened in the past.

When we seek to understand the meaning of our individual life stories, we do not actually begin with birth or infancy, even though written autobiographies might start there. Rather, we view early childhood in the light of later experiences that are formative or pivotal. Likewise, Israel's life story does not begin with the time of Abraham or even the Creation, although the Old Testament starts there. Rather, Israel's history had its true beginning in a crucial historical experience that created a self-conscious historical community—an event so decisive that earlier happenings and subsequent experiences were seen in its light. That decisive event—the great watershed of Israel's history—was the exodus from Egypt. Through the ages, the story of the deliverance of slaves from bondage, and their march through the wilderness toward a promised land, has had a powerful appeal to the religious imagination of many oppressed groups and individuals. It is the paradigmatic biblical story of salvation and deliverance.

Exodus 1–24, a passage that speaks of the exodus and the birth of the nation of Israel, is less concerned with what happened historically and more concerned with the meaning behind these events. This is not to say that the narrative does not describe actual events, but to emphasize that it describes them theologically. While providing interesting stories about Moses and the Israelites, the exodus account focuses not so much on Moses as liberator of the people but on God's redemptive role. God, not Moses, is the primary actor. The broader story— beginning with the classic account of deliverance from Egyptian slavery and including the covenant enacted on Mount Sinai and the subsequent wilderness experience that led to the conquest of the Promised Land—is not recorded for its own sake. Rather it provides a clue to who God is and how God acts toward humanity, particularly toward those who are downtrodden and oppressed.

Despite his upbringing in Pharaoh's court, Moses identifies with the Hebrew slaves, an impulse that led to his slaying an Egyptian taskmaster. Forced to flee, Moses took refuge in "the land of Midian," an area of the Sinai Peninsula occupied by shepherds. There he marries the daughter of a Midianite priest. While tending the flocks of his father-in-law, Moses came upon "the mountain of God." Moses's encounter with the God of the ancestors (Exod. 3:13) in that sacred place and his role in the ensuing encounter with the pharaoh is one of the masterpieces of religious literature. It was in the Midianite wilderness that God discloses essential aspects of the divine nature, including (1) God's personal name (Yahweh), which, literally untranslatable, has come to be associated with *God's creative activity* ("I am", "I cause to be") and (2) *God's redemptive activity* ("I will be with you"; see Exod. 3:12) on behalf of Israel.

Yahweh appears to Moses with memorable words: "I have observed the misery of my people . . . I have heard their cry . . . I know their sufferings, and I have come down to deliver them . . . and to bring them to a good and broad land, a land flowing with milk and honey . . ." (Exod. 3:7–8). In a fundamental declaration of faith, the ancient Israelites affirmed that their history originated in a marvelous liberation from oppression, declaring climactically the mighty deeds of God on their behalf. The verbs of the narrative sweep to a climax: God heard, God saw, God rescued.

The primary purpose of the exodus narrative is to glorify the God of Israel, the "divine warrior" whose strong hand and outstretched arm wins the victory over Pharaoh and his armies. The text heralds five interlocking biblical themes: (1) *divine love* (when things on earth get bad, God's love is greater still); (2) *divine mercy* (God is always "for us," never "against us"); (3) *divine initiative* (God always takes the initiative in restoring that which is broken, forgotten, or lost); (4) *divine sovereignty* (God is completely in control, even to the point of hardening Pharaoh's heart); and (5) *divine freedom* (while disclosing the divine name, God nevertheless retains the divine freedom that eludes human control: "I will be gracious to whom I will be gracious, and will show mercy on whom I will show mercy. But you cannot see my face; for no one shall see me and live"; Exod. 33:19–20).

As we learn from the third commandment, God's name is not to be taken in vain (Exod. 20:7), meaning that God cannot be manipulated or influenced magically. This commandment, read contextually, is less a prohibition against using God's name as a curse and more against attempting to use worship or religious ritual to manipulate or control God in a possessive sense. The God who speaks to Moses is the Lord, not the servant of the people. From this time forward, the question "what is God like?" would be answered in concrete historical events. That is precisely the point of the conquest with Pharaoh, the plagues against Egypt, the crossing of the sea, the guidance through the wilderness, and the conquest of the Promised Land. Because God is sovereign, God controls history, the powers of nature, and on occasion, even the human heart. In describing the pharaoh, the text states repeatedly that God hardened Pharaoh's heart, but also that

Pharaoh hardens his own heart. The narrator tells the story in a way that allows for human obstinacy while ultimately glorifying the God of Israel. Pharaoh is given freedom, but not so much that he can exceed the bounds of God's sovereign control (see Rom. 9:17–18).

The exodus account is firmly embedded into the story of Israel's theological history. It is part of the narrative that runs from Genesis 12 to 2 Kings 25. The first nineteen chapters of Exodus tell the story of the Israelites' bondage in Egypt and their deliverance by Yahweh. It describes the call of Moses and his powerful encounters with Pharaoh. It presents the story of the plagues on Egypt, culminating in the visit by the angel of death and the institution of the festival of the Passover. Next, Moses leads the Israelites out of Egypt and through the sea. The book of Exodus then describes their journey in the wilderness until, in chapter 19, the Israelites arrive at Mount Sinai, where God calls them into covenant relationship. The Ten Commandments in Exodus 20 and the laws that follow are part of this story.

The book of Leviticus records additional priestly legislation, presented as part of a dialogue between God and Moses. The book of Numbers picks up the narrative in the second year after the exodus (Numb. 1:1) and describes the Israelites' journeys and wanderings for the next forty years (Numb. 33:38). Central to this story is the forty years of wandering that result from Israel's fear of entering the Promised Land, based on a negative account by ten of twelve spies sent to report on the land (by comparison to the Canaanites "we seemed like grasshoppers"; Numb. 13:32–33). The book of Deuteronomy records a series of speeches attributed to Moses just prior to Israel's entry into Canaan. In the overall story, a new generation has replaced the fearful generation punished by God for their refusal to enter the land. Deuteronomy (the word means "second law" or retelling of the law) represents a restatement of the covenant God made with the previous generation on Mount Sinai forty years earlier. The events of Deuteronomy flow into the book of Joshua, where the story continues without interruption.

The Covenant at Sinai

Exodus 1–24 deals with two series of events: the deliverance from Egypt and the making of the covenant at Sinai. These two accounts are intertwined, the first a preparation for the second (see Exod. 3:12), and the second based theologically on the first. A small literary unit at the beginning of Exodus

19 stresses the essential connection between these traditions. This passage (Exod. 19:4–7), occurring right after the notice of Israel's arrival at Sinai, portrays God as carrying the people, like an eagle lifting its young, toward the mountain rendezvous: "I bore you on eagles' wings and brought you to myself. Now therefore, if you obey my voice and keep my covenant, you shall be my treasured possession out of all the peoples. Indeed, the whole earth is mine, but you shall be for me a priestly kingdom and a holy nation."

An earlier story, narrated in Exodus 18:13–33, describes a conversation between Moses and his father-in-law, Jethro, called "a priest of Midian." Jethro, observing Moses in his role as arbitrator of disputes among the people, recommends to Moses that he divide the people into groups of ten, hundreds, and thousands, designating leaders to judge the disputes that arose at each level. Installing judges in this manner would alleviate the onerous task of adjudicating all disputes, more than any one leader could or should do. Jethro's recommendation resulted in an appellate court of sorts, with Moses as the court of final appeal. For this plan to work, however, Moses and the people needed an objective standard on which all decisions would be based. That is what is described in Exodus 19 and in the entire Sinai experience.

As Moses led the people to the foot of the mountain, God called Moses to come up the mountain. The priests were told to await consecration, and Aaron, the high priest, was told to accompany Moses on his journey. The high priest first, and then the lower ranks of the priesthood had to be validated. When the preparation was complete, God spoke. The law thus came from God through Moses to Aaron and the priests. In that manner the law was revealed and recorded. Those who judged the people did so according to that single standard of the revealed Torah. It began with the great moral principles we call the Ten Commandments, but it stretched out into the intimate details that governed the lives of the people until it covered almost every conceivable human experience: Sabbath day restrictions, kosher dietary laws, circumcision requirements, purity rites, and so forth. The Torah, thought to spell out God's will for God's people, served Israel as both constitution and bylaws. It formed the heart of Judaism, the foundation of the Jews' covenant with God.

At Sinai the people of Israel experienced what Moses had sensed earlier at that same sacred mountain—that God wished to relate to humanity through a covenant community, a people with a special vocation: the ordering of life according to God's sovereign demands. Here we find a unique characteristic of Israel's faith: the strange combination of the universal and the particular. God's sovereignty knows no limits ("the whole earth is mine"; Exod. 19:5), yet out of many peoples God singles out one people, not for privilege but for a task. They are to be a "priestly kingdom" (Exod. 19:6), that is, a community separated from the world and consecrated to the service of God (see 1 Pet. 2:5, 9–10).

History in the Old Testament is the history of a covenant relationship. This relationship is initiated and established by God, the sovereign Lord (Suzerain); as vassals, humans respond to it and bind themselves in obedience. The covenant involves not only obligations toward God but also obligations toward the other members of the community. The legal stipulations are binding, yet not static. They can be adaptable to new cultural circumstances, but the basic principle remains constant: persons are absolutely responsible to one another (Second Table of the Law, commandments 5–10) because they are absolutely responsible to God (First Table of the Law, commandments 1–4).

As early as the Genesis creation account (see 1:28—2:3), humans are given cultural mandates to guide communal life. Though the word "covenant" does not appear in the creation narrative, theologians speak of God's relation with Adam and Eve prior to their departure from the Garden as the covenant of creation. Like God's call (election) of Abraham, basic to the covenant of creation is the creation mandate God gives to Adam and Eve, whereby they are to be God's servants on earth. Unlike the *Enuma Elish*, where humans are depicted as servile by nature, creating society to protect themselves from capricious gods, in Genesis 1 humans are depicted as divine image-bearers, vice-regents with God, and God institutes creation ordinances for their wellbeing. These ordinances include family (procreation and marriage; 1:28), labor (work is not a curse but a blessing; 1:28), and worship (the Hebrew verb for "rest" [*shabath*], is the basis of the word "Sabbath," the day of rest. As God rests from the labor of creation, so the Sabbath completes the workweek, thereby establishing a pattern of work followed by rest. As this passage suggests, duty and pleasure are complementary, not antithetical; 2:1–3).

The concept of realizing and acting upon one's ordained position as God's co-worker (vice-regent) is called stewardship. The covenant of creation binds all humans to God and to one another. It entails that, as image-bearers, humans are to reflect God's concern for all of life. That includes using wealth and property for the benefit of the entire community. The Bible provides many examples of how this occurs, stressing the welfare of the poor (the fatherless, widow, and sojourner; the book of James in the New Testament powerfully summarizes this concept in 1:27: "Religion that is pure and undefiled before God, the Father, is this: to care for orphans and widows in their distress . . ."). In Deuteronomy 24:19–22 God instructs the Israelites to harvest their fields only once a season; what remains is reserved for the needy. Leviticus 23:22 commands farmers not to harvest their land to the borders, but to leave the produce at the edges for the poor. The Bible also contains strict regulations regarding lending practices (Exod. 22:25–27), provides for an impartial judicial process (Deut. 16:18–20), and for paying the poor and needy worker on the day they earn their hire (Deut. 24:14–15). Partiality and bribery are denounced, and the Hebrews are warned to protect strangers and foreigners in their midst, for God protected them while they were strangers in Egypt (Exod. 22:21–24). As Deuteronomy 16:20 makes clear, the concept of stewardship embodies the principle of justice, and, indirectly, of righteousness and steadfast love: "Justice, and only justice, you shall pursue, so that you may live and occupy the land that the Lord your God is giving you."

Ethical responsibility is motivated by gratitude for what God has done. Nevertheless, the Mosaic covenant contains a conditional element: "*If* you will obey my voice and keep my covenant . . ." (Exod. 19:5). Faithfulness to the covenant yields blessing, betrayal brings judgment. This element of the covenant would become central to the great prophets of Israel, for despite God's faithfulness, Israel would be unfaithful. While there are consequences for betrayal, the biblical story places the accent on divine grace. The following biblical pattern unfolds: God establishes the covenant; humans break the covenant; God restores the covenant. Hence, the covenant is re-enacted and re-established.

The Prophetic Task

The most fully developed law covenant in the Old Testament is the Mosaic covenant described in Exodus 19–23. This covenant provided the laws and ordinances by which Hebraic society was to function. It governed the relationship between God and the Hebrews and determined the code of conduct with the Israelite society. Although covenant law at times was altered, the basic principles upon which it rested did not. In the Old Testament, covenant statutes are based upon justice, righteousness, and steadfast love.[1]

1. The segment on justice, righteousness, and steadfast love is adapted from Hoffecker

In the Old Testament, the term justice (*mishpat*) denotes the rights and duties of each party to fulfill their obligations under the covenantal law. These laws, however, refer not only to the vertical relationship with God, but also to the horizontal relationship between humans, that is, to society as a whole. Whereas the Hebrew word for justice refers to the rights and duties of covenant participants, the Hebrew word for righteousness (*zedek*) pertains to the conduct or attitude of the covenant people. It is often used of God and humans maintaining appropriate conduct in all matters of life, social and religious. Ultimately, righteousness is an attribute of God, namely, God's perfection in all areas of covenantal conduct. Because humans are not perfect or consistent in their conduct, the Old Testament understands human righteousness not as a human attribute but as a human response. Noah "found favor in the sight of the Lord" (Gen. 6:8) and Job was "blameless and upright" (Job 2:3) not because they were perfect but because their lives largely reflected the righteousness of God.

If justice and righteousness were the only covenant principles, the relationship between God and humanity would remain strictly legal. The divine-human relationship, however, transcends impersonal legal and moral codes of conduct, for it is based on the concept of *hesed*, a Hebrew word usually translated as "loving-kindness" but better understood as steadfast love or loyalty, a covenant love that presupposes the mutuality of relationship: "For I desire steadfast love and not sacrifice, the knowledge of God rather than burnt offerings" (Hos. 6:6). The covenant love of Yahweh is a faithful love, a steadfast unshakeable maintenance of the covenantal relationship. Both parties must have a deep love and loyalty for the other. As with the other principles discussed, human beings are to build a *hesed* relationship not only with God but with each other as well.

These principles, and their accompanying laws and application, provide the basis for Israelite society. The Hebrews, both individually and communally, were to abide by these principles and regulations in order to maintain a proper relationship with God and with one another. The Israelites' failure to live by these basic principles, however, led to injustice at all levels of society, a state of heart and mind that resulted in prophetic condemnation.

The task and vocation of biblical prophets are often greatly misunderstood. Popularly viewed, the role of the prophet is to predict future events. Modern scholarship, however, downplays this understanding of the role

---

and Smith, *Building a Christian World View*, 2:158–60.

of prophets. Biblical scholars now understand the prophetic role as having involved three distinct yet related tasks, each with a different temporal focus: (a) prophets were predictors of the future (*foretelling*); (b) they were reformers who kept alive the Mosaic past through continuous appeal to the theocratic ideals expressed in the covenants (*retelling*); and (c) they were social critics who spoke out boldly and without compromise against current disobedience and disbelief within the social, religious, and political establishment (*forthtelling*). Of the three tasks, the most significant was forthtelling and the least significant was foretelling. Biblical prophets rarely, if ever, made open predictions about the future, and when they did so, the predictions were linked to their role as social critics, which focused on the consequences for unrepentance. The prophet's futuristic role was associated primarily with the certainty of the coming of the Lord, a coming to make things right through judgment and reward.

The prophets predict that in the end there will only be a remnant who will be faithful, hence only a portion of the people will experience covenant blessing. The prophets are often considered to have been messengers of doom, because they proclaimed a message of judgment. The truth is that before there can be good news, there must be truthtelling. Like God's *opus alienum* ("strange deed") in Isaiah 28:21, where God judges by fire his own people as a means to judge their enemies, the redemptive work of God is alien, more like the work of a surgeon—who uses a scalpel to cut living tissue, even stuffing gauze into the wound to keep the incision open until the blood flows red and the poison is gone—than like a parent, who uses "tough love" to discipline a child. The analogy applies to John 3:16, which can be revised to read: For God so loved the world that he bled—until his blood flowed red—that whosoever accepts this love may live in God's presence eternally.

The story of the Old Testament is the record of Israel's failure to live by covenant principles. Because God's people broke their covenant with God, they were eventually conquered by an invading nation, Babylon, and were taken into exile. But all hope is not lost. In the latter years of Israel's history the prophet Jeremiah promised that God would do something new in the future, once again restoring the people to proper relationship with God and one another.

The Deuteronomistic History

The Pentateuch ends with Moses dead and Israel camped on the east bank of the Jordan, poised to conquer the land of Canaan. A central theme of the biblical tradition is the promise that Israel would soon possess that land. The narrative of the books of Joshua, Judges, Samuel, and Kings (these books make up the "Former Prophets" in the Hebrew Bible) pick up that theme. Together they are part of a larger work called the Deuteronomistic History because of their close connection with the book of Deuteronomy, which functions as a sort of theological and thematic preface to that historical narrative. This historical tradition was finalized in the kingdom of Judah during the time of king Josiah, probably by the prophet Jeremiah and his scribe Baruch.

Covering Israel's history for over six centuries, the Deuteronomistic History is the earliest extended historical narrative known from ancient times. Three themes are prominent in that account: (1) the exclusive worship of Yahweh as a prerequisite for Israel's continued possession of the Promised Land (idolatry will result in divine punishment); (2) the centrality of the city of Jerusalem as the only legitimate place of worship; and (3) the unconditional covenant with David, whereby Yahweh establishes the dynasty founded by David.

The Period of the Judges and the Tribal Confederacy

The books of Joshua and Judges continue the Deuteronomistic presentation of Israel's history in the Promised Land of Canaan, but they do so from differing perspectives. The book of Joshua presents an ideal picture of Israel united in worship of Yahweh alone, united also under the leadership of a divinely designated successor to Moses in fighting against their enemies. The book of Judges provides a more realistic assessment of life in Canaan, relating how the Israelites repeatedly failed to live up to the ideals of monotheism and the confederacy, while providing a less militaristic and more incremental approach to territorial acquisition.

The period of the judges follows a neat pattern that illustrates a basic theological conviction: Incomplete obedience yields incomplete victory. This cycle or pattern, repeated seven times throughout the book of Judges, consists of four elements that follow one another consecutively, as outlined in Judges 2:11—3:16: (1) Disobedience (idolatry); (2) Punishment (oppression by enemies); (3) Repentance (remorse); and (4) Deliverance (God raises a judge and the land enjoys rest).

The pattern usually begins with a formulaic introduction: "Then the Israelites did what was evil in the sight of the Lord" and ends with "So the land had rest _____ years." In each instance the Israelites tended to move away from Yahweh during times of relative prosperity. While the pattern does not do justice to the complexity of events in the period of the judges, it is instructive, for history teaches that the downfall of a people often begins not with external military pressure, but with internal moral and spiritual decay. The Deuteronomistic historians emphasized the central truth that Israel's vitality and solidarity lay in united loyalty to their God. When covenant faith was strong, Israel was in a better position to cope with the inrush of foreign ideas and armies. In like manner, when covenant faith was weakened under pressure from the surrounding culture, Israel became easy prey to economic, political, and military crises.

In addition to the consequences of worshiping other gods, another topic of the Deuteronomistic historians in the book of Judges is kingship, which they disparage. In the earlier part of the book kingship is experimented with and divinely rejected (see the story of Abimelech in Judges 9), and four times in the book, including its final verse, we are told: "In those days there was no king in Israel; every man did what was right in his own eyes." Rather than human kingship, the book of Judges advocates divine kingship: "The Lord will rule over you" (Judg. 8:23). One would be correct to call this a theocracy, but that term, meaning "rule by God," is elastic, so flexible as to be relatively meaningless unless accompanied by some account of what practical shape the divine rule takes. The term theocracy can refer to a society controlled by a caste of priests, to divine rule, or to a vague notion of "one nation, under God." The particular shape that the rule of Yahweh took under the judges was none of the above but was in part determined by the pact between God and the Israelite tribes.

One of Israel's preeminent features was its organization into twelve tribes. This pattern, read back into the ancestral period, became fundamental to Israel's understanding as a worshiping community. Other groups in the area, such as the Ishmaelites (Gen. 25:12–16) and the Edomites (Gen. 36:10–14) apparently followed similar tribal organization. Such a league of tribes may have had a practical reason for adherence to the number twelve. For instance, this number made it possible for each tribe to bear the cost of maintaining a central shrine for one month of the year. Roughly similar institutions existed among the ancient Greeks, where separate city-states joined themselves by pact to support the shrine at Delphi. Such a league was called an amphictyony, from the verb meaning "to live in the neighborhood" of a shrine, and this term is now widely used to describe Israel in the days of the judges. It appears that a confederation of this sort was instituted at Shechem, which for a while seems to have been the center of the Israelite confederacy. Later the central sanctuary was located at Shiloh, some ten miles to the south of Shechem, where the ark was kept and where the tribes assembled for religious festivals. Throughout the biblical period the tabernacle (the shrine of the covenant) was the center of Israel's religious life, for it contained the Ark of the Covenant, a box-like object that contained various cultic articles, including a copy of the Ten Commandments inscribed on tablets of stone. It is the presence of this ark that answers our previous questions about how God's will was made known to the people.

The Bible indicates that the ark was considered the point at which the heavenly and earthly spheres intersected. Apparently, the ark played a key part in making known the will of God. In Numbers 7:89 we learn that Moses went into the tabernacle (tent of meeting) to speak with God, and he would hear the voice of God speaking to him from the top of the ark. It was here at the ark that God occasionally issued orders. Though the exact means of this disclosure is never mentioned, this seemed unproblematic for the writers of our texts. This association of revelation with the ark continues from the period of wilderness wanderings until the end of the period of the judges. Scholars indicate that the tradition of a portable shrine, with the ark as its most holy object, goes back to earliest times and even has a prototype in the mythology of the Canaanites.

To say God communicated with Israel at the ark is not to say that Israel was controlled by the priests who officiated at the tabernacle. During this period, the prophetic office had not yet been instituted, the priests were primarily officiants, and no shrine had a monopoly on divine oracles. However, while God could not be controlled, the divine sovereign was believed to be present, and present for communication, at the place where the covenant tablets were preserved.

While Israel was unified by the worship of Yahweh at central sanctuaries and shrines, the unifying factor was not the league or confederacy between the tribes but their common association with the covenant. How close was this federation? How much unification of action did it bring about, and how were inter-tribal affairs regulated? While the evidence is scanty, we know that the tribes had chiefs, and it is likely that from time to time, perhaps at religious festivals, these chiefs and other tribal leaders met to discuss matters that involved more than one tribe. But this organization was hardly elaborate. When Joshua addresses the assembly at Shechem, we see that he speaks "for me and my household" (Josh. 24:15) and addresses those present as individuals and heads of families. The league with God involves the smallest social units. In the days of the judges, then, freedom of action and responsibility before God was in the hands of families, clans, and tribes.

What then of the status of the individual Israelite under the covenant? The above information leads us to believe that there was a fundamental equality of status so far as Yahweh is concerned, or to put it more accurately, an equality of responsibility. This egalitarianism is also reflected in the economic status of the people: The typical Israelite lived in a village and worked his own few acres. Land was held as a direct fief from Yahweh and was inalienable, meaning that it was an act of impiety against God and one's ancestors to sell or trade one's inheritance. Israel's social system was radically different from the Canaanite and Syrian city-states in the Late Bronze Age, ruled by kings and maintained by a wretched class of serfs. In early Israel there is a deliberate rejection of the rigid social order that oppressed the poor to maintain an elite.

Democratization of religious responsibility meant that covenant traditions were kept alive in the individual family. This is a feature so characteristic of modern Jewish and Christian life that it takes an effort to recall that in the ancient Near East much of religion was a matter for the state: the gods were the gods of the city and priestly specialists preserved the liturgy and mythology of the temple. From earliest times, of course, there were shrines in Israel with specialist priests and even a central shrine that had special functions in preserving and transmitting the covenant. But together with this, the head of the individual family was charged with teaching his son the sacred statutes and ordinances (Deut. 6:6; 6: 20–24).

This decentralization had its advantages, but without modification it would have left Israel at a disadvantage in two important activities: in war and in the exercise of justice. Ultimately, the tribal league failed over these two problems, but in the two centuries or so of its existence it developed a characteristic way of dealing with war and wrongdoing through the figure of the judge. The title derived from the type of leadership that characterized the Israelite theocracy between the death of Joshua and the establishment of the monarchy. The title "judge," though we retain it because it is tradition, is misleading. The term might be rendered better as "savior" or "deliverer." The judges were charismatic individuals who arose during time of crisis. While they were primarily military figures, who led pan-tribal armies against common enemies, some also had judicial functions, adjudicating conflicts and resolving problems in the absence of a king. There was no process by which one ran for judge, nor did one succeed a parent, though there were experiments along that line. Instead, it was a matter of a person's character. Overall, the way the judges functioned reflects Israel's basic religious and social convictions: The person who is followed is the one in whom Yahweh's spirit has manifested itself.

The Establishment of the Monarchy

Few parts of the Bible are as dramatic as the accounts of the establishment of the monarchy in the books of Samuel and the beginning of 1 Kings. These chapters narrate how Israel transformed itself from a loose confederation of tribes into a nation with a dynastic monarchy and a permanent temple in Jerusalem. The narrative is advanced by accounts of a series of personal conflicts between Samuel and Saul, the first king of Israel; between Saul and David, who succeeded him as king; and between David and his sons. Together with the books of Kings, the books of Samuel record the history of the kingdoms of Israel and Judah from the beginning of the monarchy until the fall of Jerusalem in 587 BCE. In their current form they are part of the larger work of the Deuteronomistic historians. As such, they include traditions shaped and edited with a distinct theological perspective, viewing the vicissitudes of the people not from the interplay of social or political activities but from the action of the divine covenant partner, who either rewards or punishes Israel in accordance with its observance of the law given to Moses.

Unlike Saul, 1 Samuel portrays David as an heroic figure, viewed as the legitimate successor to the divinely rejected Saul. David comes to prominence as a court musician (1 Sam. 16:17–23) and then by slaying the Philistine giant Goliath (1 Sam. 17). Anointed king by Samuel, David took Saul's daughter Michal as his first wife in order to establish a claim upon Saul's throne. He began his reign in the southern city of Hebron, ruling there for seven years. Desiring a greater centralization of power, he captured the old fortress of Jerusalem, a neutral site bypassed by Israelite forces during the earlier occupation of Canaan, and made it into his capital. The city, naturally fortified and ideally located on the boundary of the Southern and Northern tribes, came to be known as "the city of David" (1 Sam. 5:9).

In order to capture the allegiance of all Israel, David brought to Jerusalem the Ark of the Covenant, shifting the religious center of Israel from the confederate sanctuary of Shiloh to the royal shrine in Jerusalem. Establishing his throne on the religious sanctions and Mosaic traditions of the tribal confederacy, David laid the groundwork for the theocratic fusing of religion and politics. With the ark stationed in the tent of meeting, David joined together the two major cultic objects inherited from Mosaic times. Thus the city of David became Zion, the city of God.

His defeat of the Philistines, followed by successful wars against Moab, Ammon, Edom, Amalek, and Aram (Syria), led to a treaty with the Phoenician king, Hiram of Tyre. David came to be recognized as the ruler of an empire that stretched from Phoenicia (southern Lebanon) to the borders of Egypt, and from the Mediterranean Sea to the desert of Arabia. Never before or after did Israel exceed this zenith of political power.

Having established his capital, David designated Abiathar and Zadok as chief priests and guardians of the ark, appointing some of their sons as priests to work with the Levites in administering Israel's religious rituals. David also called upon the guidance of the seer Gad, who advised him to purchase the threshing floor of Araunah on which to build an altar to God. This property, adjacent to his palace, would become the site of Solomon's temple. To help govern, David also selected Nathan the prophet, adding the prestige of the prophets to his cabinet.

David's innovations marked the beginning of "royal theology," the view that God had made a special covenant with David, promising to establish David's throne securely though all generations (2 Sam. 7:1–17). This passage, placed immediately after the establishment of the capital in Jerusalem and the ark's transfer there, sets forth for the first time the Deuteronomistic ideology of kingship. It opens with David's desire to build a temple (a "house") for Yahweh. The prophet Nathan expresses his approval, but Yahweh has other plans, which are transmitted to David through the prophet: Yahweh does not want a temple, but rather wishes to establish a covenant with David and Israel, guaranteeing the security of Israel and the dynasty ("house") of David unconditionally and in perpetuity. According to the prophetic word, a temple will be built by David's successor (Solomon), who will be regarded as God's son, punished if he "commits iniquity" but never to lose God's "steadfast love" (*hesed*), phrases that reflect a covenant relationship.

It should not be imagined that the extremely high view of the monarchy presupposed in the covenant with David was held always, everywhere, and by everyone. During his reign David occasionally fell short of the ideals, enacting harsh economic practices that forced his subjects into work camps. Such practices, coupled with personal indiscretions like his affair with Bathsheba, caused his popularity to wane and led to a revolution by his son Absalom. In time, however, his weaknesses were forgotten and his greatness extolled.

Solomon's reign was a different matter. He is remembered for his wisdom, which enabled Israel to attain its greatest outward splendor, resulting in strong foreign relations, commercial growth, and an elaborate building program, including the erection of the lavish temple in Jerusalem. However, the last days of Solomon also began a period of inward decline, characterized by complacency, religious apostasy, and indulgence in polygamy (Solomon erected shrines for his seven hundred wives and three hundred concubines, many of whom were non-Israelites, and he is said to have participated in idolatrous practices). Despite his accomplishments, Solomon's reign is presented by the Deuteronomistic historians as a moral disaster, a primary example of failure to live up to Israel's theocratic ideals.

On his death, Solomon's empire split into two kingdoms, southern Judah and northern Israel. While Judah kept the capital of Jerusalem with its temple, the kings of Israel retreated to the northern city of Samaria. With their control of the strategic pass of Megiddo, they were more cosmopolitan and more inclined to take an interest in other cultures and religions than were the more introverted rulers of Judah. The ten northern tribes did not favor a hereditary principle, for though Judah was ruled throughout her history by one dynasty, no royal line managed to maintain itself for more than a couple of generations in the north.

The Northern Kingdom fell to the Assyrians in 722–721 BCE, following a lengthy siege. In accordance with Assyrian policy, inhabitants of Israel were deported and captives from elsewhere were relocated there. During this time many refugees migrated south and settled in Judah, which survived the onslaught through diplomacy, the payment of tribute, urban fortification, and, according to the biblical record, through divine assistance (see Isa. 37:33–35). It was only a matter of time before its demise would come as well. After more than a century of vassal to Assyria, the Southern Kingdom fell to the Babylonians in 587–586 BCE.

Periodically throughout Judah's history, particularly in times of national crises, there was a deep nostalgia for the brief Golden Age of David and Solomon and a longing for it to return. The thousand-year-period between David and Jesus Christ (viewed as the "Son of David"), served effectively as a preparatory millennium of Christian history, for that span of time established two key notions that would shape Christian thought and imagery, namely (1) *Kingdom hope*: the hope for rule by God, so important in both the Old and New Testaments, and (2) *Messianic hope*: the hope for a Davidic ruler that would guarantee the promissory terms of the Davidic covenant. After the end of the Davidic dynasty, elements of the royal ideology continued to play an important role in later Jewish and Christian traditions. The earliest Christians applied the language of divine sonship to Jesus. One of the titles used for him was "Christ," a Greek term that translates the Hebrew *mashiah* ("messiah," meaning one who was "anointed" or consecrated for an exalted office such as prophet, priest, or king). Royal theology also survives in the hope for a restored or new Jerusalem, in which the promises attached to the city would be fulfilled.

The Babylonian Exile

During the last two decades of its history, the kingdom of Judah was caught in a power struggle between imperial Egypt and Babylon, each striving to fill the power vacuum left by Assyria, whose capital at Nineveh had fallen to the Babylonians in 612 BCE. Josiah, the last great king of Judah, had died in 609, killed while attempting to prevent Egypt from bolstering the declining Assyrian empire in its struggle with Babylon. Jeremiah the prophet, viewing Babylon as a tool of God's power, was accused of being a traitor and condemned to a dungeon. In 587 the Babylonian king Nebuchadnezzar attacked and destroyed Jerusalem and its temple, deporting many of its inhabitants to Babylon.

The fall of Judah, with its utter destruction of Jerusalem and the temple, brought to an end political, social, and religious life in Judah. The culture shock caused by deportation, the problem of adaptation, and their resentment against God for letting it happen made this the strongest test the Jews had undergone. Their survival required nothing less than the reinvention of their identity.

Before the fall of Jerusalem, Jeremiah and Ezekiel uttered menacing oracles to lead the people of Judah to repentance; after the fall, these prophets proclaimed oracles of hope. Jeremiah promised a new covenant (Jer. 31:31–34), and Ezekiel, a new beginning (Ez. 37:1–14; also chapters 40–48). Using the typology of the exodus, the prophet known as Second Isaiah reignited the confidence of the people, assuring them of imminent delivery from captivity. Cyrus II of Persia would be God's "messiah" to deliver them (Isa. 45:1–3).

In 539 BCE the Persians under Cyrus defeated the Babylonian army. Cyrus, a tolerant and enlightened leader, issued an edict liberating the Jews from captivity and permitting repatriation. It is a tribute to Jewish tenacity and vitality that the Mosaic faith not only survived the exile but was immeasurably deepened and enriched. Though some Jews must have capitulated to the pressures of Babylonian culture, others were bound more closely to their tradition and community. Surprisingly, the sense of belonging to the covenant community was intensified, rather than weakened, by life under captivity. In the exile the people devoted themselves to preserving the Torah, studying and searching the tradition intensely for its meaning while preserving their scripture in writing for future generations. The exile was thus a time of religious activity and of concentrated and consecrated attention to Israel's religious heritage. Considerable editing of the prophetic and historical literature was done in this period by anonymous priests and redactors. The role of the priests, no longer sacramental, became one of teaching and preserving Torah. To them the tradition was not just a museum piece from the past, but a living tradition through which God spoke to their contemporary situation. Whatever the origin and early stages of the Pentateuch (the Torah), it may be regarded as certain that its final compilation took place during the Babylonian exile. The Deuteronomistic History, compiled in the years before Jerusalem fell, was also brought into final shape at this time.

Another benefit of the exile was the realization that God could be worshipped anywhere, even in a foreign land and apart from the temple. Undoubtedly, a number of prayers in the book of Psalms were composed during the exile by unknown individuals who cried to God "out of the depths" (Ps. 130:1). It is likely that the institution of the synagogue originated during the exile as well. The presence of these organized local assemblies would become essential to later survival, when the Jews came to be scattered throughout the countries of the Dispersion (the Jewish Diaspora).

The Postexilic Restoration

The sudden and surprising collapse of the Babylonian Empire and the rise of the Persian Empire (539–336 BCE) gave the Jewish people a new lease on life. Cyrus, the enlightened Persian ruler (550–530), permitted those Jews who so desired to return to their homeland and reconstitute their community life under cultural and religious autonomy. There could be no native monarchy now, for the Persians allowed no such independence. So the temple and its priesthood became the center of Jewish identity for the next five hundred years, forming an institution that would remain until the destruction of Jerusalem in 70 CE.

The first task of the returning exiles was to rebuild their temple, then the walls of Jerusalem. A century later, Ezra (a priest and a scribe) inspired the struggling Jewish settlement in Jerusalem to accept the Torah as its constitution. The Torah now proved an indispensable instrument for uniting and governing the Jewish community. Though a priest, Ezra instituted a major reform that stripped the priests of their religious and intellectual leadership, leaving them only in charge of the conduct of the temple ritual. Instead of a hereditary priesthood, which all too often exhibited the marks of decadence and moral corruption, the spiritual leadership of the people became vested in scholars. Recruited from all classes, they represented a non-hereditary, democratic element. The creative impulse in Judaism was henceforth centered in the synagogue, in which all Jews were equal and which became at once a house of prayer, study, and communal assembly.

The importance of this revolution, unparalleled in ancient religion, can scarcely be exaggerated. Ezra's successors, the scribes and rabbis, not only preserved the Torah but also gave it new life. By their painstaking study and interpretation of the biblical text they endowed the Jewish tradition with some of its most noteworthy characteristics—its capacity for growth and its fusion of realistic understanding and idealistic aspiration. Their activity made the Bible relevant to the needs of later generations confronted by new problems and perils. They contributed not only to the survival of the Jewish people but also to the background from which Christianity arose, for they formulated many of the basic teachings shared by Christianity and Rabbinic Judaism.

During the Second Temple period, both the Law and the Prophets became scripture, a sacred core of authoritative books to which the entire people looked for guidance. As we know, the Law, which was the province of the priest and later of the scribe, and the Prophecy, which was the experience of the prophet and later of the apocalyptist, did not exhaust the range of spiritual activity in early Judaism. A third strand was supplied by Wisdom, which was cultivated by the sage or the elder. Wisdom was essentially an intellectual discipline, concerned with the education of upper-class youth. The sage was a professional teacher whose function was to inculcate in his pupils all the elements of morality aimed at achieving worldly success. Wisdom had a timeless quality, transcending time and culture. Though ancient sages reflected on problems of society as they knew them, these were human problems found in varying forms in every society.

According to the historian Charles A. Beard, one of the lessons of history can be summarized by the proverb, "The bee fertilizes the flower it robs." This is particularly true of the Jews during the exile and the restoration period. Although the experience of change and dislocation seemed bitter to many at the time, the people came to realize that God was working for good. While the surrounding culture was regarded as a threat to Israel's faith, the exile also awakened a new world-consciousness, enlarging Israel's faith to an extent never before seen, not even in the cosmopolitan age of Solomon. The exiles realized that they must look beyond their own community to the whole civilized world, if they would behold the glory and majesty of God's purpose in history. The time was ripe for a deeper understanding of the conviction that Israel was called to be God's agent in bringing blessings to all the nations of the earth.

This new understanding of Israel's special place in world history was magnificently expressed by an unknown prophetic writer in the latter part of the book of Isaiah, beginning with chapter 40. This anonymous poet, called Second Isaiah or Deutero-Isaiah, has been acclaimed as one of the greatest writers and poets of the Hebrew scriptures, a visionary with a distinctly universalistic vision.

The view that world-shaking events may have a double and seemingly contradictory effect on people's lives also characterized a small but highly literate and influential group of Palestinian Jews living in Judah under Persian rule during the fourth and fifth centuries BCE. These sages flourished during this "Golden Age of Wisdom," a peaceful era of two hundred years aided by a common lingua franca (Aramaic) across the Persian Empire, a new sense of Jewish identity, and a new internationalism. During this period the books of Job and Ecclesiastes were written and the wisdom material found in the book of Proverbs was collected and finalized.

In the centuries after the return from Babylon, the Jews in Palestine were repeatedly faced with the prospect of more powerful cultures overwhelming their own and overpowering them. The period of the Restoration (also known as the Second Temple period), which followed the return from exile, was challenging and difficult for the tiny, modest, and insecure Jewish community, surrounded as it was by a welter of foreign peoples—Samaritans, Edomites, Moabites, Ammonites, Philistines, and later, Greeks and Romans. The small Jewish settlement was a tributary of the great Persian, Ptolemaic, Seleucid, and Roman empires, which arose in succession and for five centuries held sway over the Jewish community in this part of the world.

Most difficult was the coming of the Hellenistic kingdoms, following Alexander the Great's dramatic conquest of the eastern Mediterranean world in the 330s. First to rule the land were the Ptolemaic pharaohs of Egypt, followed by the Seleucids of Syria. The worst challenge to Jewish identity emerged during the rule of the Seleucid king Antiochus IV Epiphanes, who tried to force Greek customs on the Jews and who threatened the religious life centered on the temple in Jerusalem. From 167 BCE the Jews fought back, first under the leadership of Judas Maccabeus. The Maccabean rebels suffered terribly in this war, but they succeeded in winning independence (142–63) for Judea under a dynasty of native rulers, known as the Hasmoneans. The period of independence proved to be only a brief interlude, ending with the surrender of the Hasmonean state to the Roman general Pompey in 63 BCE. Finding no convincing or compliant Hasmonean candidate for a Jewish throne, the Romans installed Herod as king in 37 BCE, ruling as vassal for more than three decades, until his death in 4 BCE. Herod, the son of a Jewish mother and a non-Jewish father, had been related by marriage to the final Hasmonean ruler. His father Antipater, an Idumean governor, had earlier sided with Julius Caesar. After Julius Caesar was assassinated, Herod emerged as the person most likely to rule Palestine, due to his political pedigree and his loyalty to Rome.

The Jews despised Herod, not only because of his pedigree but also because he ruled as a cruel tyrant. Called "the Great" for his magnificent engineering feats, Herod rebuilt the temple at Jerusalem with unprecedented magnificence, making it one of the largest sacred complexes in the ancient world. He also built forts, such as Masada and Herodium, established Caesarea as the capital and main seaport of his kingdom, and installed foreign innovations such as Greek-style sporting contest, gladiatorial combats, and horseracing. At his death, Herod's kingdom was divided among his surviving sons. Galilee, the northern region of the land, was ruled by Herod Antipas (4 BCE–39 CE). Archelaus, entrusted with the southern portion of the kingdom, proved a disaster and was removed by Rome in 6 CE, replace with a procurator (Roman governor), one of whom was Pontius Pilate (26–36 CE), best known for his trial of Jesus.

During this period, at least four sectarian parties developed within Judaism, including Sadducees, Pharisees, Essenes, Zealots, and other lesser groups. Though they tolerated one another, each saw itself as the most authentic expression of Jewish identity. Likewise, each took a distinguishable stance toward Rome and the Hellenistic world.

The Sadducees, the elite of Jewish society, controlled the priesthood and the banking establishment. As members of the aristocracy, they appear to have been conciliatory toward the ruling Roman authorities, and it is likely through them that many Hellenistic ideas entered Judaism. They disappeared from history following the destruction of Jerusalem and the temple in 70 CE.

The Pharisees were a pietistic movement composed largely of laity. Recruited from the middle orders of society, they had a large following among the masses. Concerned with maintaining the distinctive practices and beliefs of Judaism, they could be faulted for being legalistic and for their rigid interpretation of the Sabbath laws. During the first century CE, both Jesus and Paul would be identified as closer to the Pharisees than to any other religious grouping. Significantly, it was through the Pharisaic wing, primarily as espoused by Paul, that many distinctive Christian doctrines emerged, including divine inspiration of scripture, election and predestination of believers, bodily resurrection of the dead, and belief in spirit beings. Combining conservative and progressive elements, this group alone, of the chief religious Jewish sects, survived the destruction of Jerusalem in 70 CE, becoming the basis for Rabbinic Judaism.

For the group known as the Essenes, however, even the distinctives observed by the Pharisees were not enough to keep them from cultural pollution. Concerned with purity, they left ordinary society and set up separate communities, with their own literature and traditions (believed to be the writers of the Dead Sea Scrolls, they are the subject of great scholarly interest). Believing that matter and pleasure are evil, they focused on ritual baptisms, stated periods of prayer, and the continuous reading and study of the Hebrew scriptures, all preparatory for an eschatological war with Rome, which they believed would usher God's long-awaited messianic kingdom. In 68 CE, as a result of the destruction of Qumran, their Dead Sea community, by the Roman armies, they joined the Zealots in active combat.

The Zealots, heirs of the Maccabees, emerged as a definite party by 6 CE, when the Romans took a census in Palestine for the sake of taxation. The movement grew in response to ongoing acts of Roman aggression. They held a militant version of the Essene theme of separation, feeling the only solution to severe Roman rule was to fight fire with fire, replicating the Maccabean tradition of violent resistance. It was they who gave impetus to the disastrous Jewish revolts against Rome (in 70 and in 132–135 CE) that would shatter Jewish life in Palestine. Out of that destruction emerged the Jewish sect that became Christianity, a world religion in its own right, inspired by the Jew, Jesus of Nazareth.

The Birth of the Apocalyptic Mindset

Despite the burdens of poverty and taxation and the lure of the Hellenistic (Greek) way of life and thought, the Jewish masses held fast to their trust in the righteousness of God. They could no longer believe, however, that the reign of God would take place in history through normal human processes. Only a supernatural cataclysm could rout the forces of evil and usher in the era of peace. Hebrew prophecy was reframed, emerging in radically altered form as apocalyptic. This new perspective described the ultimate conflict between the forces of light and darkness and foretold the final triumph of good over evil, a triumph that must surely be imminent.

Apocalyptic literature, with its promise of the advent of God's supernatural messenger, a messiah or anointed king, was initially rejected by the official custodians of normative Judaism. They were aware of the dangers of such mystical and extravagant hopes and of the despair likely to arise in the wake of unfulfilled expectations. Ultimately, however, the doctrine of a supernatural messiah became the faith of Pharisaic Judaism and of fringe groups such as the Essenes and other messianic sects whose hopes for a supernatural deliverance grew stronger as the tyranny of Roman rule became increasingly intolerable. Among them were the Christians, who began as a Jewish sect but who differed from other sects in their recognition of Jesus of Nazareth as the heaven-sent Redeemer.

The movement from classical prophecy to apocalyptic can be traced within the book of Isaiah, from its inception in the message of the eighth-century prophet Isaiah of Jerusalem (chapters 1–39), to the message of the so-called Second Isaiah during the exile (chapters 40–55), to the message of the so-called Third Isaiah, dated to the postexilic period and found at the conclusion of the book (chapters 56–66). To appreciate the theological significance of this shift, we turn to the message of Second Isaiah, which represents the transition from prophecy (First Isaiah) to apocalyptic (Third Isaiah).

Like a pastoral theologian, Second Isaiah offers comfort to a dislocated, suffering people whose faith in God has been strained to the breaking point: "Comfort my people, says your God. Speak tenderly to Jerusalem, and cry to her that she has served her term, that her penalty is paid, that she has received from the Lord's hand double for all her sins" (Isa. 40:1–2). The substance of the "good news" that is to be carried from heaven to earth is that the time of the coming of God's dominion is near. Like the former exodus from Egyptian bondage, God is about to do a "new thing," which will be so wonderful that the former things pale in significance: "I am about to do a new thing, now it springs forth, do you not perceive it?" (Isa. 43:16–19). The heart of Second Isaiah's message is the proclamation that the new creation is happening in the present as God conquers the chaos of the Babylonian exile and makes a path through the sea for his redeemed to pass over and return with singing to Jerusalem (Isa. 51:10). The prophet has taken creation completely out of the realm of mythology. For him creation is a historical event in the now. Here is a faith that turns not to the archaic past, longing for the good old days, but stands on tiptoe, facing the new age that God is about to introduce.

Study Questions

1. In your estimation, who is the primary protagonist in Israel's history? Support your answer.

2. Do you agree with the author's choice that the Babylonian exile is this epoch's turning point? Why or why not? Is there another event you consider more significant? If so, what is it? Support your choice.

3. In this epoch, does "the church" live up to its nature and destiny as God's new creation? Why or why not?

4. Explain the meaning of the statement that "the exodus and the story of the birth of the nation of Israel are less about what happened historically and more about the meaning behind these events."

5. What does the exodus teach about God's nature, purpose, and motivation?

6. At Sinai, Israel is described as a "priestly kingdom," a designation also used of the church in 1 Peter 2:5, 9. What does it mean to be a "priestly kingdom," and how does this meaning shape the identity and vocation of today's church?

7. What is a "cultural mandate," and which mandates does God give to humanity in Genesis 1? How are these mandates related to the biblical concept of stewardship?

8. According to the text, which of the following should we consider the primary role of a prophet, (a) to predict the future, (b) to keep alive the theocratic ideals, or (c) to challenge injustice in society? Support your answer.

9. What is the Deuteronomistic History? When was it finalized, and what are its chief elements?

10. Explain the role of the Ark of the Covenant in biblical times. Since we no longer have the ark today, how can contemporary believers know the will of God?

11. Describe the role of King David in establishing the Israelite monarchy? What is "royal theology," and how did it function in Israel's self-understanding? How did royal theology influence Christianity?

12. What lessons did the Jews learn during the Babylonian exile, and how did this experience impact postexilic Judaism?

13. How did the rise of apocalyptic thought impact Jewish hopes and Christian origins?

Part 2

Transformation

(4 BCE–1500 CE)

Chapter 3

Phase 3: New Israel (4 BCE–100 CE)

Disciples, Apostles, and Converts

Significant Event: Paul's conversion and subsequent missionary career to the Gentiles.

Turning Point: The Easter event (the resurrection—however understood—of Jesus). One can make a good case for other events, such as the birth of the church; the conversion and subsequent missionary activity of Paul; the literary activity that resulted in the New Testament; and the destruction of Jerusalem by the Romans in 70 CE, a monumental historical event that profoundly impacted the Jewish religion and affected Jewish-Christian relations politically, sociologically, and theologically. However, without Jesus and the events following his crucifixion, the rest would not have happened—or mattered.

Like attempting to cover the history of Israel in one chapter, doing so for the first Christian century is equally daunting. Here too we will be selective regarding subject matter (identifying eight historical and ecclesiastical themes) and deliberate in perspective (focusing on the church as the Israel of God). The following concepts and events helped shaped the early Christian conception of faith, governance, and vocation:

1. The new covenant

2. The historical Jesus

3. Literary responses to Jesus

4. The life, death, and resurrection of Jesus as eschatological events

5. The conversion and ministry of Paul

6. The church in society

7. The church separates from Judaism

8. The church as God's new creation

Early Christians insisted that the Hebrew Bible they read did not belong exclusively to the Jewish community; it belonged also to them. They could say, as did Paul: "For whatever was written in former days was written for our instruction, so that by steadfastness and by the encouragement of the scriptures we might have hope" (Rom. 15:4). Nevertheless, what was happening in their time seemed so radical and comprehensive as to constitute a "new covenant" (2 Cor. 3:6), a new beginning for Judaism and the world.

The New Covenant

In the book of Jeremiah, the prophet speaks of two epochs: the time of the Mosaic covenant, which ended in human failure, and the time of the new covenant, when the divine *torah* (law, teaching) is written on the heart, resulting in such personal knowledge of God that religious teaching would no longer be necessary.

At the time of his prophetic call, Jeremiah realized that God's word had the double aspect of judgment and renewal, doom and promise. The first effect of the divine intention was judgment: "to pluck up and to pull down, to destroy and to overthrow" (Jer. 1:10). To be sure, judgment was not the final word, for God's intention was also "to build and to plant," but rebuilding would come only after destruction. Considering himself a second Moses, in fulfillment of God's promise to Moses in Deuteronomy 18:18 ("I will raise up for them a prophet like you from among their own people; I will put my words in the mouth of the prophet, who shall speak to them everything that I command"), Jeremiah announces a message of doom. This was not a message he had devised, nor one he wished to deliver. Questioning Jeremiah's vocation and viewing him as a traitor, his detractors sentenced him to a dungeon for announcing the fall of Jerusalem.

But the prophet never lost sight of the truth that God's purpose was not just to destroy and overthrow. Jeremiah understood that the false had to be removed before the new could emerge (Jer. 24:6; 42:10). He would have been at odds with his deepest conviction and with the great prophets who preceded him had he not clung steadfastly to the vision of the New People and the New Age that lay beyond catastrophe.

Even in isolation from his nation and his people, Jeremiah knew that individuals experience God's "healing" or salvation within community. Thus, when Jeremiah looked to the horizon of God's future, he spoke of a New Community. The deepest rift in the people's history—the tragic separation of "the house of Israel" from "the house of Judah"—would be overcome, for God's love, working through the discipline of judgement, would make a new beginning for both Israel and Judah. Through their distress, not despite it, the people would be saved (Jer. 30:7).

This vision of the restored community of Israel is profoundly expressed in Jeremiah's prophecy of the new covenant (Jer. 31:31–34), a prophecy that eventually gave the name to the canon of Christian writings ("New Testament" means "New Covenant"). Several aspects of Jeremiah's prophecy seem to describe the Christian community's self-understanding as the new Israel of God (Gal. 6:16):

1. Unlike the covenant at Sinai, which marked the beginning of the divine intention for Israel, this covenant is new in that it pertains to the consummation of the divine purpose. The consummation of God's plan, however, is not in an abstract afterlife or in a distant place far removed from the concrete realities of time. Rather, God's New Age will be realized on earth and in history.

2. Like the first covenant, this covenant is the result of God's initiative.

3. Unlike the covenant with Moses, which had been broken, this covenant inaugurates a new history, a new relationship with God.

4. The covenant will be new in the sense that it will fulfill the original intention of the Sinai covenant. This covenant will be written upon the heart, not upon external tablets, and it will find expression not through obedience to religious ceremonies and written laws but through a personal response to the liberating voice of God.

5. The new covenant will create a new community—God's people—whose relationship with God will be based on trust and loyalty that cannot be broken.

6. The new covenant, like all covenants of promise, will rest upon divine forgiveness, not upon human effort. Such forgiveness, however, must be preceded by God's "discipline," which shatters human pride and self-sufficiency and results in gratitude and thanksgiving.

Early Christians, even those of Jewish descent, considered themselves to be living in the "last days": "Long ago God spoke to our ancestors in many and various ways by the prophets, but in these last days he has spoken to us by a Son, whom he appointed heir of all things, through whom he also created the worlds" (Heb. 1:2). Note the sharp separation of sacred history into two periods. This setting of new against old is defined by the mode of God's revelation: In the past revelation came through prophetic mediators, now it has come through a Son, the one through whom the plurality of previous modes of revelation is channeled, the antitype in whom is fulfilled a host of types. To say that Jesus Christ is "heir of all things," as elaborated by the author of Hebrews, means that multiple features of Old Testament religion must be seen as prefiguring this single individual.

For Christians, the relationship between the Old and New Testaments is one of continuity and discontinuity. Like two partners joined in marriage, neither is a substitute for the other, nor are they independent of one another. Rather there is relative independence, whereby they complement one another. For Christians, the gulf between the testaments is bridged by Jesus Christ, whose person and work establishes a deep discontinuity with Israel's scripture and, at the same time, a deep continuity in the purpose of God. The discontinuity is expressed in the Gospel of Matthew: "You have heard that it was said to those of ancient times . . . but I say unto you" (5:21–22, 27–28); the continuity is expressed in the same Gospel: "Do not think that I have come to abolish the Law or the Prophets. I have come not to abolish, but to fulfill" (5:17). In short, both testaments are theologically necessary if the church is to hear in the human words of the Bible the word of God.

The mystery of the relation between the testaments seems consonant with Paul's discussion in Romans 11 about the relation between the Jewish and Christian communities. In the face of Israel's rejection of Jesus as the Messiah, Paul grapples with the "mystery" of God's election that includes both Jews and Gentiles in "the Israel of God" (Gal. 6:16), declaring, "All Israel will be saved" (Rom. 11:26). God is thereby faithful to the promises made to the ancestors of Israel and extends the meaning and power of those promises to all who have faith.

The Historical Jesus

The central theme of the New Testament is a person, Jesus of Nazareth, a wandering preacher of the first century who has changed the course of history. Whether Christian or not, all who live in the Western world have been influenced by the teachings and life of this individual. Early disciples envisioned Jesus as the climactic historical figure, the Messiah who brought the long-awaited messianic kingdom of God, a rule that by ending evil and suffering would usher in an age of bliss. Later followers and even unbelievers would view Jesus' historical role as pivotal, representing its midpoint. Ernst Renan, famous nineteenth-century scholar, maintained this view when he wrote: "All history is incomprehensible without Christ"; also Napoleon, who confessed toward the end of his life: "This man, Jesus, vanished for eighteen hundred years, still holds the character of men as in a vise"; and H. G. Wells, who once declared: "I am an historian. I am not a believer. But I must confess, as an historian, that this penniless preacher from Galilee is irresistibly the center of history."

Although we cannot be precise about the length of his life or even the duration of his ministry, scholars maintain that Jesus was born around 4 BCE, shortly before the death of Herod, and that he died by crucifixion around 30 CE. Jesus began a brief itinerant ministry in rural Palestine that lasted from one year to no more than three years. It reached a limited number of people and ended in apparent failure, with his crucifixion by Roman authorities. The New Testament is a response to Jesus of Nazareth, whom Christians call Christ, and to a cluster of events scholars call the "Christ event," centered on his birth, death, and resurrection.

According to the Gospels, Jesus began his career as a religious teacher in Judea, where he was baptized by John the Baptist in the Jordan River. John seems to have regarded himself as forerunner of the Messiah, and Christians came retrospectively to consider him as the forerunner of Jesus Christ. Jesus settled in Capernaum on the Sea of Galilee, and his preaching centered in that area. There he named his first disciples, the Galilean fishermen Peter and Andrew from nearby Bethsaida, and James and John, the sons of Zebedee. Other disciples followed, at least twelve, according to the developing Christian tradition that the church represented the "New Israel," a counterpart to the twelve tribes of Israel. If one totals the number of disciples named in the Gospels, they add up to more than twelve, but that is not a concern, for Jesus was not interested in founding a separate religion, which already had priests, liturgy, and a sacrificial system.

In addition to the twelve male disciples, the Gospels indicate that Jesus also had women followers. Women, together with men, would go on to have leadership positions in the church during the apostolic period, including as prophets, deacons, elders, and even apostles (see Rom. 16:7, where Paul numbers Junia among one of the apostles). The Gospels names women among the band of Jesus' followers (see Luke 8:1–3) and as those to whom Jesus first appeared after his resurrection, including Mary Magdalene, prominently featured in John 20:1–18.

Following his death and resurrection, the disciples are included among the apostles, trustees entrusted to carry out Jesus' legacy. The makeup of this band of disciples, including fishermen, tax collectors, and even a zealot, indicates that Jesus was embarking on a deliberate task, one found in America's motto *e pluribus unum*, namely, to take a motley crew and create *koinonia* (fellowship), to create out of many one *ekklēsia* (church). Like Israel of old, the nucleus of this "new Israel" would transcend political, social, and economic differences (see I Cor. 1:26–29). Most of the apostles disappeared rapidly. Some, like Peter, were said to have been martyred in Rome during the reign of Nero (54–68 CE). James the Just, "the Lord's brother," presided over the church in Jerusalem until he too was martyred, probably in 62 CE. Some, like John, "the beloved disciple," lived a long life, dying, according to tradition, during the reign of Trajan (98–117 CE). It would be Paul, not one of the original apostles, who would become the first significant Christian thinker and the decisive Christian missionary. According to tradition, he was martyred in Rome, perhaps about the time of Peter. Out of reverence and respect for the apostles, many of the books of the New Testament are attributed to them, even though it is clear that some of these books were written long after their death.

The human Jesus must have been a figure of great power and originality. In him a force of immeasurable magnitude began to operate in this world, unleashing a movement that has lasted through twenty centuries and is on the rise globally. When a person of such eminence appears, who can apprehend that person totally? One observer will see one aspect, another a different aspect; and even the collection of their observations cannot yield the whole person. Of course, no one can know another person completely. Even after years of marriage, husbands and wives often discover aspects of one another's being of which, up to that moment, they had been ignorant. This being so, it is not surprising that, when Jesus of Nazareth appeared, no single mind could encompass the whole of him, no single artist could paint the definitive portrait. What we have in the New Testament is a collection of fragments of memory and interpretation concerning Jesus, extruded through longstanding Jewish hermeneutical processes. Early Christians, believing that in Jesus all of God's promises were fulfilled (2 Cor. 1:20), added to this tradition, searching the Hebrew scriptures for passages that could be interpreted christologically.

At quite an early period in their corporate existence, before they called themselves Christians, the fellowship of disciples of Jesus in Jerusalem followed what they called the Way—the way of faith and life initiated by Jesus (see Acts 9:2; 19:9; also 18:25). This expression was not unprecedented in Judaism; it is found, for example, in the ancient Jewish writings known as the Dead Sea Scrolls as a designation for the Qumran community's faith and life, and may be understood as a shortened version of "the true way" or "the right way." As companions of the Way, the followers of Jesus found themselves assessing the place of Jesus in God's unfolding purpose for humanity. With increasing clarity they saw his identity and role foreshadowed in the Jewish scriptures, especially as he had taught them how to understand those scriptures.

Literary Responses to Jesus

We actually know very little of the historical Jesus, for our knowledge of his life comes from the Gospels. To understand Jesus properly, we must understand the Gospels, four versions of the life of Jesus composed between 70–95 CE. Like all scripture, the Gospels are theological treatises. They were not written primarily to convey factual information about Jesus, but rather to inspire loyalty and engender belief. They neither dropped from heaven fully written, nor were they written by eyewitnesses.

The Gospel story grew and developed over a period of forty to sixty-five years. When Mark wrote the first Gospel around 70 CE, approximately forty years or two full generations had passed since the crucifixion. Prior to Mark's Gospel many of the most familiar aspects of the Jesus story were unknown. Paul, who wrote letters between 50–60 CE, wrote mostly about the "Easter experience." He shows no knowledge of figures such as John the Baptist or Judas Iscariot, or even of events in the life of Jesus such as his virgin birth, baptism, temptation, or transfiguration. Furthermore, Paul does not seem to be acquainted with any of the parables or miracles of Jesus.

The virgin birth of Jesus, exalted to prominence in the Apostles' and Nicene Creeds of the third and fourth centuries, was not part of primitive Christianity. Missing from Mark's Gospel, the virgin birth was a ninth-decade addition to the tradition, found first in Matthew's Gospel (c. 80 CE). Mark has no knowledge that Jesus ever preached the Sermon on the Mount, or that he taught the disciples what came to be called the Lord's Prayer. Matthew and Luke (c. 85) expand the tradition, nearly doubling the content of Mark, while introducing new characters, adding teachings, and expanding the number of parables. When the Fourth Gospel appeared (c. 95), its author added new ideas to the growing story. John alone suggests that Jesus is a preexistent being, though on two occasions he refers to Jesus simply as "the son of Joseph" (John 1:45; 6:42). There are no parables in John's Gospel, and miracles have been turned into "signs." Christianity is clearly evolving. Once we recognize how the story grows, it is hard to literalize its parts.

The New Testament is best understood as the early Church's response to the historical Jesus (who he was, what he said and did), envisioned as five widening circles of response leading from "the Jesus of history" to "the Christ of faith," that is, from the experience of Jesus *by his disciples* to the confession of him *by the church*. Most periods seem to have lasted approximately twenty years, with occasional overlap.

1. The period of *the earliest disciples* (27–30 CE): this includes their involvement with Jesus in ministry and their return to fishing and other occupations following his crucifixion.

2. *The oral period* (30–50): the years between the date of the crucifixion and the first letter written by Paul are years of silence, from which no writings have survived. During this period, characterized by preaching and proselytizing activity on behalf of the early followers of Christ, the "Jesus material" (including sayings of Jesus and stories about Jesus) circulated as single and detached units. Some scholars argue for the existence of proto-gospels and for the possibility the passion narrative

reached a fixed form at an early period, but these assumptions cannot be corroborated with literary evidence.

3. The period of *the Pauline epistles* (49–64): this phase includes Paul's missionary travels and the authentic letters of Paul, Christianity's earliest written documents.

4. The period of *the Gospels* (65–95): this material, while going back to actual events in the life of Jesus, represents an expanding tradition of faith. To the Gospels should be added the book of Acts, written by the same author as the Gospel of Luke. Acts can be viewed as a sequel to the Gospels in that it describes the spread of early Christianity through the work of the apostles. While few details from this period can be verified historically, for believers they convey truth.

5. *The church* conscious of itself as society (80–100): this period overlaps significantly with that of the Gospels; literarily it features the writing of the latest books of the New Testament, including disputed letters of Paul (such as the Pastorals), the General Epistles, and the book of Revelation.

The Life, Death, and Resurrection of Christ as Eschatological Events

The New Testament is saturated with the belief that something new has happened in the history of humanity, in and through the life and death of Jesus Christ, and above all through his resurrection from the dead. Like their Old Testament counterparts, the followers of Jesus were shaped by an event so profound that it continues to be celebrated as decisive for Christians around the world. The early Christians found in Easter a correlation with the exodus—a path from darkness to light, despair to hope, inability to possibility, bondage to freedom—and with creation, for the resurrection constituted a new beginning for humanity.

In order to make sense of the New Testament, we need to begin with Easter, for Easter is central to Christianity. Whatever occurred on that first Easter, it had incredible power. Before the Easter experience Jesus' followers forsook him and fled. After the Easter experience they were willing to die for their conviction that whatever their understanding of God, it had to include Jesus of Nazareth. This shift in God consciousness revolutionized the theology of a group of Jewish people so dramatically that the world has never been the same. In addition, the Easter event led Jewish Christians to create Sunday, a new holy day, different from yet fulfilling the notion of the Jewish Sabbath.

While the line between the eschatology of Jesus and that of the church cannot be clearly drawn, it seems likely that Jesus thought in the framework of Jewish apocalyptic, though purging it of features such as nationalism, revenge on enemies, and desire for a sensuous paradise. While he seemed to have conceived his messianic role to be that of Isaiah's Suffering Servant, quite likely he also related himself to the figure of the coming Son of Man, Daniel's heavenly figure who would appear on the clouds at the consummation of history (Mark 14:62; see Dan. 7:13–14). In any case, early Christians clearly believed that the appearance of the Messiah in the role of the Suffering Servant was an eschatological even. It was their conviction that already the *eschaton* (the final and decisive event) had entered history, giving assurance of the near approach of the Day of Judgment and "the time of universal restoration" (Acts 3:20–21). The cross was God's sentence of judgment upon human sin and all the powers of darkness, but God's victory in the resurrection had already made possible a "new creation" for those who were in Christ (2 Cor. 5:17).

While later Christians focused on the vision of a second coming of Christ, it is important to recognize that in the early Christian message the center of gravity lay not in the anticipation of Christ's return but in the proclamation that Christ's "first coming" was itself an eschatological event. The New Testament places the emphasis on the victory that has already been won in the cross and resurrection and shuns any attempt to pry into the mystery of the future, which lies in the sole authority of God (Acts 1:7; Matt. 24:26). Oscar Cullmann expressed this matter aptly using an analogy from World War II. Speaking of the invasion at Normandy, known as the Decisive Day (D-day), he noted that the decisive battle in a war may occur at a relatively early stage of the war, and yet the war continues. While the war continues until Victory Day (V-day), the tide turns on D-day, guaranteeing the final outcome. As a result of Christ's resurrection, early Christians were assured that the goal of history had been achieved proleptically by Christ's victory over death. The End would merely vindicate the faith of the present.

At the cross, one of the seven last sayings of Jesus is "It is finished" (John 19:30), a statement not of resignation but of accomplishment. At a certain point the earthly career of Jesus of Nazareth came to an end, and what he accomplished would not be done again or anew. Nevertheless, with

God every end is a new beginning. The end of Jesus known in the flesh is the beginning of Christ known in the Spirit. It is faith in this living Christ, encountered through the living Spirit, that keeps New Testament hope alive.

The dominant theme in the preaching of Jesus—indeed the center of his mission and message—is the coming of the kingdom of God. While the phrase "kingdom of God" is rare in contemporary Jewish writings, it is widely regarded as one of the most distinctive aspects of the preaching of Jesus. Because almost everywhere in the Old Testament the idea of the kingdom is related to the people of Israel and the rule of the house of David in Jerusalem, Jesus is at pains to divest his teaching of this former understanding of the nature of the kingdom. What Jesus proclaims is the immediate sovereignty of God, who will take control of the destinies of all humans, restore humanity to what God had intended it to be, and overthrow the evil powers that had led astray human beings from their proper destiny.

In Mark's Gospel, Jesus' first act upon returning from his sojourn in the wilderness is to proclaim the coming of the kingdom (Mark 1:15). Here Jesus is picking up where Second Isaiah left off half a millennium earlier. Isaiah had envisioned a day when God would finally bring justice to the world, when the long-suffering faithful could rejoice at the end of oppression. Jesus shared Isaiah's anticipation but was more specific about when this time would come: "Truly I tell you, there are some standing here who will not taste death until they see that the kingdom of God has come with power" (Mark 9:1). His audience was to repent and "believe in the good news."

Whatever Jesus envisioned in his proclamation about the kingdom, it was going to be on earth. Despite Matthew's preference for the expression, "kingdom of heaven," it is clear that the concept, as Jesus used it, refers to the destiny of good people on a new, improved earth. It has nothing to do with the souls of dead people ascending to heaven.

In New Testament teaching the coming of the kingdom is always dependent on divine initiative, never on human achievement. Humans may enter the kingdom; they may proclaim it and inherit it (Matt. 25:34; 7:21), but they can neither earn it nor bring it forth. Because the word "kingdom" suggests a geographical region or realm, which is misleading in this context, scholars prefer the term "kingship" or "kingly rule of God."

According to the New Testament, Christians are kind of hybrid creatures who live in two dimensions. They are citizens of the present age while at the same time living under the dominion of Christ's kingdom.

As Paul put it somewhat paradoxically, Christians live "in the flesh" (human nature) as well as "in the Spirit" (the new dimension introduced by Christ). Awareness of this dual citizenship led early Christians to say that they were "strangers" in the historical era on earth (Heb. 11:13). Ever since the New Testament period, Christianity has had to steer between two dangers: the temptation (1) to withdraw from society, on the assumption that Christ's kingdom is not of this world (John 18:36), and (2) to make a too easy identification of the kingdom with something in this world, such as the institutional church or the ideal human society. However, the essential message of the New Testament is this: The kingdom is not of this world, yet it has been manifest in this world through the life, death, and resurrection of Christ. Although God's kingdom is a higher order than any political reality or human ideal of the present age, it has influenced and penetrated the kingdoms of this world—not as a tangent touches a circle but as a vertical line intersects a horizontal plane. The task of the church is to bear witness to this "vertical dimension" of history and, in so doing, to seek to leaven and redeem society in the name of Christ. This attitude toward society is not one of "detachment" but of "transfiguration," involving a rhythm of withdrawal and return through worship and action, faith and good works.

The tension between the "already" and the "not yet" nature of the kingdom is evident also in Paul's eschatology. At several points Paul emphasizes that the coming of Jesus inaugurates a new era or "age," which he designates a "new creation" (2 Cor. 5:17). While the presence of this new age can already be experienced, for Paul the ultimate transformation of the world is yet to come. Viewing the resurrection of Jesus as eschatological event, for it confirms that the "new age" is truly present, Paul also looks ahead to the future coming of Jesus Christ in judgment at the end of time. Another theme of Paul's eschatology is the coming of the Holy Spirit. This theme, which builds on a long-standing aspect of Jewish expectation, sees the gift of the Spirit as a confirmation that the new age has dawned in Christ. One of the most significant aspects of Paul's thought is his interpretation of the gift of the Spirit to believers as a "guarantee" or "first installment" of ultimate salvation (2 Cor. 1:22; 5:5).

Emphasis on the kingdom is found in all genres and strands of the New Testament literature. It is introduced in a number of different contexts quite naturally and as though it formed part of the ordinary vocabulary of Christian thought. As one might expect, the book of Revelation also speaks of the kingdom. There the fulfillment is said to be close at hand, leading the expectant church to affirm: "The kingdom of the world has become the kingdom of our Lord and of his Messiah, and he will reign for forever and ever" (Rev. 11:15).

The church is aware of living in an interim, "between the ages." It cannot bring in the kingdom; it can only testify to its reality, living by the spiritual and ethical principles established by Jesus. Because the citizens of the kingdom belong to a community of believers and are not isolated individuals, they are responsible to maintain the four "notes" or marks of the church, that is, its four defining characteristics as noted in the creeds of Christendom:

- *One*: the unity of the church.

- *Holy*: the purity of the church (to be "holy" is to be set apart for and dedicated to service).

- *Catholic*: the universality of the church (every Christian is part of an inclusive and welcoming whole).

- *Apostolic*: the faithfulness of the church to its founding principles.

Through discipleship, the church models God's "new creation," exhibiting the presence of the kingdom of God to the world, thereby fulfilling individually and communally the cultural mandates associated with the covenant of creation (see Gen. 1:26—2:3). These ordinances, instituted for human wellbeing, include family, labor, and worship. The covenant of creation binds all humans to God and to one another. It entails that, as image-bearers, humans are to reflect God's concern for all of life.

The Conversion and Ministry of Paul

One of the heroic figures in the life of the early church, the apostle Paul emerged from being an arch-persecutor of Christians into an unrelenting missionary of the gospel. The impact of Paul upon the church was both widespread and permanent. His influence was fourfold:

- The first great theologian of the church.

- The first full-time missionary to the Gentiles.

- The founder of numerous congregations in Asia Minor, Greece, and Macedonia.

- The author (actual or alleged) of a group of letters that now comprise one-fourth of the bulk of the New Testament.

Paul is sometimes called the second founder of Christianity. As the first great theologian of the church, he was both a practical theologian—in that he addressed specific needs arising in the church—and a task theologian. To him belonged the unique task of developing or disclosing a theology for the Gentile church, indicating how Gentiles would be brought into full participation in the fellowship of Christ, what Paul refers to as "the body of Christ" (Rom. 12:5; 1 Cor. 12:13, 27; cf. Col. 1:18; Eph. 4:4) and "the Israel of God" (Gal. 6:16; cf. Rom. 11:25–26).

The first full-time missionary to the Gentiles, Paul helped bridge the gap as the church became less Jewish and more Gentile in its makeup. Jesus had performed a revolution in religion, recognizing in Judaism a rich spiritual treasure, resulting in a distinct system of worship, a religious way of life, and a high ethical outlook. Yet that treasure was not available to everyone, for Judaism was an ethnic and deeply exclusive faith. Jesus believed himself to be not simply a teacher of truth but the Messiah, through whom God's eternal purpose for Israel and the nations would be fulfilled. This meant that Jesus undertook the task of liberating the spiritual treasure of Israel's faith for humanity. However, his ministry was almost exclusively to Jews, and his faithfulness to God led him to the cross. The work of Christ became entrusted to his followers, who would be empowered by the Holy Spirit to continue the mission Jesus had begun. It is in Paul and his work that we see the task being accomplished. Paul took the work of Christ and set it free from possession by any one ethnic group, sect, or clique. In so doing, Paul remains the classic exponent of the idea of freedom in Christ and of the universality of God's plan for all humanity (see Rom. 3:29–30; Gal. 3:14; 5:1; cf. Eph. 3:6).

Paul also founded new congregations during his missionary travels, providing exhortation, encouragement, and support through letters and personal visits. He helped heal doctrinal and moral difficulties in his churches, providing a form of moral instruction known as *paraenesis* (see, for example, 1 Thess. 4:1–12), such as one might expect to see in the philosophical letters of his day. His letters to the church of Corinth deal with numerous practical issues they were facing, helping later Christians more fully understand the nature of the Christian life.

While not all of Paul's letters remain, by the end of the first century they became preserved through a collection that marks the church's initial

Christian canon (see 2 Pet. 3:15–16). As part of scripture they became the most famous and influential set of letters ever written, impacting every major Christian thinker and practically every major revival. Central in the conversion of Augustine and Luther, they held a critical place in their life and teachings. During the Reformation, Calvin patterned his famous *Institutes of the Christian Religion* on Paul's letter to the Romans. While Paul had no idea he was writing scripture, there is no denying that he considered his writings to be invested with special authority, and furthermore, that he expected his readers generally to recognize this as factual (1 Cor. 2:16; 7:17; 14:37–38; cf. 2 Thess. 3:14).

The Church in Society

Every verse of the New Testament presupposes the new people of God, a new community called the church. From the beginning, Christians were described as "the body of Christ," followers of Jesus who showed by their lifestyle that they were a part of the new order that Jesus had announced and that they believed had now arrived. Theologically, the church was a microcosm of the transformation that God's new order would bring for the whole world. To be in the church was to have a foretaste of life as God's new people. Socially, the church in the Roman Empire was an alternative society, based not on selfishness and greed and exploitation, but on the new freedom and fellowship that Jesus had announced: freedom to love God and to love and serve others (Mark 12:29–31). As the church expanded across the Mediterranean world, it was indeed a new society—a context in which people of diverse social, racial, and religious backgrounds were united in a new and radical friendship. Because they had been reconciled to God, they found themselves reconciled to each other.

Jesus conceived his mission to be that of calling the remnant of Israel—twelve disciples, corresponding to the twelve-tribe structure of Israel—to covenant faithfulness. And when the meaning of Jesus' life, death, and resurrection came upon these disciples with overwhelming power at the festival of Pentecost (Acts 2), a powerful movement emerged, rightly termed the Age of the Spirit. This small community became a dynamic and militant church, with a message that "turned the world upside down" (Acts 17:6) and a gospel that was carried enthusiastically to the ends of the earth. The Acts of the Apostles gives the story of the emerging church. The expansion was amazingly rapid. Within ten years of the death of Jesus, there were

Christian communities throughout Palestine and Syria; in twenty years, across Asia Minor and into Greece; and in twenty-five years, in Rome.

Christian expansion, as narrated in the book of Acts, resulted in a twofold shift: geographically, the center of the church gravitated from Jerusalem to Rome; ethnically, the church's identity shifted from Jewish Christians to predominantly Gentile Christians. According to Acts, the church expanded because it fulfilled faithfully its two tasks in society: to evangelize, that is, to serve as Christ's witnesses "to the ends of the earth" (Acts 1:8; see also Matthew's Great Commission in 28:19–20), and to live by the ethics of love and mercy that Jesus had taught.

While stressing the newness of the church, we must also keep in mind the relation of this community to the entire Old Testament heritage. In a sense, the church regarded itself as the "New Israel," for like ancient Israel, congregants had a special role in history. The Old Testament narrates how a people was formed to be the bearer of God's purpose in history and the instrument of God's saving work. Israel was not primarily a race or a nation but a covenant community created by God's action. Having delivered Israel from slavery in Egypt, God made them a covenant people. Through many tumultuous years, God educated and disciplined them in order that they might understand more deeply the meaning of their special role.

It was Second Isaiah who understood most profoundly Israel's place in God's worldwide purpose. According to this prophet, Israel was called to be a "light to the nations" (Isa. 49:6) and a servant whose sufferings would benefit all humanity (Isa. 49:3; 53:4–6, 11–12). However, in the intervening years, this expansive vision was obscured. The last two centuries before Jesus witnessed a resurgence of Jewish nationalism that led in time to wars with Rome. In 70 CE the Romans destroyed the temple, leveled Jerusalem, and removed the last vestiges of Jewish statehood.

Thus, in the fullness of time, God acted once again to reconstitute the community of Israel—no longer bound by ethnic or nationalistic limitations but open to all people, Jew and Gentile alike, on the basis of faith. The new community did not establish a clean break with the people of God whose life story is portrayed in the Old Testament. Rather, as Paul puts it in his important discussion in Romans 9–11, the community is a "remnant chosen by grace." It is, so to speak, a "wild olive shoot" grafted onto the olive tree (Israel); and the "branch" (Gentile Christians) is supported by the roots that reach down deeply into God's choice of Israel and God's faithful dealings with this people (Rom. 11:17–24).

Though the early church regarded itself as the true Israel, outwardly it differed little from the numerous synagogues that existed in Jerusalem. Like other members of the synagogues, its members took part in the regular worship of the temple (Luke 24:53; Acts 2:46; 3:1), observed the Jewish festivals, and in general kept the Mosaic law. Although some parallels can be drawn with the ancient Hebrew temple observances, the church in the New Testament was more similar to the Jewish synagogue (a learning center) than to the temple and its cultic activities. The first Christians, themselves Jews or proselytes to Judaism, modeled church worship after synagogue worship. This pattern included readings from scripture, prayer, preaching, and singing. The service closed with a distinctively Christian addition, the breaking of bread (the Lord's Supper or Eucharist), the central mystery at the heart of Christianity (see Acts 2:42). At first, homes of believers served as the places of worship; only later did Christians build church structures comparable to Jewish synagogues. The cross became the central cultic object, rather than the Ark of the Covenant or Torah scrolls. The cross served as a sign of Jesus' crucifixion and resurrection and symbolized the meaning of these events. The first day of the week (Sunday), which commemorated Jesus' resurrection, replaced the Jewish Sabbath as the primary cultic season. In addition to the regular activities of worship and education, which helped to unify the new Christian community, the basic cultic acts were baptism and the Lord's Supper.

Such worship and religious practices did not emerge without problems, however, and new leaders were required. Initially, the disciples of Jesus (the Twelve) became prominent leaders of the Jerusalem church, with a smaller number—consisting of Peter, John, and James "the Just"—exercising greater influence. A somewhat larger group, known as apostles, became the preeminent figures in the spread of Christianity. This group included the Twelve, but the total company of apostles was more numerous. What made a person an apostle was a personal commission by Jesus (the Greek word *apostolos* means "one sent"). Apostles were ambassadors of the risen Lord, understood to have extraordinary authority in the church.

In the world beyond Jerusalem, the church generally assumed the form of a synagogue, that is, a congregation. The Greek word for church (*ekklēsia*) means a group of people called together. It is one of the words used in the Septuagint to designate the assembly of the people of Israel. Because the Jews chose the word *synagogē* for their assemblies, it is quite likely that the first Christians deliberately, and to avoid confusion, rejected the term adopted by the Jews and chose the other. Almost from the start, church congregations were governed by elders (Greek, *presbuteros*), one of whom was chief. With the passage of time, the office of chief elder evolved into that of bishop. Ephesians 4:11 lists prophets, evangelists, pastors, and teachers after apostles among the spiritually gifted leaders of the early church. Apostles stand first in 1 Corinthians 12:28, followed by prophets, teachers, miracle workers, healers, helpers, administrators, speakers in tongues, and interpreters. In keeping with the order of both lists, Paul assigned particular honor to the office of prophet (see 1 Cor. 14:1–19). While the authority of the apostle was derived from a connection with Jesus, that of the church prophet was entirely charismatic. As the church developed, the authority of the apostles was passed from the apostles to the bishops through apostolic succession, an authority initially not concerned with the passing of power but of correct teaching. Over time the charismatic offices in the church waned, whereas apostolic authority was deemed irreplaceable.

As developed by Paul, the church presupposes a faith community that is the source of social unity. All life, whether politics, economics, education, or religion, stands under the covenant relation to God. Within that conception, every believer has a part to play. Whether Christians meet together for worship or fellowship, all members are indispensable for all have something to contribute (see 1 Cor. 14:26–33). As a result, Paul asserts that every Christian has a distinct *charism*, a ministry that is not restricted by either ordination or some other special experience, but which is given to all by the work of the Spirit in the lives of believers (1 Cor. 12:7).

In the church, all members are of equal importance, and that includes equality of women with men. Because Paul's letters contain conflicting statements about the place of women in the church's life (due in part to later editorial activity), the recommended starting place for discussing Paul's own view is Galatians 3:28: "There is no longer Jew or Greek, there is no longer slave or free, there is no longer male and female; for all of you are one in Christ." Despite statements to the contrary, generally seen as interpolations (see 1 Cor. 14:33b–36) or post-Pauline (see 1 Tim. 2:11–15), the early Christian movement clearly affirmed sexual equality, prompting Thomas Cahill to call the primitive church "the world's first egalitarian society." Likewise, Cahill declares Paul's statement in 1 Corinthians 11:11 (that "in the Lord woman is not independent of man or man independent of woman") to be the clearest affirmation of sexual equality in the entire

Bible—indeed, the first in world literature.[1] Paul happily worked alongside women, some of whom were his close friends (Phil. 4:2–3). His most extensive list of greetings to Christian leaders includes many women (Rom. 16:1–15), and he refers to at least one of them as "apostle" (Junia, Rom. 16:7). Furthermore, when Paul advises the church at Corinth about the appropriate way to behave, he takes it for granted that both men and women should pray or prophecy in public worship (1 Cor. 11:4–5). In 1 Corinthians 11:1–16 Paul uses rabbinic arguments where it suits him, moving in two directions simultaneously: conserving tradition by upholding the custom of head-covering, yet breaking with tradition in allowing women to participate in worship. The whole frame of reference is determined by Paul's insistence that men and women have the same freedom and opportunity to play a full part in the life of the church.

The same point also comes out clearly when Paul discusses marriage in 1 Corinthians 7. Some of what he writes is obscure, no doubt because of its specific reference to details of the Corinthian situation. However, the general principle is clear: Men and women relate to each other not through domination but by mutual love and service.

For Paul what determines a person's function in the church is the endowment of God's Spirit. In God's new society, social distinctions such as gender, race, and social class are irrelevant. The heart of the gospel is freedom: freedom from guilt, from the Law, from sin, and from all that would inhibit the development of one's God-given potential. To be set free by Christ is to be released into a new world in which people can find their own true identity, relating to each other in freedom and fellowship because they are related to Christ himself. The final transformation, however, is yet in the future, when the "glorious freedom of the children of God" will be fully realized (Rom 8:21). In the meantime, the church stands as a testimony to that future hope, and as the context in which people can serve one another as they love and serve God.

The earliest church was undoubtedly charismatic. These early believers were dominated by their experience of the Holy Spirit at work among them, so they gave little thought to the problems of organizing the infant church. They believed the Holy Spirit was the only organizing force they needed. This understanding of Christian fellowship became central for Paul and quite likely for other apostles as well. The authentic picture of a church in the New Testament is of groups of Christians acting together in

---

1. Cahill, *Desire of the Everlasting Hills*, 148.

a spirit of mutual love and friendship. When Paul wrote to the church at Rome some twenty years after the events at Pentecost, there seems to have been no organized hierarchy. Yet over the next century, even within the next half-century, this changed dramatically.[2]

The New Testament church was not a perfect body. In 1 Corinthians, Paul addresses many flaws, among them sectarianism, divisiveness, perfectionism, superiority, insincerity, arrogance, immorality, liturgical improprieties, and eucharistic malpractice. Paul rebukes some members, while condemning sinful behavior. Further dissension appeared later in the apostolic churches, mainly over "false teaching." Nevertheless, the emphasis is on unity, particularly in essentials. In worship, secular and social distinctions were to be abolished (Gal. 3:28; Philem. 16), although women were kept subservient to men, at least in some of the churches (1 Cor. 14:34; 1 Tim. 2:11–12).

While inequality is condemned, there was apparently no advocacy yet for the liberation of slaves. Many Christians, in fact, were slaves, for in the Roman Empire slavery was the foundation on which the entire economic structure of society rested. Slavery, as we know, was so ingrained in ancient imperial societies that it would take some eighteen hundred years before abolition was addressed. New Testament church members were drawn from all levels of society. Some, having positions of importance in the secular community, were wealthy enough to own slaves and to have houses large enough for meetings to be held there. But these were a minority.

From the start, one serious problem threatened the church's survival: the terms on which Gentiles could become Christians. At first, it was unclear whether Gentiles should be required to keep the Old Testament laws, either in whole or in part (Acts 10:1—11:18; 15:1–35; Gal. 2:1–10). In the end, however, Gentiles were accepted without on the grounds that Jew and Gentile had been reconciled to one another through the death of Christ (Eph. 2:13–18). Christ is the vine, they are the branches (John 15:1–11); the church is the olive tree, to which the natural branches (Israel) have been grafted and the wild branches (Gentiles) engrafted. God's work of election, as Paul and other early Christian writers stressed, is not based on ethnicity, gender, or merit but on grace.

2. This topic is addressed in Chapter 4: "Catholic Christianity."

The Church Separates from Judaism

While Christianity initially may have functioned like an appendage of Judaism, by the year 70 it was moving out on its own. The move to independence from Judaism was accelerated by Roman destruction of the Jewish temple and the cessation of the sacrifices that had played such a large role in Jewish worship.

Prior to the fateful year 70, Judaism tolerated varieties of opinions within its fold. Between the years 30 and 70, Jewish followers of Jesus continued worshiping in the synagogues. During that period, it was quite clear that Jewish people began incorporating Jesus into their faith story. Within the synagogues, Jewish Christians were at best an enriching new tradition and at worst a minor irritation. However, when the survival of the Jewish faith tradition was at stake, their level of toleration dissipated perceptibly. Acrimony grew between Jews committed to Jesus and traditional Jews who claimed orthodoxy for their convictions, tying their claims to the belief that the God they worshiped could be found only in the unchanging completeness of the Torah. The shift o a survival mentality set the stage for heightened negativity to develop. After the fall of Jerusalem, many followers of Jesus, both Jewish and Gentile, began to interpret the Roman defeat of the Jews and the loss of the temple as God's punishment of traditional Jews for their rejection of Jesus. Thus the stage was set for hostility. Echoes of this rising hostility can be found overtly in the Gospels, particularly in Matthew (21:43; 23:31–38; 27:25). As rhetoric heightened, the lines around what Jews could tolerate within Judaism tightened considerably so that Jewish Christians, offended by this increasing hostility, began to move more and more into Gentile circles.

From that point on, fewer Christians wished to identify with the rigidly orthodox survival mentality that began to characterize Judaism, while fewer Jews wanted to see any aspect of the Jesus tradition left within their faith traditions. Somewhere in the late 80s a split occurred between the synagogue and the followers of Jesus. We can sense the pain of that split in John 9:22, which states that "the Jews had already agreed that anyone who confessed Jesus to be the Messiah would be put out of the synagogue."

Once that split had occurred, Christianity began to move more and more into the Gentile world. Because the Gospel of Matthew was written during this separation and the Gospel of John shortly thereafter, the

Fourth Gospel's blatant negativity toward orthodox Jews (John 8:44) and its descriptions of exclusion from the synagogues reflect that final fracture (John 9:22; 12:42). By the start of the second century, Jewish Christians faded into increasingly Hellenized and Gentile circles, and thereafter Jewish Christians ceased even to think of themselves as Jews, while those who claimed Jewish identity became more firmly entrenched in their tradition. By the middle of the second century there were hardly any Jews left in the Christian movement. "The common ground between Jews and Christians, once so powerful, became nonexistent. This hostile negativity toward Jews and all things Jewish has remained dominant in Christianity to this day."[3]

The Church as God's New Creation

Of the many passages in the New Testament that deal with the calling and mission of the new community, 1 Peter 2:4–10 is one of the most instructive. It establishes the notion that the church is a "spiritual house" built upon the foundation of Jesus Christ, the "living stone." On this assumption, the church is not essentially a social organization or a human institution that can be analyzed sociologically, but is rather a creation of God, who has chosen the rejected stone (the crucified Jesus Christ) as the foundation.

The place of the church in the movement of God's purpose for the world, from creation to consummation, is developed with majestic splendor in the epistle to the Ephesians. In addition to describing the church in terms of the image of the temple, of which Jesus Christ is the chief cornerstone (Eph. 2:19–22), a second image is used, the distinctively Pauline image of the body, of which Christ is the head (2:16; see 1:22–23; 4:15–16).

The theme of peace is sounded in 2:17, the words "to you who were far off" and "to those who were near" echoing God's great promise to Abraham in Genesis 12:4: "in you all the families of the earth shall be blessed." While we usually think of peace as the absence of war, in the Bible "peace" has a more positive meaning, pointing to a state of harmony, wholeness, and welfare within the community. It is a basic biblical premise that there cannot be right relations within the community unless human beings are in right relation with God, for when separated from God, people are at odds with one another as well as with themselves. Thus, the command about loving God precedes the other commandments and supplies the basis for loving the neighbor.

3. Spong, *Liberating the Gospels*, 53.

As Old Testament prophets looked away from the fractured society of Israel, they anticipated the coming of the age of the Messiah, when the barriers of separation would be overcome and human beings would be brought into a new relation with God, with one another, and with the natural environment. In Ephesians love is not a commandment but a new reality in human relationships that has been initiated by God's prior love through Jesus Christ. The church is a fellowship of love, the highest endowment of God's Spirit (see 1 Cor. 13:13; 1 John 4:7–21).

The theme of the unity and faithfulness of the church in the world is elaborated in John 17, Jesus' so-called "high-priestly prayer." In his final prayer, two prepositions are important: "out of" and "into." God has summoned a people for Christ "out of" the world (John 17: 6). Indeed, the New Testament word for church (*ekklēsia*) literally means "called out" and suggests the idea of God calling people out of the world into a new and unique fellowship. However, the church is not taken out of the world into a detached life, but rather is sent "into" the world (John 17:15, 18).

The church is God's new community in the world. As God's mission for the world, the church has inherited the vocation to be a light to the nations and the instrument of God's healing of the brokenness of society. This cannot be done without unity, and so above all, Jesus' prayer is for the unity of the church: "that they may be one, even as we are one" (John 17:11, 22). And this unity is to be the most convincing demonstration to the world that Jesus has been sent by God as the Way, the Truth, and the Life (John 14:6).

Study Questions

1. In your estimation, is there anyone beside Jesus and Paul whom we might consider the chief protagonist in the apostolic period? Support your answer.

2. Do you agree with the author's choice that the Easter event (the death and resurrection of Jesus) is this epoch's turning point? Why or why not? Is there another event you consider more significant? If so, what is it? Support your choice.

3. In this epoch, does "the church" live up to its nature and destiny as God's new creation? Why or why not?

4. Discuss the chief qualities that characterize Jeremiah's "new covenant." In your estimation, to what extent does the first-century church embody these qualities? To what extent does the twenty-first church embody these qualities?

5. Do you agree with H. G. Wells's assessment that Jesus Christ is "irresistibly the center of history"? Support your answer.

6. In your estimation, how fluid was the oral period in terms of the expanding Jesus tradition (in other words, how creative were the early Christian preachers and teachers with regard to the expanding Jesus tradition)?

7. If the first coming of Christ represents an eschatological even, to what extent should Christians focus on the second coming of Christ?

8. If the church's responsibility is to unify people and not divide them (see Ps. 133:1), is that goal achievable in today's society? What can you say and do to bring about greater unity in your local church and in your local community?

9. What was the role of the Holy Spirit in the first-century church? What is the role of the Holy Spirit in the twenty-first-century church?

10. How does the New Testament both encourage and discourage women leadership in the church? Should all Christian denominations pave the way for the equality of women and men in ministry and in administration?

11. How did the fall of Jerusalem change the church's perception of its relationship to Judaism? Given their common origins and their ensuing separation, how can Christians work with Jews to overcome suspicion and animosity?

12. Which biblical image or model of the church do you find most attractive? Why?

Chapter 4

Phase 4: Catholic Christianity (100–325)

Mystics, Bishops, and Intellectuals

Significant Event: The ascendance of Constantine to imperial power, marked by the battle of Milvian Bridge, which signaled Constantine's emergence as a pro-Christian emperor.

Turning Point: The Edict of Milan (also called the Edict of Toleration), which brought to an end official Roman persecution of Christians, paving the way for Christendom.

Among the many important ecclesiastical developments and events during the second and third centuries, the following helped shape the early Christian conception of faith, governance, and vocation:

1. The growth and expansion of early Christianity
2. Conflict with Rome, including imperial persecution of Christians and martyrdom
3. Christian heterodoxy (heresy)
4. Christian response to culture, persecution, and heterodoxy: apologetic literature
5. The shaping of Christian orthodoxy through canon, episcopacy, and creed
6. The ascendance of Constantine to imperial power

As we examine this phase of church history, the second and third centuries CE, we need to be aware that the historical evidence for this subapostolic period is scarce. Historians and theologians are thus required to fill in with imagination, speculation, or informed hunches what went on during the period after about 110, when the New Testament documents were completed. The result is that historical accounts of this period are dependent upon the stance of the interpreter. There was as yet no orthodox church or tradition, and the diversity within the developing church was greater than that in the church today. To oversimplify, it is possible to describe a Roman Catholic, an Orthodox, and a Protestant interpretation of early Christian history, each of which depends on basic assumptions concerning the way that God guides the church. Catholic interpretations of the early church are likely to emphasize the role of early bishops in constructing the institutions, organizing the sacred writings, and guiding the worship of believers; Orthodox interpretation are likely to emphasize patterns of prayer, evolving habits in using the New Testament, and consensus dependent upon creedal statements and ecumenical councils as the crucial shapers of early Christian history; and Protestant interpretations are likely to stress the foundational role of the New Testament writings and to be more willing than either Catholics or the Orthodox to find flaws in early church practices or decisions. It is important to remember that these perspectives represent shades of difference. Christians are almost universally united in believing that the early church was built upon an apostolic foundation, that is, on the work that God began in the apostles through the presence of Christ and the power of the Holy Spirit.

The Growth and Expansion of Early Christianity

The church's identity from a primarily Jewish to a Gentile phenomenon is an interesting story, requiring a self-definition appropriate for a missionary religion expanding throughout the Mediterranean world. Expansion required stable conditions, made possible by the *pax Romana*, a period of Roman peace established by Caesar Augustus that lasted from 27 BCE to 180 CE in the Roman Empire. This two-hundred-year period saw unprecedented peace and economic prosperity throughout the empire, providing political and social stability and making possible the easy movement of ideas and people. The pervasive Hellenistic culture that accompanied the expansion of Roman political power made a common form of the Greek language available to all those living under Roman rule. A deep moral and religious hunger characterized much of the populace during this period, favoring a religion that offered high moral standards and the power to attain them. People sought hope and meaning through membership in one or more of the many religious cults that permeated the empire. Longing for the assurance of personal immortality, many sought companionship in fellowships that combined religious with social purposes.

As Christianity began its spread across the Mediterranean world, it was moving into areas of competition. The religious movements of the early empire included a wide range of options, from ecstatic cults to staid philosophical groups wrestling with religious issues, and from the imperial cult offering the emperors divine honors to small gatherings of devotees of various deities. Both church and synagogue, which were launched along organized lines in the second and subsequent centuries, were examples of this social phenomenon as well as beneficiaries of the widespread yearning for these forms of group identity.

The dispersion of Jews throughout the Roman world meant that not only Jews but also "God-fearers" (Gentiles who were attracted to Jewish beliefs and rituals and regularly attended synagogue services), came into contact with Christian missionaries, who used Jewish synagogues as a base of operations for their travels.[1] The Christianity that spread from Judea with astonishing speed after the year 70 was able to take advantage of these existing conditions.

During the second half of the first century, a distinction arose between itinerant and local ministries, which resulted in a two-tiered structure of authority consisting of:

- Leaders with local authority (i.e., with oversight of individual congregations): these included presbyters (elders), "bishops" as Eucharistic celebrants, and "deacons" assisting in liturgy, with administrative and social duties.

- Leaders with universal authority (i.e. with ministry to all churches): these included apostles, prophets, and teachers.

---

1. See Acts 10:2; 13:16, 26, 43, 50; 16:14; 17:4, 17; 18:6–7; English translations often render the technical Greek terms for "God-fearers" as "devout."

By the end of the first century (the close of the "apostolic" period), the church became more institutionalized. After the death of the apostles, leading cities such as Jerusalem, Antioch, Alexandria, Ephesus, and Rome became vested with greater status, their bishops with greater authority. Worship was now guided by trained clergy, and a fixed liturgy developed for the Lord's Supper. Baptism was no longer administered as a spontaneous expression of faith in Jesus, but as the culmination of catechetical instruction. This teaching often took place during Lent, followed by the baptism of converts on Easter. We may trace four main reasons for these changes in the early church:[2]

1. *Church growth*: the early church grew at an amazing rate, due in part to evangelistic efforts like those of Peter and Paul, but also to the fact that the church exhibited a remarkable ability to meet social and human needs. Leaders were needed, with specialized training, to meet these needs.

2. *Heresy and orthodoxy*: the charismatic approach was open to abuse as well as to false or abusive leaders. The need for a clearly delineated sense of tradition may have been the single most important factor that led to the development of a hierarchical church in the second century, which resulted in an ordained clergy and in the development of a canon of authoritative scripture.

3. *Social change*: like any organization, the church has no future unless it plans for the future. Growth requires planning, adaptation, and economic resources. The early church seems to have had elements of institutionalism from the start, including rites for initiates (baptism) and for members (the Lord's Supper), and it was conscious of having traditions to hand on to future generations. Its leaders had great authority and were, at least on some occasions, paid by other church members. As long as the church saw itself as operating through the power of the Holy Spirit, change seemed unnecessary. But once it became suspicious of the exercise of charismatic gifts, due to their misuse, it was a short step from that to the institutionalized church.

4. *Frustrated hope*: the earliest Christians expected Christ's imminent return. The Christians at Thessalonica became so excited about the fact that Jesus was to return that they neglected work in order to prepare

2. Drane, *Introducing the New Testament*, 398–406.

for this great event. Paul rebuked them for this, though he shared their sense of expectation (1 Thess. 4:13—5:11). While early Christians expected the arrival of God's visible kingdom, this did not occur, and the prospect of a future return of Jesus diminished over time (2 Pet. 3:8). Eventually Christianity came to terms with the fact that it needed to settle down for the long haul.

In the final analysis, the church became an institution not out of conviction but out of practical necessity. Because of church growth, heresy, social change, and frustrated hope, the charismatic ideal no longer seemed a practical way forward.

During the second and third centuries of the Common Era (up to 313), Christianity was threatened by conflict within (orthodoxy versus heterodoxy) and without (conflict with other elements of society, such as pagan philosophers, and imperial persecution by the Roman state). At its inception, the period was characterized by great diversity of beliefs and practices, some Jewish, some pagan, and others uniquely Christian, but by the end of the period, Christianity was searching for agreement and unity. Unity demanded a universal version of the church and over time there developed a term of great resonance for Christianity, the word "catholic," from an ordinary Greek adjective for "general," "whole," or "universal." Bishop Ignatius of Antioch provides the first known use of the term in his letter written to the Christians of Smyrna, in the early second century. Since he did not bother to explain exactly what he meant by the "catholic church," he evidently expected his readers to be familiar with the expression. This was a momentous development, for Christians have never abandoned their hope for unity, despite their general inability to sustain it at any stage in their history.

Conflict with Rome: Imperial Persecution of Christians

The Jewish revolt against Rome during 66–70 had devastating consequences, not only for Judaism, but also for the Jewish-Christian movement. Before succumbing to the Romans, the Jewish rebels massacred the Sadducee elite, whom they regarded as collaborators with the Romans. The Jewish Christian church chose this moment to distance itself from the world of Jewish nationalism, kept out of this struggle by fleeing from Jerusalem. They regrouped in the town of Pella in the upper Jordan valley and maintained contact with other like-minded Jewish Christian communities in the Middle East. In the course of the capture of Jerusalem, the great temple complex went up in flames, never to be restored; its site lay as a wasteland for centuries. The name of the land was changed to from Judea to Palestina (land of the Philistines) to symbolize the utter extinction of the Jewish nation. Between 132 and 135 Jewish patriots rose again in revolt, only to suffer even greater devastation. The Roman victors, determined to quench Jewish rebellion once and for all, erased the name of Jerusalem from the map and created a Roman colonial city in its place, Aelia Capitolina (*Aelia* after the family name of Emperor Hadrian, and *Capitolina* after the newly-built temple of Jupiter, the chief god of the Roman pantheon as worshipped on the Capitoline Hill in Rome). On the site of the Jewish temple a pagan temple was erected, and Jews were forbidden under pain of death to set foot within Jerusalem.

The catastrophe for Jerusalem left the Jewish leaders determined to make peace with Rome, for the sake of preserving their religion and giving it greater coherence. Like the Jewish Christians, the Jewish survivors regrouped away from the former capital on a former estate of the Herodian royal family at the town of Jamnia, on the coast near Gaza. Here the Pharisaic wing shaped the future identity of Judaism, establishing a legal and academic center of Judaism and finalizing the canonical process for the Jewish Bible. The synagogue would replace the temple as the center of Jewish life and liturgy.

The growing coherence in Judaism meant that by the end of the first century CE the break between Christianity and Judaism was official. The Roman imperial authorities unwittingly encouraged this separation by imposing a punitive tax in place of the voluntary contributions that Jews had previously paid to the temple. For Roman officials, it became important to know who was and was not a Jew. Despite their rebellion, tax-paying Jews continued to enjoy the status as an officially recognized religion (*religio licita*). Christians who finally broke their link with Judaism could avoid the special tax, but they would find themselves adrift politically, without official recognition and protection. For their independence they would pay dearly. In the long-run, however, it represented their redemption.

In the Roman Empire, the church was a small body in the midst of what it regarded as a largely hostile world. In the first century, when there was no systematic state persecution, suspicion and hatred were shown to the Christians in isolated and sporadic fashion. Their faith forced them to withdraw from many accepted everyday practices connected with the worship of other deities. They became a close knit group, separated from others. At the beginning, they shared their possessions (Acts 2:44–45), but this practice soon disappeared. As they attempted to preserve the purity of church life and disciplined those whom they thought transgressed in behavior or belief, the Christians exhibited many of the qualities of a sect. At the same time, Christians were active in preaching and evangelism, resulting in strong churches, which developed almost exclusively in urban areas.

Yet in order to grow and expand, the new religion of Christianity needed more than the generally favorable social conditions made possible by the *pax Romana*. Christian claims about a "crucified Messiah" or about the existence of non-Jews who became "children of Abraham" by faith (Gal. 3:7) offended Jews deeply and drew their opposition. Similarly, the empire had its own objective and would not stand by patiently when upstarts insisted that Jesus, not Caesar, should be called Lord.

With the official bestowing of divinity on Emperor Julius Caesar after his death, there was a growing disposition to treat the emperors as manifestations of the divine, especially in the eastern Mediterranean. Although Nero (54–68) seems to have made some effort to promote his own status as divine, it was not until Domitian (81–96) that an emperor announced that he was to be addressed as *Dominus et Deus* ("Lord and God"). Roman persecution, which flared under the emperors Nero, Domitian, and Marcus Aurelius before being exerted systematically by the emperors Decius and Valerian (mid-third century), reached its climax in the time of Diocletian (start of the fourth century).

Martyrdom

Tertullian, a second-century church father, wrote, "The blood of martyrs is the seed of the Church," implying that the martyr's willing sacrifice leads to the conversion of others. The theme of martyrdom is prominent in early Christianity, beginning with the New Testament writings and lasting until the so-called Edict of Milan in 313, when Emperor Constantine legitimized Christianity with legal sanction.

In the Judeo-Christian tradition, martyrdom goes back to the uprisings of the Maccabean period, when Jewish heroes resisted efforts by the Syrian tyrant Antiochus IV to eliminate distinct Jewish religious practices. The elderly Eleazar and his seven sons publicly refused to submit when threatened by death, even when one after the other were publically executed before the others. Convinced that God would reward with future resurrection those who remained loyal, their witness was conceived as a witness to the faithfulness of God. This conviction inspired the followers of Christ.

According to the book of Acts, at his final meeting with his followers the risen Lord promised that they would receive power when the Holy spirit had come upon them, and would become his "witnesses" throughout the world (Acts 1:8). The Greek word for "witness," *martys*, became significant for Christians of the second and third centuries, living under the threat of Roman persecution, which could happen suddenly and without warning. The oppression of Christians included personal and social penalties such as expropriation of property, economic marginalization, exile, and even death. For Christ's followers, martyrdom found embodiment in the innocent suffering and death of Jesus. The New Testament depicts Jesus as the witness to God in the face of death: "For this I came into the world, to testify (or to bear witness) to the truth" (John 18:37). At his last meal with his followers, Jesus tells them, "You must bear witness as well" (John 15:27). Elsewhere Paul speaks of Christians as "bearing in their body the death of Jesus" (see 2 Cor. 4:10), and if they are thus conformed to Christ in his death, they can hope to share in his resurrection. First Peter, written during the final decades of the first century, enjoins Christians to embrace suffering, for in so doing they are "sharing Christ's sufferings" (4:13) and that of fellow believers: "for you know that your brothers and sisters in all the world are undergoing the same kinds of suffering" (5:9).

The first widely recognized saints in the Christian tradition consisted of martyrs and confessors (the latter consists of those who confessed Christ in the face of persecution but not actually to the point of death). The tradition of martyrdom in Christianity began with Stephen, a Hellenistic Jew chosen by the apostles to continue their preaching mission and to care for the poor (Acts 6–7). Because of the boldness of his witness, the Jewish leaders put him to death by stoning. In addition to Stephen are Peter and Paul, who according to tradition were killed in the local persecution in Rome under Nero.

During the second and third centuries, three highly visible Christians bore witness in a way that glorified martyrdom as the perfect expression of discipleship. Ignatius, bishop of Antioch, was arrested during the reign of Trajan (around the year 107) and was taken captive to Rome, knowing his fate would take him to death in the arena, ravaged by wild animals. He wrote seven letters to churches in Asia Minor, begging Christians not to intervene. He saw martyrdom as the completion of his discipleship and wrote, memorably, "Let me be ground by the teeth of the wild beasts that I may become the bread of Christ."

Polycarp was the bishop of Smyrna, one of the churches to whom Ignatius wrote. He collected Ignatius's letters and then wrote a letter exhorting the Christians in Philippi. Said to have known John, the last of the disciples of Jesus, Polycarp was executed in 155, his death celebrated by a writing called *The Martyrdom of Polycarp*. A third notable martyr was the Christian philosopher Justin, later known as Justin Martyr. Condemned as a Christian by a fellow philosopher, he suffered martyrdom under Emperor Marcus Aurelius in 165. His trial before the Roman prefect was recorded and still exists. When the emperor ordered him one final time to offer sacrifice to the gods, and thus avoid death, Justin refused.

In addition to these well known examples, evidence exists for the arrest, imprisonment, and execution of numerous unknown Christians as well. A letter written from churches in Gaul (including present-day France and other surrounding regions) attests to the suffering and death of a considerable number of Christians there under Marcus Aurelius in the year 178. *The Acts of the Scillitan Martyrs*, written around 180, provides evidence of the martyrdom of twelve North African women and men. Another literary work, the *Martyrdom of Perpetua and Felicity,* narrates the account of two Christian women in North Africa, one of high status and the other of low status. The account was written around 203, close to the events of their imprisonment and death. In 225 Origen of Alexandria wrote *Exhortations to Martyrdom*, an elaborate and passionate statement concerning the ideal of martyrdom. Like Perpetua and Felicity, Origen's father died as a martyr in the persecution of 203. During his lifetime Origen also underwent torture, dying as a confessor.

It is common today to associate persecution and martyrdom with the catacombs, a vast labyrinth of subterranean galleries just south of the city of Rome. From the second century CE onwards, Roman Christians began burying their dead in these large underground chambers. Here early Christians not only buried their dead, but they held memorial services and celebrations of anniversaries of Christian martyrs. Contrary to popular thought, however, Christians did not use the catacombs as hiding places or for secret worship, for during times of persecution the catacombs were closed by Roman authorities. Christians worshipped in the catacombs because of their association with martyrs and because early Christians were buried there (primarily on account of their predominantly lower-class status, since most had been slaves).

In ancient times, Etruscans had buried their dead in underground chambers, so Christians, because of their belief in the resurrection, revived the practice because they did not wish to cremate their dead. Originally, catacombs were located outside the boundaries of the city because Roman law forbade burials within city limits. Cut into the soft volcanic rock of the Roman subsoil, these chambers were easy to dig, yet were remarkably stable. Narrow steps connect as many as four levels, superimposed one below the other. There are forty known subterranean burial chambers in Rome. Saint Callixtus's catacomb, named for Callixtus, a canonized saint, is one of the largest, having over twelve miles of underground passageways. Callixtus served as pope from 217 to 222, when he was martyred for his Christian faith. Initially many Christians desired to be buried in chambers alongside martyrs, but the practice of catacomb burial declined after 380, when Christianity was declared the official state religion.

Conflict Within: Christian Heterodoxy (Heresy)

Throughout religious history, people who disagree or dissent from the norm have been called heretics. The term "heresy," meaning "choice" in the Greek language, usually refers to a person or movement that "stands apart" or deviates from orthodoxy. When a dominant group or religion labels a movement "cultic" or an individual "heretical," this usually indicates amnesia or a short memory, for at its source, almost every distinct movement goes back to someone branded "heretic" on account of novel thoughts or innovative ideas. In the Judeo-Christian tradition alone, Abraham would have been a heretic to the religions of ancient Mesopotamia; Moses to the Egyptians; Jesus and Paul to Judaism; Martin Luther to Catholicism; John Wesley to Anglicanism; William Wilberforce to slavery; Elizabeth Cady Stanton and Susan B. Anthony to patriarchy; Martin Luther King, Jr. to racism; and so forth. Heresy, not apathy, drives history. In the grand scheme of things, nonconformists spark newness and change.

Throughout the first four centuries of the church's existence, a running debate occurred between people who called themselves Christians. This debate focused on beliefs (doctrines), but it also impacted morality. The debate culminated in the great church councils that began in the fourth century, where the "official" position emerged as orthodox and the rejected views were declared heterodox (heretical). Doctrinal debates centered on the areas of Christology (the deity of Christ, his two natures, the incarnation), the Trinity, and soteriology (the redemptive work of Christ, as well as the relation between faith, grace, and good works). Other areas of debate included the nature of revelation and inspiration (the orthodox position culminated in the selection of the twenty-seven books that make up the New Testament), anthropology (how humans are unique, how they relate to God, and the influence of sin on their nature), and eschatology (views regarding the end of the world, the resurrection of the dead, and the afterlife).

More serious than religious opposition from Judaism and persecution from Rome, the early church's internal struggles were caused primarily by minorities who wanted to remain free and charismatic in their interpretation of Christianity. The majority opposed heterodox beliefs and practices, favoring factors that would define orthodoxy, such as apostolic succession, institutional authority, and a binding notion of "the faith."

The second-century heresies were mainly three: Montanism, Gnosticism, and Marcionism (which was an outgrowth of Gnosticism). Montanism became known about 170 as a group of enthusiasts who gathered around Montanus, a Phrygian visionary attended by Prisca and Maximilla, women prophets who had left their husbands to follow him. He proclaimed that the end of the world was at hand, and thus was the first prominent person in a long line of millenarian fanatics who have appeared in church history ever since. However, his chief claim was to lead a spiritual elite directly guided by the Holy Spirit, which was called to restore the church to primitive purity. The sect was puritanical in nature and imposed rigorous discipline on its followers.

Marcion, whose father was bishop in Pontus (in northern Asia Minor), knew Christianity from an early age. However, he had a profound dislike toward both Judaism and the material world. About 144 he went to Rome, where he gathered a following. Excommunicated for his unorthodox ideas, he founded his own church, which lasted for several centuries as a rival to the orthodox church. He argued that the Creator God of the Old Testament, responsible for the evil, material world, was quite different from the God and Father of Jesus, who is love. The Father's purpose was that there be only a spiritual world, whereas the God of the Old Testament, either through ignorance or out of an evil intent, made this world and placed humanity in it, a theme one finds in many Gnostic writings as well. This perspective led

Marcion to reject the Old Testament and to replace it with his own canon, a truncated New Testament canon that included the epistles of Paul—according to Marcion, Paul was one of the few who truly understood Jesus' message—and the Gospel of Luke. All other ancient Christian books were said to be tainted by ignorance. As to the many quotations from the Old Testament in Luke and Paul, Marcion explained them away as interpolations—the work of Judaizers seeking to subvert the original message.

Marcion posed a great threat to the church, for he rejected or radically reinterpreted the doctrines of creation, incarnation, and resurrection. He also organized his own church with its own bishops and scripture. For a number of years, this rival church achieved a measure of success, and even after it was clearly defeated, it persisted for centuries.

Perhaps no greater threat was posed to the church's self-understanding and authority during those early centuries than by the spirituality of groups that modern historians call Gnostic, for their reliance on various forms of secret wisdom (*gnosis*). Toward the end of the second century the Christian apologist Irenaeus listed 217 forms of Gnosticism, many of which borrowed liberally from Christian doctrines or practices. Gnosticism was so prevalent in the Greek and Roman worlds that it affected pagan religions and philosophies as well as Judaism and Christianity.

Gnosticism, a cluster of religious views centering around the issue of salvation (Gnostics emphasized that redemption comes through special knowledge or insight), was perpetuated by its own apostles, prophets, and teachers, as well as through a vast literature that purported to contain special teachings that Jesus supposedly gave to his disciples and that were to be kept secret and shared only with enlightened (redeemed) individuals. In an attempt to eradicate these heterodox systems, distinguished bishops and other church leaders began to write apologetic works against these views, calling for the destruction of all Gnostic literature. Nevertheless, some of these documents survived, including fifty-two texts discovered by Arab peasants in 1945 in a remote area of Egypt known as Nag Hammadi. These texts, buried between 350–400 CE, probably by Gnostic Christian monks, include texts dating from the early second centuries. Scholars believe some writings, such as The Gospel of Thomas, may incorporate traditions as old as or older than the Gospels of the New Testament.

While Gnostic sources are post-Christian, some scholars claim that Gnostic beliefs predate Christianity and may even have influenced Christianity, since Gnosticism flourished during the second century CE. Some

Pauline scholars have suggested that the central problem Paul dealt with after the Apostolic Council stemmed from Gnosticism. There is no question
that some of the scandals that arose in Paul's Corinthian churches point
to Gnostic-like behavior and belief.[3] There is little question that incipient
Gnosticism was present in first-century churches, but full-blown Gnosticism did not appear until the second and third century, borrowing from
Christianity while distorting it.

The Gnostic worldview, as it affects Christianity, revolves around four
factors:

1. *Cosmological element*. Most Gnostic systems begin with a philosophy
   of strict dualism. The cosmos is represented by two realms that oppose one another: the divine realm of light and the demonic realm of
   darkness. Life and death, truth and falsehood, salvation and the ruin
   of human life, are anchored in the cosmos. There is a distinct qualita-
   tive difference between matter (viewed as evil) and spirit (viewed as
   good). The world and all things visible in the universe are characterized as darkness and evil and are under the control of evil spirits.

2. *Theological element*. Gnostics distinguish between two deities. The primary God, who dwells in the abode of light and is Light, is unknown.
   A second god (craftsman or demiurge), lesser and evil, fashioned this
   world, trapping particles of light in the darkness of matter.

3. *Anthropological element*. Humans consist of body (flesh) and soul
   (soul and spirit are sometimes further distinguished), two elements in
   conflict with one another. Within (some) humans is a spark or particle
   of light, placed into humanity during the primeval period by the demiurge. Apart from enlightenment, humans remain ignorant of their
   true (godlike) inner nature. Once redeemed, the spark must escape
   back to its source, the unknown God.

4. *Christological element*. Christ is understood to be a divine messenger
   (actually God, for all beings of light are emanations [hence begot-
   ten] of God, hence God). Jesus is a redeemer (Savior) who provides
   knowledge (gnosis) about the unknown God and the divine element

---

3. A partial list from 1 Corinthians includes (a) the presence of the "Christ-party"
(see 1:12), (b) esteem of "wisdom" (1:17), (c) sexual freedom leading to immoral behavior (5:1; 6:12–20), (d) devaluing the earthly Jesus (12:3), (e) emphasizing glossolalia
(speaking in tongue) over other gifts (13:1; 14:1–5), and (f) denying the resurrection of
the body (15:12–19).

to those who by origin are divine. In Jesus, Christ only appeared human in order to deceive the forces of evil and in order to penetrate the realm of darkness with secret insight and knowledge.[4]

Another area in which Christians and Gnostics disagreed was the role of ethics. Although some Gnostics lived according to high ethical standards, often stressing asceticism and living like hermits in order not to be contaminated by the world's pollution and deception, many lived like libertines (see I Cor. 5:1–13), considering ethics superfluous. It was representatives of this latter group that caused Paul such difficulties in Asia Minor and Greece, and are clearly his antagonists in 1 and 2 Corinthians. Whereas orthodox Christians saw evil embodied in immoral practices, Gnosticism saw evil within human nature, primarily in spiritual ignorance. Hence the solution involved gaining insight and ignoring (and even overindulging) the flesh.

The Shaping of Christian Orthodoxy through Canon, Episcopacy, and Creed

During the second century, the church stood at a crossroads. Could it draw clear lines between true worship of Jesus Christ and the era's multitude of Greek, Roman, and Middle Eastern philosophies and mystery religions that also featured revelations from a high God and appeals for dedicated moral life on earth? The answer is affirmative, but the journey was long and arduous before Christian orthodoxy prevailed.

An umbrella of protection was needed, broad enough to accommodate the masses, yet specific enough to deal with deviant belief and behavior. Many Gentiles, formerly pagan, began joining the church. Most were illiterate, in a state of spiritual infancy, and not yet ready for the freedom Paul had spoken about in Galatians (see 3:23–26; 5:1). Like all adolescents, they needed guidance and protection. By the year 112, Ignatius, leader of the Christian church in Antioch of Syria, urged fellow believers to "follow the bishop as Jesus Christ followed the Father." On his way to martyrdom in Rome, he wrote letters to the churches of Asia Minor and to Rome. In each letter, he calls for submission by the members to the bishop and the

4. This view, which denies the humanity of Jesus Christ and argues that Christ only "appeared" to be human, was held by some of the dissidents in the Johannine churches. Called docetism, this view is condemned as "the spirit of antichrist" in I John 4:1–6 (see also 1 Cor. 12:3; 2 John 7; Col. 1:22).

elders and requests respect for the deacons. In his letter to Polycarp, bishop of Smyrna, Ignatius declares, "Let nothing be done without your approval." His injunction revealed the emergence of a system of church organization constructed around locally powerful bishops.

By 150 CE, a fairly well-defined rule of governance by bishops was firmly in place, and catholic orthodoxy—meaning a universal rule of faith binding upon all Christians—was taking shape. While oversimplified, the following chart describes the evolution of church government:

- First century: several "bishops" or "elders" in each congregation.
- Second century: one bishop over one congregation.
- Third century: one bishop over several congregations.
- Fourth century: some (metropolitan) bishops over other bishops.
- Fifth century: one bishop (the bishop of Rome) exercising, or attempting to exercise, authority over all others.

The function of the bishop in early Christianity was fourfold: (1) administrative, (2) liturgical, (3) pastoral, and (4) apologetic. The first line of defense, bishops were the primary protectors of the faith.

By the time of Ignatius there circulated among the expanding Christian congregations two collections of Christian documents, one consisting of the four gospel accounts of the life of Jesus as attributed to Matthew, Mark, Luke, and John, and the other containing copies of the letters credited to the apostle Paul. Soon Christians would add to these the Acts of the Apostles and other sacred writings, set alongside the Hebrew Bible to provide written guidance for the church.

A series of compositions, classified as church orders because they devote themselves to the regulation of the common life, were written during the second and third century. They also show how the roles of the clergy were developing. The authority of the bishop increasingly appears as supreme within the church, particularly in worship. Below the bishop are various lower clerical orders, including acolytes, exorcists, lectors, deacons, priests, and widows. While the clergy is sharply contrasted to the laity, until around the year 1000 it was common for priests to be married. The earliest rulebook, the *Didache* or the *Teaching of the Twelve Apostles*, originated from Syria around 100 CE. This brief book provides instructions for baptism, the Eucharist, and for hospitality of traveling evangelists, among other items. More complex are the *Didascalia Apostolorum* or the *Teaching of the*

Apostles, originating in Syria during the third century, and the *Apostolic Constitutions*, eight volumes from the fourth century.

In roughly the same period that witnessed the evolution of an episcopal system of church organization and a scriptural record of Christ and the early church, there also appear short, concise summaries of what it meant to be an orthodox Christian. These creeds (from the Latin *credo*, "I believe"), proved immensely useful both as a way of marking out the boundaries of Christian faith and as an introduction for inquirers or the children of believers. Some creeds were baptismal, formulated as a way to teach catechumens (converts undergoing instruction).

The statement of faith known as the Apostles' Creed, used widely in the Western churches as a baptismal statement, illustrates the creed-making process. The earliest version, often called the Old Roman Creed, goes back to 140 CE, though it was not until the eighth century that the creed is quoted in its present form. The title first appears around 390, and soon after a legend circulated that it was the joint composition of the apostles, each contributing a phrase or concept. The creed, divided into three parts or articles, follows a Trinitarian pattern; the first relates to God, the second to Christ, and the third to the Holy Spirit. The major portion is devoted to the second article, for that was the most controversial, but each article protects the church against heretical teaching.

The earliest heresies tended to overspiritualize Jesus, thereby detaching Christianity from history. The Gnostics, for example, viewed matter as evil, something the first article rebuts, affirming that God was "maker of heaven and earth." The basic conviction of the Greeks was that truth was changeless, and hence not tied to events, which were unreliable. The second article emphasizes the historicity of the Christian faith, grounding it in a series of historical events. The emphasis of the third article is participation—making experiential the subject of the first two articles. The Holy Spirit makes the difference between a living and a dead faith. According to the Apostles' Creed, faith that is not experienced is not faith.

Together with the episcopate and the canon of scripture, the early creeds became the anchors that stabilized the church in its early subapostolic history. The importance of creed, canon, and episcopacy for the development of orthodox Christianity cannot be overestimated, but behind each word lies a historical process complex as it was important.

Christian Response to Culture, Persecution, and Heterodoxy: Apologetic Literature

Apologetic literature had its roots in Judaism. Such literature arose among Diaspora Jews like Philo of Alexandria and Josephus, who responded to anti-Semitic charges of misanthropy with historical and philosophical treatises that demonstrated how the Jewish law and the Jewish manner of life was actually philanthropic.

Following the destruction of Jerusalem in the year 70 and its reconstitution as a Roman colony in 135, Christians continued their claim to be the New Israel, although the issue for Christians about obeying the Jewish cultic laws died out with the destruction of the Jerusalem temple and the emergence of Rabbinic Judaism. Although Jerusalem continued to be an important center of the church in the eastern Mediterranean, it was at Caesarea on the Palestinian coast and at Alexandria in Egypt that the vitality of the cultural life of the church was most evident. These cities were centers of Greco-Roman culture and learning, and in both cities the Christians took on the task of coming to terms with the challenges from culture. In each place, Christians developed schools for the instruction of their leaders that helped shape the life and thought of Christianity for centuries. By 180, a school existed in Alexandria for the intellectual training of leaders of the church, headed by two of the early church's greatest scholars, Clement and Origen. There they pursued the claim that through Jesus, God had brought to fruition the fuller and final disclosure of the divine plan for the human race.

In Rome and Carthage, the major centers of Roman culture in the western Mediterranean world, the issues that dominated the thought of the church differed. For them, the central concern involved the identity of the church, specifically, defining Christian orthodoxy. Important for the church was the developing attitude toward the Christian movement on the part of both the political and the intellectual leaders of the Roman world. Speaking for Christianity were some who had been trained in the best methods of the Greco-Roman intellectual tradition, providing reasoned explanations for what Christians believed and taught. The Greeks called this strategy an *apologia*, which means a "rational defense" for one's position (the New Testament also encourages apologetic defense of one's beliefs; see 1 Peter 3:15; Titus 1:9; Jude 3). Four Christian thinkers whose extensive writings provide the fullest picture of this effort are Justin Martyr, Origen, Irenaeus, and Tertullian.

A native of Palestine, Justin explored the major philosophical options of his day before turning to an investigation of Christianity. He wandered about the Mediterranean world as a Christian philosopher, finally settling in Rome, where he founded a Christian school. His two major writing that have survived are both apologies, the first addressed to a Jewish rabbi (*Dialogue with Trypho*), and the other to Gentiles (*Apology*). In his first work, Justin claims that the new covenant established by Jesus has displaced the covenant with Israel described in the Bible, supporting his contention that the church is now God's instrument to bring the light of God's knowledge to all nations. His *Apology*, addressed to Emperor Antoninus Pius (138–161) and to the Roman senate and people, describes Christianity as a rational search for truth and invites dialogue on philosophical grounds. In a third apology (actually an appendix to earlier ones), Justin counters the false charges that have been brought against the Christians. He notes that the bravery of the Christians in the face of persecution had been an important factor that originally attracted him to that faith.

Origen was one of the most brilliant thinkers in the history of Christianity. When he was ten years old, his father was killed during the persecution of the church by Emperor Severus (193–211). Origen wished to follow his father in martyrdom, but his mother kept him safe in the house by hiding his clothes. Trained in both secular and Christian learning, he quickly excelled, developing special competence in the languages and contents of the Jewish and Christian scriptures, so that at the age of eighteen he began to preside over the Christian school in his native city, Alexandria. By means of allegorical and figurative interpretation of the scriptures, Origen was able to show the correlation, as he saw it, between Greek philosophy and the Bible. In 232 he moved to Caesarea, where his program of teaching and writing was so colossal that he had stenographers on hand during his lectures to record his discourses. He was among those tortured during the persecution of the church under Decius (249–251), and died from those injuries in 254.

Origen's greatest contributions were his detailed commentaries on the Bible and an extended apologetic response (*Contra Celsum* and *The First Doctrine*) to an earlier attack on Christianity by Celsus, a Roman philosopher of the later second century. It is clear that Celsus knew the New Testament writings, as well as the claims that were being made in the second century by various competing Christian groups, such as the Gnostics and the followers of Marcion. Using the tactic of a scornful critic, Celsus's attack featured a fivefold critique: (1) Christians rely on miracles, which can be equated with magic; (2) Christianity was a low-class movement, appealing to the ignorant and the gullible, who were obsessed with healing and prophecy rather than with wisdom and philosophical truth; (3) Jesus was not divine, but the illegitimate offspring of a Roman soldier. Claiming allegiance to a resurrected Lord, Christians actually worshipped a powerless corpse; (4) the Jewish-Christian view of God, revealed to a minor race of people and thereby excluding from participation the majority of the human race, is preposterous and unacceptable; (5) the Jewish-Christian scriptures, embarrassing when read literally, had to be interpreted allegorically to cover up their improbable teaching. Celsus's alternative to the Jewish-Christian perspective was to disavow their doctrine of God, affirming that there is only one god behind the many names. He maintained that there is, and always has been, a single god accessible to humanity through reason. There were, Celsus acknowledged, some admirable moral truths affirmed by Jews and Christians, such as love of one's neighbor, but these insights were already present in the writings of the Greek philosophers, as were the teachings of other religions. Christians were foolish to employ the human, fleshly Jesus as their basis for understanding the divine purpose for the cosmos.

A major figure among the Christians of the late second century was Irenaeus, who worked to consolidate Christian orthodoxy. Born at Smyrna around the year 130, he was ordained bishop of Lyons in Gaul in 178. Anxious to reconcile Christians in the eastern and western Roman worlds and to establish principles on which such unity might be affirmed and maintained, Irenaeus wrote *Against Heresies*. This major work not only attacks false teaching, but it also offers a full declaration of what Irenaeus considered the essence of authentic Christian faith. Like the philosophical insight of which Origen wrote, faith has an intellectual content that can be defined with increasing clarity. Nevertheless, false teachers who deny aspects of the faith that Irenaeus has identified as orthodox are threatening this unity of faith. Included among these heterodox groups were Gnostics, who denied that creation is good or that the God of Jesus is the creator of the universe. To support their heretical views, Gnostics were producing rival writings to the New Testament, including gospels, apocalypses, acts, and letters attributed to various apostles.

In his definition of orthodoxy, Irenaeus argued for a threefold approach to tradition: the canon of scripture, the rule of faith, and the authority of bishops. In countering heresy, Irenaeus argues for the necessity of a literary canon, a standard by which books could be used to define Christian teaching and practice. He refuted Marcionites, Gnostics, and other sectarian teachers with specific citations from the Old and New Testament, indicating which compositions he was using and thus showing which are truly authoritative and which are rejected. Using this method, Irenaeus represents an important stage toward the final formation of the New Testament canon. Unlike the heretics, who take only one Gospel as their norm, Irenaeus insisted that there are four, just as there are four winds and four corners of the earth. The one gospel message rests on four pillars, "breathing immortality on every side and enkindling life anew in human beings."

Irenaeus also draws on the developing tradition of a rule of faith—or creed—to provide a doctrinal framework for Christian belief. Elements of a creed were already present in Judaism: "Hear, O Israel, the Lord your God is one God." Even the basic Christian claim, "Jesus is Lord," is a statement of belief. Various creedal statements appear in the New Testament, such as in 1 Timothy 2:5–6: "For there is one God; there is also one mediator between God and humankind, Christ Jesus, himself human, who gave himself a ransom for all." Likewise in 1 Corinthians 8:5–6, when Paul tells the Corinthians, "Though there may be so-called gods in heaven and on earth—as in fact there are many gods and many lords—yet for us there is one God, the Father, from whom are all things and for whom we exist, and one Lord, Jesus Christ, through whom are all things and through whom we exist." Irenaeus's rule of faith, like the Apostles' Creed, presents an epitome of the scriptural story. As such, it also provides a guide to the reading of the scriptures.

The notion of the bishops as the successors of the apostles, already found in Clement of Rome, is argued more fully by Irenaeus, with specific attention to the bishops of Rome. The institutional argument directly opposes the Gnostic position concerning secret teachings, secret teachers, and secret books. Christianity has a public creed, an apostolic tradition, and a clear canon of scripture. The consensus of the patristic period, already visible by the end of the second century, is that the unity and truth of the church, represented by the orthodox tradition, is to be maintained by the apostolic witness, the succession of leadership from the apostles through the bishops, and fidelity to an accepted collection of scriptures.

These church standards will develop more fully during the conciliar age (the ecumenical councils of the fourth through seventh centuries).

Another kind of response to the mounting pressures on Christianity in the later second century was the promotion of the idea that God would intervene directly in current affairs to vindicate the church and destroy opposition. One Christian leader who came to share this point of view was Tertullian. Born of pagan parents in Carthage around 160 and trained as a lawyer, Tertullian converted in 193. Thereafter, he devoted his legal skills to the defense of Christianity. His writings were in Latin, which was a new feature in Christian literature. Until that time Greek had been the primary literary language of the Christians, and Latin the vernacular of the masses in the western Roman world. According to one analysis, Tertullian coined 509 new nouns, 284 adjectives, and 161 verbs in the Latin language. Of these, perhaps the most important is the word "Trinity" (*trinitas*).

In his *Apology*, Tertullian addressed the two major charges brought against the Christians of his day: that they do not worship the traditional gods (which is sacrilege) and that they do not offer the sacrifices for the emperor (which is treason). Instead of accepting the charge that Christians are morally and politically subversive, Tertullian argues that they follow Jesus, the embodiment of reason and power and the enlightener of the human race. As his followers, Christians are the enemies of human error, not the enemies of the human race. Defending Christians, Tertullian provides the modern reader with a vivid picture of life in the churches of the second century. They gather to pray to God for strength and guidance, for the welfare of the state and its rulers, and for the triumph of peace in the world. They live according to high moral principles, presided over by elders, sharing the modest resources of the members. They provide support for burial of the poor, for orphans, for the aged, and for victims of tragedy.

Concerned to affirm the continuity of the Christian tradition in the face of new interpretations that were arising, it is ironic that in his later years he was strongly influenced by the Montanists, a charismatic movement that claimed to have received prophetic revelations that supplemented and modified the New Testament writings.

The Ascendance of Constantine to Imperial Power

By the turn of the third century, the growing tendency in the Roman Empire to combine features of various religious traditions (called "syncretism" by modern scholars) was evident throughout all layers of society, including on the imperial level. In spite of the efforts of some emperors, such as Commodus (176–192) to relax the opposition to Christians, and even though there was a significant number of conversion of women within the imperial establishment, pressures against the church continued to mount. In 202 Septimus Severus decreed a prohibition of conversions to Christianity. An empire-wide persecution of Christians began. Instead of persecution cooling the fervor of the Christian movement, this violent imperial effort at suppression succeeded in increasing the zeal and commitment of its members. Irenaeus voiced his expectation of the emergence of a New Age and saw the death of Christian witnesses as evidence of its imminence. In the middle of the third century, the Christians' view of the impending overturn of the present order had a resurgence. Tertullian became more and more interested in the pronouncements of self-styled new prophets and their revelations about the future.

The mixture of the astonishing courage of the martyrs' convictions coupled with the intellectually impressive defense of their faith offered by brilliant thinkers such as Justin, Irenaeus, Origen, Tertullian, Clement, and Cyprian forced many thoughtful Romans to reassess their attitudes toward the resilient Christian movement. By 250, however, Rome faced multiple problems: Persians on the east, Goths on the north, economic woes, and a plague swept across the empire. Emperor Decius felt he had an answer: Rome had lost its ancient spirit, nourished by ancient values. Rome needed a revival of "true" religion, and so Decius appointed a day on which all his subjects would be required to sacrifice to the ancestral gods, followed by a signed pledge of loyalty. A magistrate would attest the certificate. Under dire pressure, some Christians recanted their faith; others experienced torture and confiscation of property; some were exiled, and others martyred. Thankfully, Decius's reign ended a year later, but within six years, Emperor Valerian renewed the persecution, though he was soon captured by the Persians. The next emperor restored personal and church properties to the Christians, and for the next four decades, the church had relative peace.

A disturbance related to the army sparked the persecution under Diocletian, the final and most violent persecution of Christians. While some Christians had served in the army, many attempted to leave, while others refused to serve in the military. Some church leaders discouraged combat, espousing love of enemies and other forms of pacifism. The conflict erupted in 303, when Diocletian issued a decree that prohibited Christians from meeting, required the demolition of all churches, the burning of all copies of the Christian scriptures, and the stripping of citizenship for Christians of high rank, forcing all others into slavery. Two fires broke out in the palace, and, as in the days of Nero, Christians were blamed. Prisons filled and stayed full even though pardon was offered to those who recanted. One observer recorded seeing nearly one hundred Christian men, women, and children on their way to slavery in the mines, their right eye gouged out and their left foot crippled. In Egypt alone, thousands of Christians submitted to death, after dreadful torture.

The martyrs who perished in this final persecution gave medieval Christians many edifying tales and legends. Martyrs include Pope Marcellinus; St. Sebastian, a Roman soldier who survived death by arrows only to be clubbed to death; St. Agnes; a gentle girl who refused to marry a pagan; and St. Lucia, a girl of Syracuse who came to be revered in Sweden. The persecutions under Galerius, who followed Diocletian, claimed as victims St. George, honored by soldiers and also by England as their patron saint, and St. Catherine of Alexandria, whose name is attached to the famous monastery at the base of Mount Sinai.

All this changed in 312, when Constantine defeated his rival Maxentius at the battle of Milvian Bridge. During what became a crushing victory for Constantine, Constantine had a dream in which he saw a cross in the heavens and the words, "In this sign conquer." A year earlier the Emperor Galerius, on his deathbed from a disease he believed was punishment from God, had decreed pardon to all Christians and toleration for their faith. In 313, Constantine's Edict of Milan guaranteed that their freedom would continue. Within a century, Christianity would become the official state religion. At the time of Constantine, perhaps one in twenty—some estimate one in ten—were Christians. A century later, most people in the Mediterranean world were at least nominally Christian.

Study Questions

1. Whom do you consider the chief protagonist in the subapostolic period (second and third centuries CE)? Support your answer.

2. Do you agree with the author's choice that the battle of Milvian Bridge is this epoch's turning point? Why or why not? Is there another event you consider more significant? If so, what is it? Support your choice.

3. In this epoch, does "the church" live up to its nature and destiny as God's new creation? Why or why not?

4. Describe the process that led to the institutionalization of the early church.

5. Discuss your reaction to early Christian fervor, which at times resulted in martyrdom. Would the church have survived without such commitment? Should Christians today maintain this kind of devotion to Christ? Explain your answer.

6. What appeal did Marcionism, Montanism, and Gnosticism have for early Christians?

7. What threats did Marcionism, Montanism, and Gnosticism present to the early church? Should today's church be vigilant in identifying doctrinal heresy and moral deviance?

8. Describe the worldview of ancient Gnosticism. Do any of its elements appeal to you?

9. The New Testament encourages apologetic defense of the faith and therefore of one's beliefs (see 1 Pet. 3:15). How prepared are you for such an endeavor? How might the study of church history provide greater proficiency in these areas?

10. Discuss Celsus's critique of Christianity. Do you find any points of his polemic pertinent? Support your answer.

Chapter 5

Phase 5: Christendom I (325–476)

Councils, Monarchs, and Popes

Significant Event: The canonical process, including the recording, selection, and preservation of the twenty-seven New Testament documents that became definitive for Christian faith and practice.

Turning Point: The Council of Chalcedon. The Fourth Ecumenical Council defined further the nature of the Trinity and resulted in the Chalcedonian Creed, which declared Jesus "fully human and fully divine." The council's judgments and definitions marked a significant turning point in the christological debates.

Among the many important ecclesiastical developments and events during the fourth and fifth centuries, the following helped shape the church's conception of faith, vocation, and governance:

1. Political events from Diocletian to Constantine

2. Constantine's contributions to Christianity

3. Arius, Athanasius, and the Council of Nicaea

4. The canonical process

5. Beginnings of the papacy

6. Augustine's theological legacy

7. Doctrinal development from Nicaea to Chalcedon

8. The decline and fall of Rome

The Christian movement started the fourth century as a persecuted minority; it ended the century as the established religion of the empire. The central figure in this transformation was Emperor Constantine, one of the major figures of Christian history. His embrace of Christianity is considered one of the most important events for the growth and development of Christianity in the West. As a result, the Christian church was joined to the power of the state and assumed a moral responsibility for Western society. During the fourth and fifth centuries, the church refined its doctrine and developed its structure. The church historian Eusebius saw Constantine's embrace of Christianity as its victory over the empire. Others believed culture enticed believers toward worldliness. As Søren Kierkegaard warned centuries later, when everybody is a Christian, nobody is a Christian.

Political Events from Diocletian to Constantine

The last major persecution of Christians had taken place under Diocletian in the years following 303. Why would Diocletian, one of the most capable and efficient emperors of the late Roman Empire, attack the church? Although a practicing pagan, for eighteen years he paid little attention to the growing Christian power. His court was full of Christian officials, and his wife and daughter were considered Christians. Impressive church buildings appeared in the principal cities of the empire. Then, suddenly, he ordered his army purged of Christians and the implementation of widespread persecution, hoping to eliminate Christianity altogether. Diocletian's strategy was obvious. The empire was under threat, culturally, economically, and politically, and Diocletian needed to unify the empire and provide for its stability. Germanic peoples on the Danube and Rhine were migrating southward. The empire, dependent on conquest for the acquisition of new wealth, was relying on dwindling resources. The economic situation was deteriorating, made worse by famine, plague, and monetary inflation. The signs of a crumbling empire were already present in 284, when Diocletian, a military commander and the son of slaves, was made emperor. He believed that by unifying the empire religiously, unity and peace would prevail. He needed a scapegoat, and he hoped that eliminating Christianity would make the empire run more efficiently.

In some respects, Diocletian was as important as Constantine for the shaping of imperial Christianity because he gave new shape to imperial politics. In order to provide for the better administration of an empire that stretched from the Middle East to the British Isles, Diocletian established a hierarchical political structure with a complex bureaucracy. The third century had seen thirty emperors claim the throne, and many others tried. To protect the empire from the anarchy created by the constant assassination of emperors, the shrewd army combatant established an effective plan for succession—the tetrarchy. He divided his realm into four administrative districts, with an Augustus and a subordinate Caesar in both the east and the west.

In 305 Diocletian abdicated the throne and the new Augustus in the east, Galerius, became emperor. He continued Domitian's policy of persecution, determined to push ahead to the complete extermination of Christianity. However, in 311, on his deathbed, he realized that his attempt to eliminate Christianity had failed. His final official act was to issue an edict of toleration, thereby ending the last and worst persecution of Christians by Rome. The axiom proved true, that darkness is greatest before dawn.

Upon the death of Galerius, a struggle for imperial power broke loose. The other Augustus in the west, Constantius (the father of Constantine), was in far-off Britain. Unlike Diocletian and Galerius, Constantius had never pushed persecution in his district of Gaul, having suspended all measures against the Christians and even showing them signs of favor. Eusebius, Constantine's biographer, spoke of Constantius as a believer in the one God, though he stopped short of calling him a Christian.

In 312 Constantine, political heir to Constantius, advanced across the Alps to dislodge his rival Maxentius from Italy and to capture Rome. When he came upon his militarily superior enemy at the Milvian Bridge, just outside the walls of Rome, he found help in the God of the Christians. His brilliant victory over Maxentius served as proof to Constantine that his success was due to the power of Christ and the superiority of the Christian religion. Constantine was now co-emperor with Licinius, the Augustus of the east. In 324, Constantine overcame Licinus to rule as the sole Roman emperor.

Constantine's Contributions to Christianity

Constantine was not baptized until just before his death in 337, but deferment of baptism was then not unusual by persons who wished to avoid having to do penance. It is probably best to regard him as Christian from 312. He did much to relieve suffering, incorporating Christian (humane) attitudes into law. Mitigating the severities of the criminal law and the law of debt, he improved the condition of slaves and discouraged the killing by exposure of unwanted children. Before Constantine, it was legal for a father to sell a child into slavery; now this became a crime. Earlier, husbands owned all property, including his wife, and divorce was automatic, occurring for trivial reasons. Constantine began new regulations on divorce, protected the wife's property rights, and made it illegal for married men to have concubines. He also reformed prisons and established hospitals.

In 313 Constantine and Licinius issued a decree of toleration for all religions, including Christianity. Called the Edict of Milan, it was based on an earlier mutual agreement at Milan in 312. Although signs of paganism endured under Constantine—including his retention of the title *Pontifex Maximus* as head of the state religious cult—he began to favor Christianity openly, becoming its protector and benefactor. He proclaimed freedom of worship for all Christians, release from exile of those who had been persecuted, and restored property to confessors and property taken from churches with funds from the imperial treasury. He also allowed Christian priests to enjoy the same exemption from taxes as their pagan counterparts; abolished executions by crucifixion; eliminated the battles of gladiators as punishment for crimes; and in 321 made Sunday a public holiday. Constantine began the practice of donating pagan temples as Christian sanctuaries, and thanks to his generosity, magnificent church buildings arose as evidence of his support. In 319 he began the construction of the first basilica of St. Peter's in Rome, on the site thought to be Peter's grave. In Palestine he commissioned a church on the traditional site of Jesus' sepulcher and another in Bethlehem, the traditional site of Jesus' birth. Christian symbols began appearing on imperial coins, and pagan symbols gradually disappeared. The state also recognized as valid decisions made by church officials for the Christian community. At the Council of Arles in 314, the church responded by making it lawful for a Christian to hold imperial office and by excommunicating Christians in the army who evaded their military duties.

Constantine's boldest and most important innovation was the founding of Constantinople in 330, a "New Rome" named after himself.

Politically, Constantine recognized, as Diocletian had, the need to establish firm control over both the Western and Eastern Empire, especially given that the west was under increased barbarian threat and the east under pressure from the Sassanid Empire (224–651), aggressive successors to the Persians and Parthians of antiquity. He chose as his new capital the site of the ancient Greek city of Byzantium. The location was ideally located on the Bosporus, a narrow waterway between the Black Sea and the Mediterranean and a natural crossroads between Asia and Europe. The city had a natural harbor, and was supremely defensible. In the future, Constantinople would become a genuine rival to the old Rome, thriving especially when the old capital was weak. Constantinople repelled all invaders for over one thousand years, until Turkish Muslims warriors finally conquered it in 1453. In 1930, the Turks renamed the city Istanbul.

Some have said "the devil joined the church when Constantine became a Christian." A symbol of the times is a Roman coin showing a deity, divine Lord Mithra, but now holding in his hand a cross. Some compromise with culture may seem harmless, such as celebrating Christmas on December 25. This day marked the Roman Saturnalia, a festival celebrating the birth of the sun god. Other mergers with popular custom were more questionable. Once the church had questioned participation in war; now this issue virtually disappeared. Once the church questioned how a rich person could enter the kingdom of God; now the church gloried in its wealth. Pomp and ceremony, modeled in part on that of the state, replaced the simpler worship of the early church. Allied with a hierarchical, imperial government, the church reveled in its own hierarchy, removing laypeople from leadership in worship and from government of the church. Indeed, the emperor would issue decrees concerning church government and doctrine.

The most dangerous effect, however, lay in the church's growing worldliness. Once the threat of persecution had weeded out all but the truly committed Christians. Now awareness of the tension between the kingdom of this world and the kingdom of God was fading. Once the lives of candidates for church membership were examined for months before they could be baptized. Soon every subject was expected by law to become a church member.

Beginning no later than the third century, holy men and women dramatically lived out their protest against worldliness. Anchorites retired to the desert to devote themselves to prayer, even seeking physical suffering to put down the flesh. Rejoiced in extreme deprivation, people like Macarius

lay naked six months in a swamp, mosquitoes and poisonous insects sting-
ing him nearly to death. Withdrawing from the sinful world to live on top of
a column, Simeon Stylites refused to come down even for his own mother's
funeral. The "desert fathers" went into the wilderness not to withdraw but
to battle Satan. Yet when they felt needed to help the world, some came
back. Twice the great ascetic Antony returned from the desert. Once it was
to strengthen Christians in persecution. What could the Romans do to him
that he had not already done to himself? He came back again to defend the
faith against the Arian heresy.

After all the intervening years, it is hard to grasp what the change in
imperial leadership meant for the church. Prior to 312, Christianity had
been outlawed and persecuted. Suddenly it was favored and pampered.
Constantine thrust it into public life, and the church responded by reimag-
ing its identity and mission. The population of the empire was by no means
yet Christian, and paganism did not immediately disappear, but the actions
of Constantine decisively placed the imperial power behind the church,
with the expectation that the church would also support imperial power.
This principle would be tested in 325, at Nicaea.

The Christianization of the empire was an uphill battle. The imperial
favor of Constantine did not mean that the empire became immediately or
totally Christian. Many individuals kept older ideals and practices alive.
Rural areas were particularly slow to convert to Christianity, and intellectuals did not capitulate easily. The famous rhetorician Libanius (314–394),
a highly influential scholar, continued to defend traditional ways, even as
he included Christians among his pupils. The efforts of Constantine's successors to impose Christianity on the populace further indicate that the
transition was difficult.

In 341 Constantius (337–361) and Constans (337–354), sons of Constantine, ruled as co-emperors (as co-Augustus) until 350, when Constantius became sole emperor. At his death he appointed his cousin Julian as his
successor. In 341 Constantius prohibited all pagan sacrifice, an indication
that the practice persisted. In 346 Constantius and Constans issued an edict
closing pagan temples. The final evidence for the continuation of paganism
was the reign of Emperor Julian (361–363). Known by Christians as the
Apostate, Julian was raised Christian, but he converted to paganism and
sought to restore the empire to its traditional polytheism. Elevated by Constantius to Caesar of the west in 355, he proved himself adept as a soldier. In
360, when he was acclaimed Augustus by his troops, he openly renounced

Christianity. While he did not persecute Christians, he promoted a syn-cretistic form of religion, restoring pagan education and pagan temples while honoring Jesus among other sages and heroes of the past. One might only wonder what might have happened if Julian had not been cut down in battle after a brief reign.

Succeeding emperors quickly and decisively restored Christian privi-leges, some allowing freedom of worship while others rejected pagan wor-ship and emperor worship. The decisive establishment of Christianity as the state religion of the empire took place under Theodosius the Great, who ruled the east from 379 to 392 and was sole ruler from 392 to 395. By 380, rewards for Christians gave way to penalties for non-Christians. In that year Theodosius issued an edict imposing Christianity on all inhabitants. He closed all pagan temples, where possible converting them to Christian worship. In 392, he declared sacrifice to the gods to be treason, punishable by death. Jews were allowed to assemble for worship, but were not allowed to proselytize or enter into marriage with Christians.

Some Christian leaders protested the increasing power of the em-peror, implicit in the Christian empire. Theodosius was taking for granted the close link between his own will and God's. In 390 a seemingly minor incident involving the imprisonment of a homosexual charioteer resulted in the death of seven thousand protestors. Ambrose, bishop of Milan, was appalled, and challenged the emperor to repent for having issued the mas-sacre. Ambrose refused the emperor communion until he had confessed his sin. In the end, Theodosius repented, taking off his imperial robes in front of a crowded congregation and asking pardon. He had to do so on several occasions until at last, on Christmas Day, Ambrose gave him the sacra-ment. It required unusual courage to humiliate an emperor—the threat of excommunication—an instrument the church would use repeatedly in its clash with the state.

In 410 Alaric, the Visigoth leader, besieged the city of Rome. For 620 years, Rome had seen no foreign invaders outside its wall. The Romans pleaded for mercy, but the Visigoths eventually charged the gates and plun-dered the city. Devastation followed everywhere—except in the churches, for Alaric proclaimed himself a Christian. A short time later the Visigoth troops withdrew, but Rome, the "eternal city," would never be the same. Shocked Romans beheld the locations where statues of the ancient gods had stood. Had they made Rome great? Would they have saved the city? Were they angry because the empire had turned to the Christian God? Refugees from Rome fled in all directions. In the North African seaport of Hippo, a bishop named Augustine provided a lasting answer, writing *The City of God* (416–422) against critics who claimed that the fall of Rome was due to the abandonment of the pagan gods. The question occupied him almost to the end of his life. From Adam to the end of time, Augustine wrote, humanity falls into two cities: the mass of the godless, united by the common love for temporal things, and the company of spiritual believers, bound together by the love of God. What drove Rome to greatness was the former. The City of God, born of grace, is the only eternal city. "There," Augustine wrote, "instead of victory, is truth; instead of high rank, holiness; instead of peace, felicity; instead of life, eternity."

Augustine's view implied the doctrine of "two swords" or jurisdictions by which God orders society. The spiritual sword of the church works to bring people under the rule of the City of God, while God uses the temporal sword of the state to restrain sin and keep order in society. Church and state are separate institutions and yet work together for the benefit of earthly order and welfare. The state has its place in suppressing crime and preserving peace, but since the state is based on the power of sin, it must submit to the laws of the Christian church.

Augustine's vision inspired many during the early Middle Ages. The present might be bad, but better things are to come. The golden age—the kingdom of God—lies not in the fading splendors of an external worldly kingdom that can only crumble and fall, but rather lies within, in the unfading spiritual love of God. Augustine's answer provided light for the dark days ahead and a philosophy for the foundation of Christendom.

Arius, Athanasius, and the Council of Nicaea

Among world religions, Christianity is distinctively preoccupied with matters of belief. While all religions espouse truth, the precise content of belief seems critical to Christians, unlike adherents of other faiths. The reason for this emphasis seemingly lies in origins. Christianity arose as a religion of choice; it began as a Jewish sect that professed Jesus as Messiah (in contrast to other messiahs) and as Lord (in contrast to other masters). Intellectual commitment is at the heart of the movement, and this commitment has specific content.

Early on, the church began to recognize authoritative scriptures, but as the author of 2 Peter 3:16 noted, there are some things in scripture "hard to understand." Was Jesus divine or human? Do Christians worship three gods or one? In what sense is God one and yet three? In the second half of the second century the theologian Tertullian coined the word "Trinity" of God. Was God, some wondered, first the Creator-Father, then became the Son, and is now the Holy Spirit? Some "modalists," as this view came to be known, taught that God had appeared in different modes throughout history. Others, called adoptionists, believed that Jesus had been specially adopted by God and imbued with the fullness of the divine presence. Neither of these views satisfied the church, since they either undercut the conviction that Jesus was a distinct person or shortchanged the fullness of his deity.

Another set of answers stressed the distinctions between the Father and the Son. Some, like Origen, argued that Jesus was "generated" from the Father, but also that this generation was "eternal." By this formula Origen hoped to preserve both the unity of the Trinity and the distinction between the Father and the Son. Some, like Arius (250–336), a presbyter[1] from Alexandria in Egypt, followed Origen's train of thought but did not share his concern for balance. He openly challenged teachers in Alexandria by asserting that the Word (Logs), who assumed flesh in Jesus Christ (John 1:14), was a lesser god that had a different nature than God the Father. The Son is neither eternal nor omnipotent. He was a lesser being—the first created Being and the greatest—but nevertheless created. Such teaching appealed to many former pagans and even to Gnostics, who taught that there is one supreme God and a number of lesser beings who do God's work. Converts from paganism found it hard to grasp the Christian belief that the Word existed from all eternity, and that he is equal with the Father. Arius made Christianity easier to understand. It seemed more reasonable to think of Christ as a kind of divine hero, greater than an ordinary human being, but of a lower rank than the eternal God. At issue were the Son's status as a divine being and the unity of the idea of God. If the Son was of a different nature than the Father, then there are at least two Gods.

When in 318 he communicated his views to his bishop, Alexander, Arius so stressed the unified, eternal character of God the Father that the Son was reduced to a lower status. The matter became contentious, for many in the church wondered how such a subordinated Christ—who was more than human, yet less than fully God—could impart salvation to

---

1. A priest; in episcopal church hierarchy, an office intermediate between bishop and deacon.

humanity. To Arius, however, the transcendence of the Father and the need to pursue logically the meaning of divine unity mattered more than anything else. From the time Arius began to air his views in 318 to the time the council met at Nicaea seven years later, a great debate arose, threatening the church's fragile unity. Arius's views were all the more popular because he had an engaging preaching style. He put his ideas into jingles, which set to simple tunes were soon being sung by adults and children alike.

Bishop Alexander was incensed. He called a synod at Alexandria about 320, and the assembled clergy condemned Arius's teaching and excommunicated him. When the populace was informed of the verdict, riots erupted in the streets of Alexandria. Arius turned to his friend, Eusebius, bishop of the eastern capital city of Nicomedia, and won his support. Thus, the theological quarrel became a test of strength between the two most important churches in the east: Nicomedia, the political capital, and Alexandria, the intellectual capital. Constantine, recognizing that the explosive issue had to be defused, decided to intervene.

As Constantine approached the end of his life, he searched for a way to unify the empire. Like Diocletian, he was equally concerned about the stability of the empire and about the difficulties created by religious strife. To Constantine, however, the best course was not to suppress Christianity but rather to exploit its potential for unity. Thus, once he had gained sole control, he set out to heal the strife that was bedeviling the church. Christians, it seems, were divided over theological issues. The same believers who had been the victims of terrible persecution under Diocletian and Galerius were now demanding that their fellow Christians be suppressed or banished from their churches over disagreements concerning points of doctrine. Constantine had no choice but to intervene.

By the year 324, that strife centered on the teaching of Arius. Thus, in 325, he called for a council to meet at Nicaea, not far from Nicomedia in Asia Minor, the church's first ecumenical council. To the council came bishops mostly from the east, including a young assistant to Bishop Alexander by the name of Athanasius, who would devote his life to defending the teaching hammered out at Nicaea. In reality, the council was over before it started, for of the three hundred bishops present, all but two eventually opposed Arius. Many of these bishops came from churches that worshipped Jesus. They had undergone persecution on his behalf; some bore the disfigurement of suffering and prison. One had lost an eye, another the use of his hands. They would accept no compromise.

Now came the hard part, designing a statement that the council could embrace but that would also exclude the teachings of Arius. The bishops who met at Nicaea were not all of one mind, but under the guidance of Athanasius, their declaration of first principles eventually (after a struggle lasting most of the fourth century) became bedrock for Christian life and Trinitarian theology. The council's essential declarations, in the words of the Nicene Creed, are as follows:

1. Christ is *true God from true God*. Jesus was God in the same sense that the Father was God.

2. Christ is *consubstantial (of one substance) with the Father*. Athanasius's insistence on the use of the Greek word *homoousios* (meaning of *same* substance) led to great controversy, both because this technical term is not found in the Bible and because many in the church preferred the assertion that Jesus was "of a *similar* substance with the Father" (using the Greek word *homoiousios*, from *homoi* "similar").

3. Christ was *begotten, not made*. This means that Jesus was not formed or created, as all other things and persons, but was from eternity the Son of God.

4. Christ *became human for us humans and for our salvation*. This phrase succinctly summarized Athanasius's concern, that Christ could not have brought salvation if he were only a creature, for only God can save.

The Nicene formula of 325 did not immediately win the consent of the church. Arius's logic continued to exert appeal, and for the next fifty years, heated debate continued. Soon after the council concluded, Athanasius, contributor to Nicene faith as well as its champion defender, succeeded Bishop Alexander upon his death. For the next fifty years, however, no one could predict who would win in the struggle with Arianism. During these decades, Athanasius was banished no fewer than five times, each banishment and return to Alexandria representing either a change in emperors or a shift in the palace ecclesiastical elite. When Athanasius and other anti-Arians made it clear that "one substance" did not deny the separate person and work of Father, Son, and Holy Spirit, the Nicene statement eventually began to win acceptance. Finally, at a council called in 381 at Constantinople by Emperor Theodosius, the assembled bishops reaffirmed the main propositions of the Nicene statement and produced the slightly modified version that is now known as the Nicene Creed. This version also included a fuller statement on the Holy Spirit, clarifying that even as Jesus was fully divine, so was the Spirit.

The Trinity continues to mystify Christians. Sometimes it is helpful to clarify by using analogies found in nature, such as the yolk, white, and shell of an egg; the root, tree, and fruit of a plant; or water in its three forms of ice, liquid, and vapor. These are all useful as illustrations, but they miss completely the personal element in the Christian doctrine of the Trinity. Since Christians traditionally view God as personal, various social analogies have been proposed. Augustine used the psychological analogy. He believed that if humans are created in the image of God, they are created in the image of the Trinity. His psychological analogy for the Trinity came from the human mind: God, he said, is like the memory, intelligence, and will resident within the human mind.

Between 325 and 381, when the Second Ecumenical Council of the church met at Constantinople, leaders in the debate clarified their use of the term "person." Two quite distinct approaches gradually emerged, one associated with the eastern, and the other with the western, churches. The eastern position, which continues to be important within the Greek and Russian Orthodox churches, was developed by a group of three writers, known collectively as the Cappadocian Fathers—Gregory of Nazianzus, Gregory of Nyssa, and Basil the Great. They settled on the formula: God is one divine Being in three persons. However, the word "person" did not mean to them what it means today. To us, a person means someone like Tom, Dick, or Jane. However, the Latin word *persona* originally meant a mask worn by an actor on the stage. Rather than focus on the nature of God, they considered how God is experienced. The western position, especially associated with Augustine, begins from the unity of God, and proceeds to explore the implications of the love of God for our understanding of the nature of the Godhead. Augustine developed the idea of relation within the Godhead, arguing that the persons of the Trinity are defined by their relation to one another. The Father is the lover, the Son the beloved, and the Spirt is the "bond of love" between Father and Son.

Ultimately, of course, analogies fall short of reality, though they are useful when finite human beings seek to speak about the mystery that is God.

Doctrinal Development from Nicaea to Chalcedon

While theologians continued to probe the mystery of the Trinity, the Christological debate continued over a century and became the primary passion in the churches of the east. Between 350 and 450 numerous heresies arose, each proposed as a means to greater clarity in pursuit of the question, "Who is Jesus Christ?"

The first position advanced and rejected was associated with a priest named Apollinaris, a younger friend of Athanasius. Using a psychological explanation, he described human nature as embracing body (the physical part) and soul (the animating and rational part). At the incarnation, he suggested, the divine Word (Logos) displaced the soul, creating a "unity of nature" between the Word (Christ) and the body (Jesus). In this manner he was able to stress the deity of Christ and the body as representing Christ's human nature. Objections arose, questioning the humanity of Jesus, and whether such an arrangement fully redeemed humanity. Without complete solidarity with humanity, could the Word secure salvation? In 381, the Council of Constantinople silenced the Apollinarian teaching as an inadequate description of the incarnation.

A second heresy was associated with Nestorius, bishop of Constantinople. Nestorius, a monk at Antioch before becoming patriarch of Constantinople, rejected a popular designation of Mary as *theotokos* (the "bearer of God"). Although he did not deny the deity of Christ, his controversial notion (called *Christokos*) maintained the absolute separation of Christ's two natures. His views made it appear that he viewed the two natures of Christ as a merging of wills rather than as an essential union. Due more to political than doctrinal reasons, Nestorius incurred the hostility of Cyril, the patriarch of Alexandria. Cyril was a distinguished preacher and theologian, but ruthless in debates. At the Ecumenical Council of Ephesus (431), called by Emperor Theodosius II, who until then had supported Nestorius, Cyril got Nestorius deposed before the late arrival of his supporters. Chaos ensued, and eventually Theodosius surrendered to pressure and expelled Nestorius. Nestorius died around 450, an exile in Egypt. His supporters, however, refused to accept his excommunication. Many fled to Persia, founding there the Nestorian Church, which soon enjoyed an active life. Nestorian missionaries traveled east, penetrating India, Tibet, and eventually China. In his autobiography, Nestorius insisted that he did not oppose the use of "God-bearer" because he denied the deity of Christ, but rather to emphasize that Jesus was born as a genuine human being with body and soul. Nevertheless, even if unfairly, the church has attributed the name Nestorius to the failure to view the divine and human natures as truly united. In modern times, liberal views of Christ are labeled as Nestorian, particularly those that affirm that if only the willpower of the human Jesus held him in a moral union with divine Word, then the difference between Christians and Christ is one of degree. According to "degree Christology," Jesus was not truly divine but only a lofty picture of humanity: Jesus is a human model but not a divine savior.

Soon after the Council of Ephesus a third heresy arose, spearheaded by Eutyches, the spiritual leader of a monastery near Constantinople. He defended the one nature in Christ (a view known as monophysitism), combining the two natures so intimately that the human nature appeared completely absorbed by the divine one. In minimizing the human nature of Jesus, Eutyches thus jeopardized the Christian doctrine of redemption.

To deal with Eutyches, Patriarch Flavian of Constantinople convened a synod, which condemned Eutyches as a heretic. Eutyches, however, found support in Dioscorus, patriarch of Alexandria, who persuaded Emperor Theodosius II to summon an imperial council. The council assembled under Dioscorus's leadership in Ephesus (449) and vindicated Eutyches, even though this council was not recognized by the rest of the church. Pope Leo called it the "Robber Council" and asked the emperor for a new council. The successor of Theodosius, Emperor Marcian (450–457), granted the request and in 451 called the Fourth Ecumenical Council of Chalcedon.

At this town near Constantinople, some four hundred bishops gathered and quickly indicted Dioscorous for his actions at the robber council. Rejecting monophysitism, the council supplemented Nicaea with a new christological statement, acknowledging Jesus Christ "at once complete in Godhead and complete in manhood, truly God and truly man." The view, known as "hypostatic union" or diophysitism, became the classic Christian position, summarized in the doctrine of the two natures, perfectly divine and perfectly human. While affirming the centrality of the two natures of Jesus Christ for the church, the Chalcedonian creed established the boundaries of christological truth, wisely noting that so long as we recognize that Jesus Christ is both truly divine and truly human, the precise manner in which this is articulated or explored is not of fundamental importance.

Many Christians in the Eastern Empire, however, rejected this position. They maintained the monophysite teaching that instead of the divine and human natures joining to form one person in Jesus, he possessed one nature in which the divine and human were indistinguishable. This teaching was an important factor contributing to the breaking away of the Monophysite Churches from the rest of Eastern Orthodoxy. Coupled with the decline of the Byzantine power in the outlying areas of the Eastern Empire, monophysite doctrine led to the Coptic Church in Egypt and to the so-called Jacobite Church of Syria, with most of its adherents in India.

Historians acknowledge that the battles surrounding the great councils were fueled as much by personal and episcopal factors as by theology. Alexandria and Antioch had long been arrayed against each other as centers of influence in the early church. This can be seen in their interpretation of scripture as well as in their Christology. While the Christian intellectuals at Alexandria emphasized the allegorical interpretation and tended toward a Christology that emphasized the union of the human and the divine, those in Antioch held to a more literal and occasionally typological exegesis and thus to a Christology that emphasized the distinction between the human and the divine in the person of Jesus Christ. Those who emphasized his divinity tended to ignore his humanity (Alexandrians), whereas those who emphasized his humanity did not deny his divinity, but simply distinguished between his divinity and humanity (Antiochenes).

Alexandria and Antioch often competed to exert controlling influence over Constantinople, important due to the presence of the Roman emperor. The various archbishops of Constantinople were often in a position to decisively tip the balance of power. To heighten an already contentious situation, the three major Eastern centers competed against one another to enlist support from the bishop of Rome, who was traditionally recognized as the key church leader in the West. Although the Roman church was never as fully engaged in detailed christological argument as Antioch, Alexandria, or Constantinople, the judgments of Rome were always deemed significant. Unfortunately, the theological quarrelling that characterized the eastern part of the Christian world eventually weakened Christianity in that region and prepared the way for the eventual triumph of Islam.

According to church historian Mark Noll, Chalcedon represented a threefold triumph: (a) of sound doctrine over error in the church; (b) of catholicity over cultural fragmentation; and (c) of discriminating theological reasoning that led to a balanced use of faith and reason. The great significance of Chalcedon for later church history was to condemn extreme Alexandrian and Antiochene theology. Chalcedon's insistence on both the integrity of Christ's person and the duality of his natures established an important guide for Christian life in the world. It failed to solve the problem of how deity can unite with humanity in a single person, however, for at the human level, that problem resists explanation.

Augustine's Theological Legacy

One of the most influential Christian thinkers of all time, Augustine was born in 354 in Tagaste, a North African town built by the Romans. Augustine's father, Patricius, owned a small farm and a few slaves. Though he was harsh and uncompromising, he was unconcerned about morality and allowed his son unlimited personal freedom. By contrast, Augustine's mother, Monica, was a devout Christian. The couple was determined to give Augustine the best education available. When he was sixteen, his father died, but due to the patronage of a benefactor, Augustine furthered his schooling in Carthage. There he fell in love with a girl who gave him a son. They lived together for thirteen years, but this experience colored his conception of sin, and it marked the depravity from which he later felt himself rescued by God's grace.

For a time he tried Manichaeism, which taught that the universe was the scene of an eternal conflict of two powers, one good and the other evil. Humans are a mixture of these elements, the spiritual part of his nature is good and the physical is evil. Salvation comes from right thinking and an ascetic rejection of physical appetites and desires. Like Gnosticism, Manichaeism taught that the spiritual Jesus had no material body and did not actually die. His purpose was to teach human beings the way out of the kingdom of darkness into the kingdom of light. Augustine remained a Manichean until the age of thirty, when he moved to Rome. Soon after his arrival in the capital, he secured a professorship in Milan. Despite great success, he was deeply dissatisfied with his life. He began to attend church, where he listened to the sermons of Bishop Ambrose. When he was thirty-two years old, a friend challenged him to answer the question, "What am I doing on this earth?" After his friend left, Augustine went out into his garden and heard the voice of a child playing nearby. When the child cried, "Take up and read," Augustine found the nearest book, a Bible, and opened it at random to read Paul's words, "Not in reveling and drunkenness, not in debauchery and licentiousness, not in quarreling and jealousy. Instead, put on the Lord Jesus Christ, and make no provision for the flesh, to gratify its desires" (Rom. 13:13–14). Instantly he was converted. The following Easter he was baptized by Ambrose.

Shortly thereafter Augustine returned to Africa, and in response to a need in the town of Hippo, he went to serve the Christians there. Four years later, amid great jubilation, Augustine was ordained a priest and a year later, bishop. For the next thirty-three years, until his death in 430, he remained in this small town, addressing the doctrinal questions of his time. Of his 230 books, the three most important are his *Confessions*, *On the Trinity*, and *The City of God*. When he first became a Christian, he sought to synthesize Greek and biblical thought. But as he grew in understanding, he differentiated more and more between its teachings and Greek ideas until his mature theological thought was consistently biblical.

When he stepped into church leadership, North African Christianity was torn by a passionate conflict between Catholics and a movement called Donatism. The movement stood for a holy church, for church discipline, and for resistance to immoral priests and unworthy bishops. Augustine rejected the Donatist's view of a pure church, arguing that until the day of judgment, the institutional church must remain a mixed multitude. Both good and bad people are in it. Augustine also set forth a different understanding of the sacraments. The Donatists argued that the validity of the sacrament depends upon the moral standing of the minister. Augustine countered that the sacrament does not belong to the priest but to Christ's grace.

If the Donatist controversy called forth his pastoral skills, the Pelagian debate called forth his theological skills. Pelagius was a British monk who came to North Africa from Rome. There he encountered Augustine, who disagreed with his view of salvation by works. Pelagius headed east, which was more receptive to his teaching. Due to Augustine's strenuous objection, Pelaguis was banished by Emperor Honorius, and in 431 Pelagianism was condemned by the Ecumenical Council at Ephesus.

What was it about Pelagius that aroused such vigorous opposition? The monk began where Augustine did, arguing that humans were created good. However, he denied that human sin is inherited from Adam. A nature created by God, he argued, is non-controvertible (does not change). Hence, at every moment, humans are free to act righteously or sinfully. Adam did introduce sin into the world, but only by his corrupting example. Humans sin, Pelagius taught, when they go against their will, but their human will remains free to choose the good, and it does so when it follows reason. Thus, there is no compulsion in sin. Sin is willing to do what our reason forbids. If it is possible for humans not to sin, as Pelagius believed, then it follows that they can work out their own salvation.

All this was in sharp contrast to Augustine's own experience. He sensed profoundly the depth of his own sin and the greatness of God's salvation. It was grace that brought him away from his sin, and only constantly inflowing divine grace kept him in the Christian life. In Augustine's view, Adam's sin had enormous consequences. In a word, Adam died when he sinned—spiritually, and soon physically. In his response to Pelagius, Augustine formulated the doctrine of "original sin," arguing that the entire human race was "in Adam" and shared his fall. Named traducianism, this view maintains that sin passes on at conception. Using the analogy of a set of scales, Augustine argued that heavy weights have been place on the side of evil. The scales (human freedom) still work, but they are seriously biased toward sin.

Pelagius was condemned for minimizing sin and dismissing the need for God's grace. Augustine's response emphasized the centrality of grace, namely, that God determines who will be saved, surrounding them with special influences, and justice condemns the rest. God is not to be accused of unfairness in choosing some to salvation. Rather God is to be praised for both justice and grace. Pelagians disagreed with Augustine's emphasis on grace, predestination, and original sin, complaining that Augustine had exaggerated human sinfulness and broken the longstanding practice of embracing human freedom.

Modern Christianity, strongly influenced by Augustine, has built heavily on this sense of human alienation from God, portraying Christ as a savior dispatched to overcome alienation. This view, known as atonement theology, reflects the idea of a fall from original goodness, a way of reading the Garden of Eden account found in Genesis 3. Atonement theology, however, is at odds with biology, psychology, and anthropology, misunderstanding the symbolic nature of the creation story. Atonement theology assumes that humans were created in some kind of original perfection, but biology indicates that life emerged from a single cell that evolved into self-conscious complexity over billions of years. If the scientific approach, which denies original perfection, is accurate, then there could never have been a fall. And if there was no fall, then there is no such thing as "original sin" from which humans need to be rescued.

Questioning atonement theology does not deny that evil is not real, or that it should be minimized. Evil is all around us, even deep within, but it doesn't stem from a mythical fall from perfection. Rather it originates in the biological drive to survive. It is this instinct, this self-centered drive, rooted in human biology, that ancient religious mythmakers tried to describe.

Jews tend to see the Garden of Eden story not as a narrative about sin entering the world, but as a parable about the birth of self-consciousness. It is, for them, not a fall into sin, but a step into humanity, human beings leaving the comfort and security of childhood and becoming adults, assuming responsibility for their freely made decisions. The primary thing one gains from eating the fruit of the tree of knowledge is insight, the ability to make freely informed decisions. To be forced out of the Garden was not a punishment for sin so much as it was a step into maturity.

In the fourth century, Gentiles were Latin-speaking legalists, not Hebrew-speaking mythmakers. As inheritors of the Greek perspective, they saw the world not as a unity but as a duality. As good was separate from evil, so God was separate from the world. Bodies and souls were antithetical concepts. Flesh and spirit, body and soul, were antithetical concepts, locked in a dualistic war. That was the matrix in which what we now call "traditional Christianity" came to be understood. This was the mindset when the councils adopted creeds, created doctrines, and formulated dogma.

Despite his controversial teachings on original sin, Augustine more fully than any of his predecessors explained how God exists as a Trinity and how God's grace is the source of humanity's salvation.

The Canonical Process

Most religious communities have a list of scriptures considered binding or authoritative. Such a collection is called a "canon," a concept derived from a Greek word meaning "measuring device" or "ruler." As applied to religious literature, it refers to the rule or standard of authority for belief and practice. Arriving at a definitive canon or binding list of scriptures involves judging the authenticity, doctrinal soundness, and communal acceptance of texts. While Jews and Christians have a "closed" canon, meaning that no books may be added or deleted from that official collection of writings, this does not mean that their religious communities always agree about which books they include in their respective canons, the form of those books, or the order in which those books occur.

By the start of the first century CE, when Christianity emerged, most Jews subscribed to the special authority of the Torah. Not all accepted the authority of the Prophets (for example the Sadducees did not), but most mainline Jews, including the Pharisees, certainly did. Jesus quoted from some of these books, as did Paul and other New Testament authors, so we can assume that all accepted them as authoritative. The third part, the Writings, was not yet completed in the first century, but one of its major components, the book of Psalms, was already in use in synagogue worship. Indeed, this book was so important that the third part of the Jewish canon could be referred to simply as "the Psalms." This usage is found in Luke's Gospel, from the late first century, which refers to "the Law of Moses, the Prophets, and the Psalms" (Luke 24:44).

It is no surprise that a faith firmly anchored in the sacred texts of its parent religion would develop scriptures of its own. Christians did develop their own scriptures, but not immediately. The first generation proclaimed its message almost exclusively by word of mouth and saw no pressing need to assemble its own sacred tradition, since it expected Christ to return shortly. As the expected return of Christ was delayed, and as the number of believers continued to expand, the need for written documents became manifest. With the passing of the first generation of Christians, the need arose to preserve those crucial stories and lessons that had given shape to their community; continuity and order were at stake.

Near the end of the first century, Christians were citing Jesus' words and calling them "scripture" (see 1 Tim. 5:18). Furthermore, some of Jesus' followers, such as the apostle Paul, understood themselves to be authoritative spokespersons for the truth (Gal. 1:8–12). Paul's letters, written occasionally to specific congregations and individuals, were reverently saved and shared with Christians in other places. Shortly thereafter they began to assume the authority of scripture, at least among some Christians (2 Pet. 3:16). In fact, Paul's authority was becoming so significant that documents written by others were being ascribed to him (see 2 Thess. 2:2; also the Pastoral Epistles and disputed letters like Hebrews, which some Bibles attribute to Paul). In the next century a host of additional gospels, epistles, and apocalypses appeared, vying for authenticity. The author of Luke's Gospel openly admits that "many writers" had preceded him in the attempt to "draw up an account of the things that have happened among us" (Luke 1:1).

By the third century, more than twenty gospels were in circulation, all claiming, like the *Gospel of Peter* or the *Gospel of Philip*, apostolic derivation. Notable among them was the *Gospel of Thomas*, consisting exclusively of isolated saying attributed to Jesus. As previously noted, the abundance of gospels was due mostly to the growth of Gnostic sects within Christianity, especially in the second century. The vast majority of Gnostics were "dualists," believing that human beings were spiritual entities trapped in an evil material world, and that they could be freed, or saved, only through secret knowledge. They shared in common a tendency to produce texts that claimed to distill new revelation. It is no coincidence that the first lists of scripture began to appear among orthodox scholars and theologians shortly after the emergence of Gnostic sects.

The process that led to the formation of the Christian canon is complex but fascinating. The four Gospels now found in the New Testament, together with the other canonical writings, may have been produced by diverse, even antithetical communities, but all were viewed to be sufficiently orthodox to make the final cut. However, during the second, third, and fourth centuries, Christians continued to debate the acceptability of certain writings. The arguments centered on three criteria:

- *Apostolicity*: the book in question had to have derived from the initial community of Jesus and his disciples.

- *Orthodoxy*; the book in question had to be valued as inspired and revelatory, that is, as derived directly from God and hence harmonious with the rest of the New Testament.

- *Catholicity*; the book in question had to be accepted and used by a wide range of communities, especially those considered authoritative or apostolic.

At first, a local church would have only a few apostolic letters and perhaps one or two Gospels. During the course of the second century most churches came to possess and acknowledge a canon that included the present four Gospels, the Acts, thirteen letters attributed to Paul, 1 Peter, and 1 John. Seven books still lacked general recognition: Hebrews, James, 2 Peter, 2 and 3 John, Jude, and Revelation. On the other hand, certain Christian writings, such as the first letter of Clement, the letter of Barnabas, the *Shepherd* of Hermas, and the *Didache*, were accepted as authoritative by several ecclesiastical writers, though rejected by the majority.

Paradoxically, Marcion, the second-century heretical Christian preacher, was responsible for the first canon of the New Testament. Unable to reconcile the Old Testament's portrayal of God as violent and vengeful with the New Testament's portrayal of God as good and loving, he created a restrictive canon that excluded all of the Old Testament and any Christian literature that had Jewish overtones. Marcion's teaching prompted a hearing before other clergy in Rome that resulted in his condemnation. Soon afterward, other church leaders began to form their own canons or lists of approved books. The most famous of these is the Muratorian Canon, dated to the church at Rome circa 190. It included the four Gospels, the Acts of the Apostles, thirteen letters attributed to Paul, Jude, and 1 and 2 John, as well some books that were later excluded, including the *Apocalypse of Peter* and the *Wisdom of Solomon*. What is unusual about the latter is that despite being a Jewish work, written prior to the birth of Christianity (in the first century BCE), it was listed as a Christian text.

Strangely, the development of a definitive canon of scripture took orthodox Christians nearly four centuries to complete. The earliest surviving list to include all twenty-seven books now known as the New Testament is from the year 367, appearing in an Easter letter written by Athanasius, bishop of Alexandria, to congregations in the eastern section of the church. In the west, the twenty-seven books of the New Testament were accepted at the subsequent councils of Hippo (393) and Carthage (397).

One highly important development was the translation of the Bible into Latin, which had replaced Greek as the language best known in the western part of the empire. About 386 an ascetic monk named Jerome took up residence in a cave in Bethlehem, where he founded a fellowship of monks. There had previously been some translations into Latin, most of them from the Septuagint, the Greek version of the Old Testament. Jerome, however was well versed in the Greek and Hebrew languages, and was determined to translate from the Hebrew and Greek originals. His work was called the Vulgate, that is, the Bible for the common people, the vulgar. Though at first many rejected it, for the next thousand years the Vulgate became the Bible throughout the church in western Europe. While Jerome rejected the apocryphal books as authoritative, they were added at the insistence of some bishops. Thus they became part of the church's canon (at the time of the Reformation, Protestants rejected the authority of the apocryphal writings on the grounds that they were not part of the original Hebrew Bible).

The Beginnings of the Papacy

Increasing instability of the empire in the west forced Christianity to engage new cultural realities and to forge a distinctively Christian culture as an instrument of civilization among converted barbarians. The Western Empire had become a shadow of its former self. In 452, Attila the Hun led his cavalry and well-armed foot soldiers out of central Asia to invade the Western Roman Empire. As he advanced on Rome, he met little resistance. The weakened Roman army kept out of range and the population fled. At a fordable spot on the Po River, Attila met an embassy from Rome. When Attila heard that Bishop Leo was there as emissary for the Roman emperor, he decided to negotiate. The contest seemed unequal, but in the end, Rome was spared. The bishop of Rome had assumed a new role and staked a fresh claim on the future.

The papacy is a controversial subject. No other institution has been so loved and so hated. Whatever one thinks of the medieval papacy, all sides agree that Pope Leo represents an important stage in the history of this unique institution. He demonstrates the papacy's long-standing capacity to adapt to different environments, developing policy for the modern world and even for the developing nations of Asia and Africa.

According to the official teaching of the Roman Catholic Church, defined at the First Vatican Council (1870), Jesus Christ established the papacy with the apostle Peter, and the bishop of Rome as Peter's successor bears supreme authority (primacy) over the whole church. Both Eastern Orthodox churches and Protestant denominations reject these claims. Whatever the claims of church authorities, history indicates that the concept of papal rule was established slowly over time. Leo was a major figure in that process because he provided for the first time the biblical and theological bases of the papal claim.

The Roman church, of course, had been prominent among the churches of the western regions of the empire from the start. The first reason is linked to the city itself. Rome was the imperial capital, and the church of Rome the largest and wealthiest church in the west. By the middle of the third century its membership approached 30,000, with a staff of 150 clerics. Tradition was also a significant factor. Beginning with Irenaeus in the second century, several early Christian writers referred to Peter and Paul as founders of the church in Rome, and to subsequent bishops as successors of the apostles.

Rome's growing influence was a part of the increasingly complex church structure emerging in the third and fourth centuries. As the church grew it adopted the structure of the empire. This meant that the provincial town of the empire became the episcopal town of the church. As the empire was divided into several major regions, so within the church people came to think of the church at Rome exercising authority over surrounding regions. The Council of Nicaea recognized the bishops of Alexandria, Antioch, and Rome as preeminent in their own areas. Jerusalem was granted an honorary primacy. Thus, by 325 the policy of patriarchates, that is, the administration of church affairs by bishops from three or four major cities, was confirmed by conciliar action.

Before his election to the papal office, Leo, a nobleman, had been sent by the emperor to Gaul to arbitrate a dispute. When the bishop of Rome died, Leo was appointed in his stead. In the sermon he preached on the day of his entrance into office, he extolled the "glory of the blessed Apostle Peter . . . in whose chair his power lives on and his authority shines forth." From that point on, the city that had once enjoyed the favor as capital of the empire, the scene of the martyrdom of Peter and Paul, now had a powerful new leader. He carried the papacy as far theoretically as it could go. His argument for the papacy was opportune—he was the right person at the right time—and convincing to a Roman audience bewildered by Rome's military and political ineffectiveness. The barbarian attacks in Italy made the imperial court located at Ravenna, on the eastern coast of the peninsula, desperate for the support of any authority that might help to keep the Western Empire together. To ensure the bishop's support, the emperor gave Leo significant authority. Thus in 445 Emperor Valentinian III issued a decree supporting the primacy of the Roman See, claiming "the only way to safeguard peace among the churches everywhere is to acknowledge its leadership universally." Leo's vision of the papacy had the support not only of the emperor but also of the bishops meeting at Chalcedon.

Significantly, the Council of Chalcedon, called to defend the true faith against false interpretations of the life of Jesus Christ, gave the bishop of Constantinople authority equal to Leo's. Constantinople became for the East what Rome was for the West.

Decline and Fall of Rome

In 455 a fresh enemy threatened Rome. This time it was the Vandals, a migrating tribe from Scandinavia driven southwestward by the Goths advancing from Hungary. The Vandals, expelled for a time from Europe, settled in North Africa, waiting for the right moment to strike at Rome. At the end of March, a hundred ships sailed up the Tiber River, manned by Carthaginian sailors. On June 2 the Vandals entered Rome, meeting no resistance. The Vandals plundered systematically, taking material treasure and political prisoners held for ransom. For fourteen days they occupied the city before withdrawing to Carthage.

In 476 Romulus Augustulus, the last emperor of Rome was deposed, bringing to an end a thousand-year era of Roman political rule. After his abdication, the Roman Senate sent representatives to the Eastern Roman Emperor Zeno, formally requesting reunion. The West, governed by Germanic rulers, seemingly no longer required an emperor; one monarch sufficed. The so-called fall of the (Western) Roman Empire raised significant questions for the church. Was its future bright or bleak? How would it react to change, by withdrawing from secular society, or through growth and expansion? For a time the future of imperial Christianity lay to the east, in the great patriarchal centers of the emerging Byzantine Empire. The church also looked northward. The conversion of barbarian kingdoms would initiate yet another phase in the history of Christendom, the establishment of the so-called Holy Roman Empire.

Study Questions

1. Whom do you consider the chief protagonist in the first phase of Christendom (fourth and fifth centuries CE)? Support your answer.

2. Do you agree with the author's choice that the Council of Chalcedon is this epoch's turning point? Why or why not? Is there another event you consider more significant? If so, what is it? Support your choice.

3. In this epoch, does "the church" live up to its nature and destiny as God's new creation? Why or why not?

4. In your estimation, how was the accession of Constantine to the throne good for the church, and how was it dangerous?

5. In what sense, if any, does it seem to you that the church is "the city of God," in sharp contrast to any "city of this world"?

6. If you had been a participant at the Council of Nicaea, on whose side would you have stood, with Arius, Athanasius, or somewhere in between? Explain your answer.

7. Compare the original purpose of the early creeds with the role they played later in the history of the church.

8. Does a standard for orthodoxy exist in the church today? If so, what is its basis of authority? How does your definition of the church affect your answer?

9. How do your beliefs square with Augustine's on original sin, predestination, and grace? On the Augustinian-Pelagian spectrum, where do you place yourself and your beliefs? Support your answer.

10. What forces were at work in the development of the Christian canon?

11. Discuss the role Leo the Great played in establishing the papacy. What role does the papacy play in our world? Should Protestants have an authoritative body equivalent to the Vatican? Why or why not?

Chapter 6

Phase 6: Christendom II (476–1095)

Latins, Byzantines, and Barbarians

Significant Event: The rise of Islam in the seventh and eighth centuries—culminating in its advance across North Africa into Spain and France—and its defeat at the battle of Poitiers in 732. Second in importance is the Great Schism of 1054, which led to the permanent division between Eastern and Western Christianity and to the eventual collapse of the Byzantine Empire at the fall of Constantinople in 1453.

Turning Point: The coronation of Charlemagne as Holy Roman emperor in the year 800, a crowning achievement for the papacy and the establishment of Latin Christendom across Europe.

Among the many important ecclesiastical developments and events during the sixth through the eleventh centuries, the following helped shape the church's conception of faith, vocation, and governance:

1. The papacy of Gregory the Great

2. Monasticism

3. Missionary expansion

4. The Holy Roman Empire

5. Eastern Christianity under Byzantine emperors

6. The rise of Islam

When the barbarians destroyed the Roman Empire in the West, the Christian church put together a new order called Europe. The underlying concept was Christendom, which united empire and church. Inspired by Old Testament theocratic society (a covenantal community under the rule of God) but likely also by centuries of Roman imperial rule, Latin Christendom began under Charlemagne in the eighth century. The road ahead, for both empire and papacy, would be uneven, rutted, and rocky. The journey would be powered by monastic zeal and missionary expansion but also threatened by a common foe, a militant faith known as Islam.

The Papacy of Gregory the Great

The previous chapter introduced the papacy, highlighting the role of Leo the Great, who contributed greatly to the expansion of papal authority in the West, not only because of his strategic role in defending Rome against invaders, but because of his critical contribution to the Council of Chalcedon, establishing papal primacy in dialogue with the patriarch of Constantinople. Expanding earlier papal efforts, Leo articulated Matthew 16:18 as a foundation undergirding the authority of the Roman bishops as successors of St. Peter. In addition, Leo obtained from the emperor an edict that defined the superiority of the pope over all other Western bishops in matters related to civil law.

Despite such weighty accomplishments, the early papacy reached its summit in the pontificate of Gregory I (590–604), also styled "the Great." One of the most revered of all popes, Gregory was thrust into the spotlight at a most inopportune time, for Rome was suffering the effects of floods, the atrocities of war, and the spread of the plague. Carts were piled high with corpses, and people were going insane. For six months no pope ruled the Vatican. When church leaders elected Gregory pope, he refused and fled. Nevertheless he returned, and was consecrated pope in 590.

An unlikely candidate for greatness, he proved a worthy successor to St. Peter. The plague continued to ravage the city, but after a public act of humiliation, led by Gregory, it seemed to subside. A later legend traced the staying of the calamity to the appearance of the archangel Michael, who placed his drawn sword into its sheath over the mausoleum of Emperor Hadrian. Since that time Romans have called Hadrian's mausoleum the Castle of St. Angelo. They adorned it with a statue of the angel, a site on the banks of the Tiber still visited by the faithful.

At his death in 604, Gregory's epitaph proclaimed him "God's Consul," for few rulers combined such executive ability with sympathy for human need. Earlier, at the age of 33, Gregory found that Emperor Justin had appointed him prefect (mayor) of Rome, the highest civil position in the city. The whole economy of Rome rested on his shoulders. Despite great administrative ability, Gregory was not comfortable with worldly power. Within a few years he stepped down from public office and spent the greater part of his personal fortune in founding seven monasteries. He distributed the rest to the poor, and at his father's death, he transformed his father's palace into a Benedictine monastery. His talents, however, were needed yet again, and in 579 Pope Pelagius II made him a deacon of the Roman church and in that capacity sent him as ambassador to the imperial court in Constantinople. Upon his return six years later, he was appointed abbot of his convent, until 590, when the plague took the life of Pope Pelagius.

Soon after Gregory's election, the Lombards laid siege to Rome. The devastation was immense, so great that everyone thought the end of the world was at hand. The church at Rome survived these attacks, however, in large measure due to Gregory's wise leadership and hands-on approach, personally overseeing Roman defenses against the attacks of the Lombards. Having secured peace, he then dedicated himself to restore order in society. He carried out complicated negotiations with the emperor in Constantinople, reformed the finances of the church, and dedicated himself to church worship. His efforts in promoting church music lent his name to the "Gregorian chants" that still influence sacred music. He was also highly regarded as a preacher and pastor, setting forth the principles for Christian ministry in his *Pastoral Rule*.

As if this were not enough, Gregory also oversaw important adjustments in the church's missionary strategy. His endeavors led to the conversion to orthodoxy of Arian Visigoths in Spain. Most famously, he sent a Benedictine monk named Augustine (later called "Augustine of Canterbury," to distinguish him from the great North African theologian) to England, which led to the conversion of the Angles and Saxons and also to Augustine's appointment as the first archbishop of Canterbury.

Gregory's pontificate established the norm for the Middle Ages, for despite his immense accomplishments, he seems to have remained a humble, pious Christian, something church leaders should emulate.

Monasticism

The topic of monasticism is controversial among Christians. Roman Catholics see the church as big enough to include both ascetics, who strive for spiritual perfection, and weak and sinful members, who strive for consistency. The church, they say, must be for all, regardless of moral attainments or spiritual failures. The Reformers of the sixteenth century felt differently. Monasticism, they said, encourages the idea of two paths to God, a higher and a lower. However, the gospel knows only one way to salvation, faith in Jesus Christ. Such faith, certainly, cannot be dead; it must be active in love for God and one's neighbor.

The desire for an extreme existence among some Christians seems consistent with elements in the New Testament that exhort believers "not to be conformed to this age" (Rom. 12:2), and with images of the first believers as sharing possessions and having nothing they called their own (Acts 2:44–45; 4:32–35). Some precedents existed in Judaism—such as the Essenes, who lived communally and on the margins of society—and in the Greek world, where philosophical schools often "lived apart" in community. The Epicureans and the Pythagoreans had a long history of "life together" outside the bounds of ordinary society, in some cases even sharing possessions.

The first form of monasticism was the lonely hermit (the word "hermit" comes from the Greek word for desert, and is a reminder that the monastic life began in Egypt, where a short journey either east or west from the narrow Nile River puts one in a rigorous desert). Antony (250–355), inspired by a sermon on Christ's words to the rich young ruler ("go, sell what you own, and give the money to the poor," Mark 10:21), took this literally and departed into the desert, living the life of solitude in a tomb. Later legends recount his battles with temptation and wild beasts, but despite such stress, he lived a full life of 105 years. His example proved contagious, for he had hundreds of imitators.

Around the year 320, a former soldier named Pachomius instituted the first Christian monastery. Instead of permitting the monks to live singly or in groups of hermits, he established a regulated common life, in which the monks ate, labored, and worshiped according to a fixed plan. From these beginnings in Egypt, the ascetic movement spread to Syria, to Asia Minor, and eventually throughout Western Europe. The monastic ideal in the East was spread through the influence of Basil the Great, who died in

379, whose *Rule of Discipline* continues to guide Greek Orthodox monasticism to this day.

The first to introduce monasticism to the West was Athanasius. In 335, when he was banished to Trier (in modern Germany), he was accompanied by two monks. The circulation of his *Life of Saint Antony* helped spread the monastic ideal. Augustine, bishop of Hippo, wrote the first western monastic rule for his community of clerics. In 415 the monk John Cassian founded a monastery near Marseille and wrote valuable books on meditation. The greatest contributor to Western monasticism, however, was Benedict of Nursia (480–550), whose *Rule* provided the constitution for Western monasticism and gave it its motto—*orare et laborare*—prayer and labor. In 529 he moved with a small group of disciples to Monte Cassino, eighty-five miles southeast of Rome, where he founded what became the most famous monastery in Europe, the motherhouse of the Benedictine order. Soon he was joined by his sister, Scholastica, who established a similar community for women. Beginning in the sixth century, Benedict's model would guide thousands of monasteries and convents throughout the world and into the twenty-first century. Benedict's only contemporary rival was the Celtic monasticism inspired by St. Patrick (c. 387–461) in the fifth century and spread by St. Columba (521–597) from the famous monastery of Iona off the coast of Scotland.

Benedictine monasteries became worlds in themselves, in which the monks committed themselves to three virtues: obedience, silence, and humility. Benedict's *Rule* also called monks to be involved in practical labor as part of their spiritual endeavors. Every Benedictine monastery included a library, and monks soon copied and read the great works of antiquity. We are indebted to them for preserving the writings of the Latin church fathers and the masterpieces of Roman literature. Monasteries also became a great missionary force, rendering immense service in the spread and development of Christianity and of civilization during the darkest ages of European history.

The study of monasticism leads to speculation about its origins and success. Conditions in the fourth and fifth centuries provided powerful motivations for the spread of monasticism. The persecutions under Decius and Diocletian took place at the same time that economic difficulties disoriented traditional patterns of life throughout many parts of the Roman Empire. Some monks, like Antony, left cities for the wilderness, departing a world in disarray. Much more important for the spread of monasticism, however, was reaction to Christendom and growing worldliness in the church. Monks came to see themselves as "athletes of God," robustly pursuing the true Christian faith. By following ideals such as self-sacrifice, hospitality to strangers, and humility, as well by promoting disciplines like prayer and study of the scriptures, the monks became the conscience of the church. They were not always perfect; at times discipline grew lax, and despite monks taking vows of poverty, the monasteries often grew immensely rich through gifts, especially of land, but the history of the Middle Ages shows constant effort toward their reform, often through the foundation of new orders designed to eliminate the corruption of older ones.

Throughout the Middle Ages, the monastic life provided one of the few venues where women were allowed to participate in the religious life. Early praise for virginity played a part, especially after the Virgin Mary became prominent in the church's liturgy and theology. Thus Hildegard of Bingen (1098–1179), an early example of female leadership in a monastic setting, became founder and first abbess of a Benedictine community on the Rhine River. A Renaissance woman, she was renowned not only for her mystical visions but also for a remarkable set of writings on scientific, theological, and musical subjects. In addition, she provided advice to kings, bishops, and leaders of other monastic institutions, as evidenced by a significant body of letters.

The rise of monasticism may well be one of the most beneficial institutional events in the history of Christianity. For over a millennium, in the period between the reign of Constantine and the Protestant Reformation, almost everything in the church that approached the highest, noblest, and truest ideals of the gospel was done either by those who had chosen the monastic way or by those who had been inspired in their Christian life by monks. Protestantism, we might recall, began with the monastic experiences of Martin Luther. Luther and Calvin turned repeatedly to the work of Augustine, the learned bishop who founded a monastic order. In fact, Luther began his adult life as an Augustinian monk. Throughout the ages, monasticism provided an alternative lifestyle that enabled Christians to express discipleship in a more radical way. Monasteries became important centers for reform and in the early medieval period of the West, monks preserved learning, copying manuscripts and preserving for other Christians a great body of teaching about the discipline necessary to be an authentic Christian.

The breadth and depth of monastic influence in the church is comprehensive. If we read scripture in our native language, we benefit from a tradition inspired by the monk Jerome (342–420). If we sing hymns, we follow the pattern established by the monks Gregory (540–604) and Bernard of Clairvaux (1090–1153). If we pursue theology, we find ourselves indebted to the monks Augustine and Thomas Aquinas (1225–1274). If we focus on Christian missionaries, we think of efforts pioneered by the monks Patrick (387–461), Boniface (680–754), Cyril (826–869), and his brother Methodius (815–885). If we are interested in the early record of Christianity in English-speaking areas of the world, we cultivate a concern begun by a monk known as the Venerable Bede (673–735). If we relish in nature and its goodness, we follow the friar Francis of Assisi (1181–1226). Monasticism was not a perfect answer to the question of how to live the Christian life, but its impact has been sizeable.[1]

Missionary Expansion

Christians focus on the expansion of Christianity westward, from Jerusalem through Asia Minor to Rome, for that is the story told in the book of Acts (see 1:8). Christianity's westward march, however, was matched and possibly superseded initially by expansion eastward and southward, into Syria, Egypt, and beyond.

Christianity's Eastward Expansion in Asia

When the followers of Jesus were first forced to leave Jerusalem after its fall in 70 CE, one of the places to which they scattered was the Roman province of Syria. Its three major cities, Antioch, Damascus, and Edessa, figure prominently in early Christian history. Indeed, one could almost say that Christianity was born in Syria, because it was in Antioch that the name "Christian" was first used for the Jewish followers of Jesus (see Acts 11:26). Under a succession of notable bishops, the church in this third largest city of the empire took root and exerted widespread influence. By the end of the fourth century, Antioch was a city of half a million people, and half of these were Christians. Early translations of the Old and New Testaments were made into Syriac, a dialect of Aramaic. Because it was related to Aramaic

1. Noll, *Turning Points*, 79.

but distinct enough to allow for a new literary tradition to emerge that was identifiably Christian, Syriac became the language of choice among Christians in eastern Syria, Mesopotamia, Persia, and eventually India, Mongolia, and China.

During the second century, Christians expanded to Edessa in eastern Syria, beyond the border of the empire, but with close ties to Antioch. The kingdom of Edessa (technically called Oshroene), a small buffer state, remained independent until its absorption into the Roman Empire in 241. The capital city of Edessa contains the remains of a second-century church building, the oldest yet discovered, built at a time when, due to persecution, no such building was possible in the Roman Empire. A legend, found at the end of book one of Eusebius's *Ecclesiastical History*, claims that the founder of the church in Edessa had been one of the seventy disciples of Jesus (see Luke 10:1).

There is good reason to suppose that from Edessa some unknown Christian continued east until he came to India. So-called Thomas Christians in India today believe that that Christian was the apostle Thomas. That may be true. The oldest literary account of the apostle's missionary work in India is found in the *Acts of Thomas*, a document of unknown origin traced through early Syriac versions to fourth-century Edessa. Whatever its historicity, evidence confirms that items found in the Thomas story are plausible. A voyage by Thomas to south India in the first century was well within the realm of possibility. Whatever its origin, we can say with some certainty that the church in India has existed from very early times.

Between the third and fifth centuries, substantial territories and populations converted to Christianity. This usually happened when the king of a client state converted and then declared Christianity the new official religion of the realm. The kingdom of Armenia, a Roman client state adjacent to Asia Minor, made Christianity the official religion under King Tiridates III in 301, making Armenia the first kingdom to officially declare itself Christian. The kingdom of Georgia, formerly a Roman province, made Christianity the official religion sometime between 317 and 327. In Yemen, at the tip of the Arabian Peninsula, a Christian teacher established a Christian school around 400.

Christianity appeared in the Sassanid Kingdom of Persia in the third century, where it underwent a forty-year persecution before enjoying temporary royal favor. An important theological school developed at Nisibis. Persia eventually became the center of Nestorian Christianity, a branch of

Christendom persecuted by orthodox Christians for its emphasis on the humanity rather than the divinity of Christ. Nestorianism ultimately became the national Persian church, and the source of further missionary expansion eastward along the trade routes to the Far East.

From Edessa, Christianity spread to another small kingdom 300 miles further east, across the Tigris River, the kingdom of Adiabene, with its capital at Arbela, near ancient Nineveh. By the end of the second century missionary expansion carried the movement to Bactria (today's Afghanistan). It may well have been from Edessa that Christianity was taken north into the kingdom of Armenia and on into Georgia, just as it was carried through Persia to India and eventually to China. The fifth century witnessed the expansion of Christianity along the Silk Road, evidenced by mass conversions of Huns and Turks in Central Asia, and in 635, a missionary named Alopen introduced Christianity to the Chinese emperor. In 638 a church was erected in the capital of Ch'ang-an, perhaps the largest city in the world at the time. This expansion is all the more remarkable when we consider that it was around this time that Christianity was introduced to the king and council of Northumbria, in northern England.

Our knowledge of this ancient expansion of Christianity eastward has forced a reconception of the early church. If we place Edessa at the western end of a region, instead of at the eastern extremity, as generally presented in textbooks, a remarkable alternative Christian story unfolds. Early Christianity:

1. Spread down the Euphrates Valley until the majority of Mesopotamia (modern Iraq) was Christian.

2. Spread through the Arab buffer states of the Persian Empire.

3. Spread to Yemen, where it was adopted by the royal house.

4. Moved steadily into Iran and northward to the Caspian.

5. Spread beyond the Persia Empire, along the trade routes, by land and by sea.

6. Spread to Central Asia and Mongolia.

7. Reached China at an early age.

The eastward spread of Christianity continued through a period that in Western church history was one of loss and decline. The arrival of Islam in North Africa and the Middle East marked the beginning of a period of eclipse in that part of the world. Church historian Kenneth Scott Latourette called the period from 600 to 1600 CE the "thousand years of uncertainty." Yet further east, from the tenth through the fourteenth centuries, Christianity experienced growth and development. Up to the fourteenth century, the expansion of Christianity continued among the shamanistic Turks who bordered the Chinese Empire. A striking and unusual feature of this period was that Christianity became the faith of nomadic peoples. In the modern period, it is hard to find examples of nomadic communities that embrace Christianity and remain nomadic.

Contrary to popular thinking, early Christian presence in Asia is not marginal or ephemeral but substantial. The study of the eastward movement of Christianity indicates that prior to 1500, when Western Christian missions to Asia began, there had already been a millennium and a half of Christian history in Asia. Surprisingly, in the thirteenth century, the height of medieval Christian civilization in Europe, there may have been more Christians in Asia than in Europe.

Christianity's Southward Expansion in Africa

Christian presence in Africa is also often distorted. Other than the early centuries of the church in North Africa, the history of Christianity in that continent is rarely discussed, and if so, it is regularly treated as a product of Western Christianity, dating to the birth of the modern missionary movement in 1792. The truth is that Africa has a long-standing continuous Christian history that both predates Western missions to Africa and Islamic presence there.

Alexandria, the Egyptian port city at the mouth of the Nile, was a thriving commercial and intellectual metropolis during the first century CE. It had a large Jewish population at that time. Early Christian tradition credits Mark with being the apostle who first preached the gospel in Alexandria. By the middle of the second century a number of schools of Christian thought flourished in Alexandria, associated with the great Christian scholars Clement (150–215) and Origen (185–254). Farther west, in parts of North Africa we know as Tunis and Algeria, there were major centers of Christianity during Roman times. Here we find Latin-speaking churches and the great theologians Tertullian (160–220), Cyprian (d. 258), and Augustine (354–430).

Christianity in Egypt was not limited to those who spoke Greek. Translation of the scriptures into various dialects known as Coptic began around 250 CE. Around that time monks and hermits began to go to the desert. These were native Egyptians who spoke Coptic and knew little, if any, Greek. At least 10 percent of the modern population of Egypt make up the Coptic church, making it one of the largest Christian minorities of any Arabic nation today. Early on, Christianity became central to Nubia. The Christian community in what is now Sudan antedated the rise of Islam by 500 years, and for the next 500 years it occupied a unique place as a Christian state on the border of the Islamic world.

The greatest success story in Africa is not Egypt or Sudan, however, but Ethiopia (ancient Abyssinia), which became officially Christian in 330, where it quickly became independent and idiosyncratic. Mixed with Jewish and Islamic elements, Ethiopian Christianity thrives to the present, one of the longest continuous histories of Christianity. Ethiopian Christianity began early in the third century with two Syrian Christians, young merchants taken captive during a raid and sold to the Ethiopian court at Axum. The two youths, Frumentius and Aedesius, quickly advanced in the king's household, where they were instrumental in converting King Ezana. Ethiopian Christianity became decidedly monophysite, emphasizing the divinity of Christ over his humanity. The Ethiopians were invited by Emperor Constantius's offer to convert to Arianism but they declined, choosing instead to come under the influence of the church in Alexandria. The task of evangelizing the Ethiopian populace fell to a group of missionary monks known as the Nine Saints, who arrived in the fifth century, fleeing the Byzantine Empire because of their anti-Chalcedonian stance. During the fifth or sixth century, the Bible was translated into the Ethiopic language, enabling a wave of evangelization to the Nubians and the Nabateans.

Christianity's Northward Expansion in Europe

The year 476 is considered the end of the Christian Roman Empire in the West. That is the year the long line of emperors inaugurated by Caesar Augustus (27 BCE–14 CE) ended, and the undisguised rule by German leaders began. No one was particularly shocked. That had come a generation earlier with Alaric and Attila. Who were these new masters of Europe? The Romans had called them "barbarians" because during earlier contact with the Romans they spoke no Greek or Latin. For the most part they were tribes from the north, originally in or near Scandinavia: Franks, Goths, Vandals, Lombards, Angles, Saxons, Bergundians, and others.

These new immigrants were tribal peoples, organized according to clans and ruled by an aristocracy of warriors. During the centuries that the Romans and Germans faced one another across the Rhine-Danube frontier, they had countless contacts with each other. During the third century, some barbarians were invited to settle on vacated lands as a buffer, and to serve in the Roman legions. By the end of the fourth century the Roman army and its generals in the West had become almost exclusively German.

The crisis of mass invasions came with the sudden appearance of a new uncontrollable force, the Huns. Late in the fourth century this wave of Asiatic people crossed the Volga and soon subjugated the easternmost Germanic tribe, the Ostragoths. The Visigoths (or West Goths) were granted asylum, settling as allies inside the empire. When corrupt Roman officials mistreated the Visigoths, they went on a rampage. The Eastern emperor tried to quell them, but in 378 he lost both his army and his life in the battle of Adrianople (in today's Turkey). This battle is considered one of history's decisive battles because it destroyed the legend of the invincibility of the Roman legions and ushered in a century and a half of chaos. Theodosius the Great was able to hold back the Visigoths, but after his death they invaded Italy, sacking Rome in 410.

The task of converting these northern peoples was enormous. Monasteries often provided the missionary monks that undertook, with considerable success, to win pagans and heretics to Catholic Christianity. To bring barbarians to a nominal adherence to Christianity was not so difficult, because they wanted to participate in the prosperity of the Roman Empire. Christianity was, in their eyes, the Roman religion. However, to instill in them Christian conduct, that was more difficult. The barbarians were brought into Christianity in two ways, directly through conversion from paganism, and indirectly through Arianism. The barbarians were not much interested in the subtleties of abstract theology. They were attracted to Arianism because of its ecclesiology and Christology. The Arians portrayed Christ as a glorified warlord, someone the Germanic warriors could admire. Another difference between the Arians and the orthodox in the West lay in the structure of the church. The Arians had no ecclesiastical center; their churches belonged to the clan.

The Arian influence began with missionary work among the Visigoths. Around the year 349 Eusebius, the Arian bishop of Nicomedia, consecrated a missionary named Ulfilas to serve as bishop to Christians in the Gothic lands. Ulfilas crossed the Danube and worked among them for forty years. The spread of Christian teachings among the Goths was greatly aided by Ulfilas's translation of the Bible into the Gothic language. From the Goths, Arian Christianity spread to other German tribes.

Some of the earliest northern peoples to convert to Christianity were beyond the borders of the empire and were not themselves German. The Irish were Celtic, and they trace their conversion to St. Patrick early in the fifth century. Captured by Irish pirates raiding the English coast, young Patrick spent six years in captivity before escaping back to England. There he had a dream in which the Irish beseeched him to return and tell them about Christ. After a time of preparation, Patrick returned to be a missionary to the people among whom he had once been a slave. For forty years he traveled widely, preaching the gospel and converting many. He and his followers began building churches. A century later the structure of the church in Ireland was predominantly monastic. Presumably the monastic community, maintaining itself on the land, fitted the agricultural communities of the Celts better than the parish-church system so common in the Roman Empire.

Ireland served as the base for the evangelization of Britain. A century after Patrick's time, an Irish monk named Columba led in the founding of a monastery on Iona, an island off the coast of Scotland. Iona, in turn, gave a new and vital impulse to the expansion of Christianity in Britain. Celtic monks from Ireland and Britain also became missionaries to the Continent. They established monasteries in Germany, Switzerland, and even in northern Italy. These became centers of evangelization and devout learning.

Ireland and Scotland had never been part of the Roman Empire, and Christianity there was taking a different form. Ireland's monastic communities included women as well as men, married and unmarried. They celebrated Easter on a different day. Their Celtic Christianity sometimes tended toward a Pelagian theology. The conversion of the Franks, influential in the establishment of the Holy Roman Empire, provided an important passage for the expansion of Catholic Christianity to Great Britain. In 596, Pope Gregory the Great appointed a monk named Augustine to head up a missionary delegation to England. Augustine and his monks began their ministry in Kent, one of the areas controlled by the Anglo-Saxon invaders of England. The local ruler, King Ethelbert, was married to Bertha, the Christian daughter of a Frankish king from the western region of the

Continent. With the support of Queen Bertha, Augustine secured a hearing from Ethelbert. The king found Augustine so persuasive that he granted land for the foundation of a monastery at Canterbury, ever after to be the seat of the English religious leader. Gregory later appointed Augustine the first archbishop of Canterbury.

The missionaries who followed Augustine worked northward, and by the time of King Oswy (the late seventh century), they converged with the Celtic followers of Columba working southward. Oswy's queen was from the south and followed the Roman practices, whereas Oswy had received his Christian beliefs from the north and observed Celtic Christianity. At the Synod of Whitby in 664, representatives of the two forms of Christianity made their case before King Oswy of Northumbria. The Celtic Christians argued their case on the authority of Columba, who had brought the faith to Scotland. The representative of Rome claimed to represent Peter, to whom Christ gave the keys. "Is that really so?" asked the king? "Does Peter guard the gates to heaven?" When the Celtic defender agreed, Oswy decided to follow Roman practices, resolving not to alienate the gatekeeper of heaven. After Whitby, the British Isles moved progressively toward Roman Catholicism.

Once rooted in Anglo-Saxon England, Christianity returned invigorated to the Continent. The most famous missionary of the Middle Ages was Winfrid, better known as Boniface. He lived until age forty as a monk in England and in 729 was commissioned to evangelize Germany by Pope Gregory II. He traveled widely in what is now France, Germany, and the Low Countries and founded a Benedictine monastery at Fulda (near Frankfort, Germany), which long remained a center for further missionary outreach. His primary task was to convert the pagan population, and in this, he had great success. In addition, he brought the British and Irish missionary monks and their converts into closer relations with Rome. Boniface became archbishop of Mainz and would have ended his career there in peace had he not been drawn to efforts with the pagans in Frisia (the Netherlands), beyond the frontiers of the Franks militarily. Boniface, now in his seventies, was preparing for worship along the coast when pirates attacked his small group, killing Boniface and the rest of his party. To his reputation as teacher, missionary, and reformer, Boniface now added the title of martyr. Of Boniface, the modern historian Christopher Dawson once wrote that he "had a deeper influence on the history of Europe than any Englishman who has ever lived."

Similarly, the missionary expansion of Christianity in Eastern Europe came about in the ninth century through the monks Cyril and Methodius, brothers by blood as well as in their vows. Their willingness to translate the Bible and liturgical materials into Slavonic, the common language of Moravia and Bohemia (now part of the Czech Republic), sealed a bond between Eastern Europe and the Greek Orthodox Church.

The Holy Roman Empire

Centuries after its fall to barbarism, the Roman Empire in the West influenced the populace. The barbarians had numerous kingdoms and fought regularly with one another. However, people still longed for the unity that once marked the empire, and they looked for a day when a revived Roman Empire might appear. As the Greeks believed that Rome had passed over to Constantinople, so the Romans and their German neighbors longed for imperial revival.

Roman Catholic influence began in the northern half of Gaul, among the Franks, the only Germanic tribe to enter the Roman Empire as pagans and not as Arian Christians. The Frankish nation, destined to greatness in the shaping of Christian Europe, was founded by Clovis (481–511), the first barbarian chief of any importance to convert to orthodox Christianity. Experiencing victory in battle after praying to Jesus Christ, he was baptized, together with three thousand of his army. Jesus was for him a tribal war-god, defended on occasion by St. Peter, whose noble exploit in his eyes was his eagerness to wield his sword to protect Jesus and to slice off the ear of the high priest's servant. In addition to St. Peter, the Franks also admired St. George, a military saint who became the patron of England.

After the death of Clovis, his dynasty began to suffer from internal weakness as royal heirs became adept at treachery and intrigue. At that time a new center of power arose from the landed aristocracy, an influential figure they called "mayor of the palace." The kingdom of the Franks experience a resurgence under Charles Martel, who became mayor of the palace in 714. Martel allowed the titular kings to retain their claim to the throne, but they were mere figureheads; the real power rested with the mayor of the palace. Charles, whose surname Martel means "The Hammer," earned a great victory over the Muslim invaders of Europe in 732, near Tours, deep within the Frankish kingdom. His victory forced them to retreat, and they never threatened central Europe again.

Martel's son, Pepin the Short (741–768) felt the time had come to legalize the power exercised by the mayors of the palace, so he turned to the pope for a ruling stipulating that whoever had the actual power should be the legal ruler. His appeal was successful, and in 751 he was crowned king of the Franks by Boniface, the missionary to the Germans. Three years later the pope crossed the Alps and personally recognized the new ruler. The pope was rewarded in 756, when a Frankish army intervened in Italy and forced the Lombards to surrender land to the papacy. The gift made the pope ruler over the Papal States, a strip of territory that extended across Italy. Around the same time, a document appeared, known as the Donation of Constantine, alleging that Constantine had bequeathed Rome and the western part of the empire to the bishop of Rome. The Donation was exposed as a forgery in the fifteenth century.

The alliance between the Franks and the papacy affected the course of European politics and Christianity for centuries. When Pepin's son, Charles the Great (known to us as Charlemagne), succeeded his father in 768, he instituted a new political order, making Europe nominally Christian for a thousand years. Charles successfully defeated neighboring rivals, including the Bavarians and the Saxons, the last of the independent Germanic tribes. He also crossed the Pyrenees and drove the Muslims further south, establishing a boundary known as the Spanish Mark, near Barcelona. Like his father, Charlemagne intervened in Italian politics, defeating the Lombards and proclaiming himself their king. He also sent ambassadors to the emperor in Constantinople. In addition to military goals, he also sought intellectual power, fostering a revival of learning and the arts. In 789 he decreed that every monastery have a school for the education of boys. He also imported scholars from Italy and Ireland and thus stimulated learning throughout the realm.

His third goal, to acquire religious power, came in 800, on Christmas Day, when he was crowned king of the Holy Roman Empire by Pope Leo III. The event took place at Rome in the church dedicated to St. Peter. The event marked a new form of Christian existence, the start of Latin Christendom. When Leo crowned Charlemagne the "new" emperor, it signaled an event that would shape Christian life in the West for the next seven or eight centuries. For the next 800 years and more, the politics, learning, social organization, art, music, economics, and law of Europe would be "Christian,"—not necessarily in the New Testament definition of the gospel—because the fate of the Western church centered in Rome has become decisively linked with the new "Roman" emperor across the Alps.

At his death, Charlemagne's empire was too vast and its nobility too powerful to last intact. From the late ninth century until the mid-eleventh century, internal and external problems steadily weakened Western Christendom. Under Charlemagne's weak successors the empire disintegrated amid civil wars and new invasions. When Vikings began sweeping out of the north, and Magyars (Hungarians) from the east, people increasingly surrendered their possessions to counts, dukes, and other local lords in return for protection. These disintegrating conditions resulted in the emergence of feudalism, a new social order in Europe. Central to feudalism was a ceremony known as the act of homage, in which the vassal promised loyalty to his lord and the lord promised his vassal protection and justice.

During the tenth century, Europe experienced almost total collapse of civil order and culture. Everywhere church property either was devastated by invaders or fell into the hands of local nobility such as feudal barons in France and kings in Germany. Bishops and abbots thus became vassals, receiving fiefs for which they were obligated to provide feudal services. This loyalty to higher lords created unusual conflicts for bishops, who looked to the pope for support. However, in the tenth and early eleventh centuries, the pope was powerless. Without imperial protection, the papacy fell into decay.

By the eleventh century the church was in a better position to influence for the better the behavior of the feudal barons. In addition to attempting to add Christian virtues to the code of knightly conduct called chivalry, the church tried to impose limitations on feudal warfare. After the German king Otto the Great revived the Roman Empire in the West in 962, some sense of unity was restored. With the renewal of the empire, however, came renewed rivalry between church and state.

During the eleventh century the controversy between church and state centered on the problem of lay investiture. Theoretically, bishops or abbots were subject to two investitures: church officials bestowing spiritual authority and a king or a noble bestowing feudal or civil authority. In reality, however, feudal lords and kings controlled both the appointment and the installation of clergy. This practice was most pronounced in Germany, where control of the church was the foundation of the king's power.

Before the church could challenge kings and emperors, however, it needed to set its own house in order. This began with a far-reaching revival within the Benedictine order of Cluny, founded in 910. The Cluniac program began as a movement for monastic reform, but in time it called for the enforcement of clerical celibacy and the abolition of simony (the purchase or sale of a church office). The ultimate goal of the Cluniac reformers was to free churches and monasteries from secular control and subject them solely to papal authority. The reform led to two significant changes: the freeing from lay control of hundreds of monastic houses, and the creation of the College of Cardinals, which henceforth elected the popes.

The person behind the reform of the papacy was Hildebrand, who in 1073 was elected Pope Gregory VII (1073–1085). Holding as his ideal the creation of a Christian commonwealth solely under papal control, in 1075 he formally prohibited lay investiture and threatened to excommunicate any laypersons who participated in its practice. This act virtually declared war against Europe's rulers, since most of them practiced lay investiture. The climax to the struggle occurred in Gregory's clash with the German king, who ruled as Emperor Henry IV (1056–1105).

In addition to forbidding lay investiture, Gregory decreed that priests must no longer be married, that emperors could not appoint popes, and that the pope, not the emperor, should appoint bishops. The German clergy rebelled at the decree against their marriage, and Emperor Henry responded by appointing a bishop in Milan. He announced that Gregory was no longer pope but a false monk. The pope excommunicated Henry and deposed him, freeing Henry's subjects from any duty to obey the emperor. Following a revolt among the German nobles, Henry appeared before Gregory at Canossa, a castle in the mountains of Italy. Dressed as a penitent, the emperor stood barefoot in the snow for three days, begging forgiveness. The pope relented and withdrew the decree. Eventually, however, Henry invaded Rome and forced Gregory to flee. A rival pope was elected to office, and Gregory died in exile. The conflict of church and state would continue.

During the late Middle Ages, when Europe longed for unity, the church attained a level of power and influence such as it has never known since. While many of Gregory's claims now appear intolerable, his successors stood for two principles that to Christianity remain incontestable: (a) the primacy of the spiritual over the secular, and (b) the idea that humans, far from perfect, can find true unity only in Christ.

Eastern Christianity under Byzantine Emperors

Of the three major divisions in Christianity today—Roman Catholicism, Eastern Orthodoxy, and Protestantism—the least known in the West is Eastern Orthodoxy. Most Protestants, if they think of Orthodoxy at all, think of it as a kind of Roman Catholicism without the pope. The differences, of course, are far greater, including the starting questions. While Protestants and Catholics generally ask the same questions—How is a person saved? What is the church? Where does religious authority lie?—Orthodox Christians start elsewhere, with holy images called icons. Found on church partitions called the iconostasis, the wall of paintings that separates the sanctuary from the nave, or hanging on walls in Orthodox homes, these images of Jesus and the saints serve as a kind of window between the earthly and the celestial realms. Viewed less as aids to worship and more as ways the heavenly beings manifest themselves to the faithful on earth, it is impossible to understand Orthodox worship apart from icons.

In Orthodoxy, the idea of image is essential to understanding how God and humans relate. Humans are created "in the image of God," bearing within the icon of God. Unlike Western Christians, inclined to understand the fundamental relationship between God and humanity in legal terms, the great theme of Orthodox theology is the incarnation of God and the re-creation of humanity. According to Orthodoxy, when humans sin, they do not violate the legal relationship between themselves and God; they diminish the divine likeness.

Salvation, therefore, consists in restoring the image of God within humanity. The major themes of Orthodoxy, then, are the rebirth, recreation, and transfiguration of human beings. This takes place within the church, viewed not as a formalized institution but as the mystical body of Christ constantly renewed by the Holy Spirit flowing through it. It is within this fellowship of love that human beings are made ready to join the preexisting communion among Father, Son, and Spirit. Orthodox believers call this process *theosis*, or deification. Athanasius, who championed Greek theology, pictured Jesus fully sharing in the corrupted world of humans so that we could fully share in the incorruptible fellowship of God: "Christ became man so men could become gods." Understandably, the language of "becoming gods" troubles Western Christians, but the language is less about humans becoming God and more about humans being transformed to become fit companions for an eternal communion with and in the triune God.

These fundamental differences were present in the Greek-speaking church early on, but the distinctively Eastern Christian faith appeared first under Constantine. Orthodoxy tends to view Constantine's reign as the climax of the evolution of the Roman Empire. Constantine's conversion was vital for the development of Orthodoxy because he created, for the first time, an alliance between state and church, and he made purity of Christian doctrine a central concern of the empire. After Constantine's victory over his rivals, God placed the emperor under the protection of the cross and in direct dependence upon Christ. Christendom took shape when the emperor came to be seen as the connecting link between God and the world, while the state was the earthly reflection of divine law.

Constantine adopted a procedure already developed by Christians to settle their differences. He called the leaders of the entire church to assemble in his presence to define the correct tradition. This procedure became a part of the Eastern Christian tradition. From the First Ecumenical Council at Nicaea (325) to the seventh, also held at Nicaea (787), it was the emperor who called the council and presided over it, either personally or by deputy. Eastern Christians today place great emphasis on these seven ecumenical councils. These councils gave us essential creeds, but they also heightened the role of the state. Religion and politics were indissolubly bound, the cross to the sword.

The symbol of a new era for the church in society was Constantinople, the new capital of the empire and the New Rome. During its thousand-year history as the center of a thriving civilization and the seat of economic and political power, Constantinople was the home of the Eastern Christian tradition and the hub of the new Byzantine civilization.

Clear evidence of the Byzantine character of Eastern Christianity appeared under a second powerful emperor, Justinian, who ascended the throne in 527. Under Justinian the unique Byzantine blend of Roman law, Christian faith, and Greek philosophy shone brightly. In Byzantine art, greatly encouraged by Justinian, Christianity expressed its distinctively Eastern style, the mundane subordinate to the transcendent.

When Justinian rebuilt Constantine's Hagia Sophia and consecrated it in 538, he claimed he had outdone Solomon. The massive dome, hung as it were from heaven, linked the finite to the infinite. The mosaics, dazzling with brilliance, portrayed Constantine and Justinian together, one offering to the Mother of God a model of Constantinople, the other a model of the Church of Holy Wisdom. The link with Constantine was appropriate, for Justinian brought the plans of Constantine to their logical conclusion, defining the future course of Eastern Orthodoxy.

Inevitably, the division of the Roman Empire resulted in the division of the church. The final dispute centered around the fact that the West added to the Nicene Creed a clause stating that the Spirit proceeds not only from the Father but also from the Son. Known as the *filioque* controversy (the Latin term *filioque* means "and from the Son"), the Greek church regarded this idea of a "double procession" of the Spirit as tantamount to God having two sons, something they found unacceptable. Centuries of theological wrangling led to the fateful events of 1054, when the papal legate to Constantinople, Cardinal Humbert, entered the great church of Hagia Sophia and placed on the altar a bull (an edict by the pope) excommunicating Cerularius, the bishop (patriarch) of Constantinople. Soon thereafter Cerularius returned the favor, excommunicating and damning the pope.

Traditionally, these events from 1054 have been called the Great Schism between the Orthodox and Catholic churches, though there were in fact at least two serious efforts in succeeding centuries to repair the breach, without success. Some historians call attention to the sacking of Constantinople by Crusaders on Good Friday of 1204, during the Fourth Crusade, as so deeply poisoning relations between East and West that it was this, rather than the events of 1054, that occasioned the final break between the two great churches of Christendom. The Latin Crusaders attempted to replace the Byzantine emperor, but they failed miserably. Within a few decades the city was regained by Orthodox emperors. Steven Runciman, historian of the Crusades, captured the sentiment in the hearts of Eastern Christians to this day when he writes, "There was never a greater crime against humanity than the Fourth Crusade." In the sweep of world history, the effects of the sack were wholly disastrous, marking the schism "complete, irremediable, and final."

In time military losses, as well as theological disputes, eroded the great empire of Constantine and Justinian. Hordes of barbarians were followed by Muslim invaders. In the late Middle Ages the original territories of Eastern Orthodoxy were reduced to western Turkey, the Balkans, and Cyprus. In 1453 the city of Constantinople fell to the Turks. After eleven centuries, Eastern Christendom was at an end, and Christians became a minority in a society run by Muslims. Today, out of the vast Byzantine Empire, only Greece and half of Cyprus are still Greek Orthodox.

Notably, around 980, in what is now Russia, the pagan ruler Vladimir I accepted the Christian faith. The magnificence of Constantinople and the awe-inspiring liturgy captured the loyalties of the envoys Vladimir sent to investigate the Christian faith. After they attended services in the great church of Hagia Sophia, the envoys told their master, "We know not whether we were in heaven or on earth, for surely there is no such splendor or beauty anywhere upon earth." While Vladimir's acceptance of Christianity seems to have been sincere, he also clearly regarded the new religion as a means of unifying his people. Soon after his conversion he brought the citizens of Kiev to the river for baptism. He also imported icons, priests, and liturgical vessels from Constantinople, granting an official tithe to the church while also assigning it public duties. Thus established, Orthodoxy took several centuries to move from urban centers into the countryside. However, when Orthodoxy won the adherence of ordinary Russians, that alliance was solidified. After the fall of Constantinople in 1453, Vladimir's successors proclaim Moscow as "a third Rome," taking as their title Tsar, meaning Caesar. The Kremlin in Russia stands today as a reminder of the inspiring Orthodox past, its onion domes pointing toward heaven.

The Rise of Islam

No history of the medieval church, whether in its Latin or Byzantine expression, is adequate without mention of the role played by the rise and westward expansion of Islam. By 570, when the prophet of Islam, Muhammad, was born, the East-West axis around which Christianity had grown was severely strained. After Muhammad received what are recorded in the Qur'an as revelations from the angel Gabriel, he gathered a small following around Mecca, in the Arabian Peninsula. In 622 rivals drove Muhammad and his followers out of Mecca, threatened by his growing power. Muhammad's retreat to Medina, known as the Hijrah, was turned into victory, however, as Arabs increasingly rallied to the cause of Allah and his prophet. In 630 Muhammad returned in triumph to Mecca. Two years later, when Muhammad died, Arabia was one-third Muslim. Two years after that, under Abu Bakr, all Arabia had turned to Islam. Within a decade, Arab armies inspired by Islamic teaching had taken Syria, Palestine, and Persia (modern Iran) and had conducted raids as far east as the borders of India. In 642 Islam entered Egypt.

The growth of Islam played a critical role in the history of Christianity. Despite internal disputes in the mid-seventh century that slowed the pace of expansion for nearly a century after Muhammad's death, the westward tide of Islam seemed irresistible. Attacks began on Constantinople, still a vigorous imperial capital, in 674. By 698 Carthage, the home of Tertullian and Cyprian, was under Islamic control. Using Carthage as a base, Islamic navies ventured forth to subdue the remaining Mediterranean region. In 711 Islamic troops of the powerful Umayyad dynasty crossed the narrow band of water at the mouth of the Mediterranean into Gibraltar. Within a decade Muslim armies had crossed the Pyrenees into what is now France. They reached Tours in 732, where they suffered defeat under Charles Martel and the Franks. The battle of Poitiers (Tours), the high watermark of western Islamic expansion, stemmed the Muslim tide, though it would take more than seven centuries for the Muslims to be driven completely out of Europe, from the Iberian Peninsula (modern Spain).

The spread of Islam over Egypt and North Africa was undoubtedly facilitated by the weakness of Christianity in those regions. Heavy taxes imposed by Constantinople, as well as plundering armies from Persia, made North Africans ready for new rulers. The centuries of Christian infighting, with wearisome strife over doctrine and contests for power, further undermined the internal strength of the Christian community. Some historians speculate that the Egyptian preference for forms of Christian theology stressing the unity of God (especially monophysitism) predisposed North Africans toward the radical monotheism of Islam.

The spread of Islam accelerated the division between Eastern and Western forms of Christianity, especially by making communication between the eastern and western Mediterranean more difficult. More importantly, geographic refocusing signaled papal willingness to give up the ideals of a Mediterranean Roman Empire in exchange for a new Roman Empire in the North. The expansion of Islam undoubtedly helped turn the attention of the papacy from the East to the North, leading in 800 to the coronation by Pope Leo III of Charlemagne as the first emperor of the Holy Roman Empire. In 800, when the Roman crowds addressed Charlemagne as Augustus, they deliberately evoked the majesty of Rome. The popes leading up to Leo III had come to realize that the old connection between Rome and Constantinople was now bankrupt. The emperor in the East could no longer secure Europe against Islam.

After the seventh century, it becomes impossible to understand the internal course of Christian history without bringing Islam fully into the equation. In the East, Islamic scruples against images played a role in how the Byzantine church defended its use of icons. A few centuries later, the spectacle of Islamic rulers in Jerusalem, combined with anguished appeals for help from the Eastern emperor, provoked the call for crusades.

Within the sphere of learning, Islam exerted a beneficial influence. While Europeans in the ninth and tenth centuries languished in feudal darkness, under disintegrating social conditions sparked by civil wars and devastating invasions, Muslim culture thrived, making advances in astronomy, mathematics, science, medicine, and the arts. When Europeans in the eleventh and twelfth centuries became curious about the philosophy and science of the ancient world, they found it more convenient to translate Arabic editions of Greek texts than to use copies of the originals locked away in Constantinople. The Western scholastic resurgence in the twelfth and thirteenth centuries also benefited from Islamic learning.

Study Questions

1. Whom do you consider the chief protagonist in the second phase of Christendom (sixth through eleventh centuries CE)? Support your answer.

2. Do you agree with the author's choice that the coronation of Charlemagne in the year 800 as Holy Roman Emperor is this epoch's turning point? Why or why not? Is there another event you consider more noteworthy? If so, what is it? Support your choice.

3. In this epoch, does "the church" live up to its nature and destiny as God's new creation? Why or why not?

4. How did influential popes like Leo and Gregory bring positive good to the church?

5. Discuss the impact that monasticism had on the church at large.

6. What potential dangers arise from the division between monastics and other Christians?

7. In your estimation, why was Christianity's early missionary expansion eastward and southward successful? Why are these chapters in Christianity so often ignored or neglected in textbooks on church history?

8. Why was Arianism attractive to the barbarians? How is the vestige of Arianism still present in the church today?

9. Define "Christendom." Discuss how it shaped medieval Europe's outlook on everyday life, including politics, social conduct, and economic conduct.

10. We begin to see in this chapter some growing cultural differences between the churches of East and West. What kinds of differences marked the two regions in their approach to theology?

11. Discuss the ways the spread of Islam changed the growth and character of the church in the seventh and eighth centuries.

Chapter 7

Phase 7: Renaissance (1095–1500)

Crusades, Colleges, and Cathedrals

Significant Event: This period contributed many groundbreaking movements and events. When Pope Innocent III issued his papal decree *Unam sanctum* in 1302, it represented the late medieval church's supremacy in society. The result, however, was short-lived. For two hundred years, the Crusades dramatically influenced medieval life, but in the end, they produced only negative results. The era also produced Francis of Assisi, still a model of the Christian life, based on compassion for all, love of nature and of all creatures, and service to the poor and disadvantaged. However, while he is widely admired, few follow his style of life. In the end, I select as most significant the development of university education in this period. With the building of great cathedrals came a new emphasis of education, its supreme task to understand and explain reality (God's revealed truth). The scholastic method confirmed the "medieval synthesis," promoting the integrity of faith and learning (philosophy and theology; reason and faith) as compatible avenues in affirming, "All truth is God's truth."

Turning Point: In my estimation, two events qualify as turning points for this era: (1) The life and writings of John Wycliffe, which challenged abuses in faith and practice, thereby anticipating the Reformers' emphasis on the priesthood of believers, justification by faith, and the authority of scriptures; and (2) the flowering of the Renaissance in Florence, Italy, which produced superior works of art, architecture, literature, and engineering, and gave birth to modernity.

Among the many important ecclesiastical developments and events during the twelfth through fifteenth centuries, the following helped shape the church's conception of faith, vocation, and governance:

1. The papacy during the late medieval period
2. The Crusades
3. The medieval synthesis and sacramental theology
4. Cathedrals, worship, and the Christian life
5. Scholasticism: philosophy and theology, faith and reason
6. Monks and mystics
7. Heretics and Inquisition
8. Renaissance

Emerging from the "dark ages," the late medieval church took the lead in rule by law, the pursuit of knowledge, and the expressions of culture. The underlying concept was Christendom, which united empire and church. It began under Charlemagne in the eighth century, but the popes slowly assumed greater power until Innocent III (1198–1216) taught Europe to think of the popes as world rulers. Later centuries, however, saw the papacy corrupted by power, and reformers arose crying out for change.

The Papacy during the Late Medieval Period

Modern times are marked by the idea of autonomous, sovereign states without religious affiliation, and by the concept of the church as a voluntary association apart from the rest of organized society. However, neither of these ideas existed in the Middle Ages. At that time, three competing views emerged regarding society and the church's role in the world: (a) the Constantinian (Justinian) view, whereby the church and state are united *under the state*, (b) the Augustinian view, which views state and church as *independent but cooperative*, neither supreme over the other, and (c) the medieval view, whereby church and state are united *under the church*. Augustine's model of the "City of God" and the "City of Man" led to the doctrine of two authorities or swords by which God orders society. The spiritual sword of the church works to bring people under the rule of the City of God, while God uses the temporal sword of the state to restrain sin and keep order in society. The Justinian model regards the state as holding both swords but lending one to the church (this model is operative in the absence of a strong institutional church). In Justinian's theory, modeled in the Byzantine Empire (but also traditionally in state churches in Europe and Latin America) God advises the emperor (ruler), whose reign thereby makes holy the empire (nation). The Augustinian model views church and state as separate institutions and yet working together for the benefit of earthly order and welfare. This view led to the American view of society, with its separation of church and state. The medieval view, implemented in the absence of a strong central government, regards the church as holding both swords but loaning one to the state. In this segment we explore the development of the medieval view.

During the twelfth and thirteenth centuries, the papacy led an admirable attempt to constitute a perfect society on earth, achieving incomparable power and majesty. Germanic rulers continued to call themselves Roman Emperors and continued to go to Rome for their coronations, but they were merely the sovereigns of a cluster of kingdoms and municipal republics that constituted the Germany of the late Middle Ages. The papacy, by contrast, built upon the reforms of Pope Gregory VII and emerged as the most powerful institution in Europe. The pope's government was truly monarchical and centralized. All bishops swore fealty to the pope, and no religious order could be founded without his authorization. The papal court in Rome heard appeals from all over Christendom, and in every country legates from Rome executed papal orders.

In the hands of a strong leader, the papacy could overshadow all secular monarchs. Such a leader was Pope Innocent III (1198–1216). Trained in canon law (church administration), Innocent III held an exalted view of his office. "The successor of Peter," he announced, "is the Vicar of Christ. He has been established as a mediator between God and man, below God but beyond man; less than God but more than man; who shall judge all and be judged by no one."

The pope's first weapon in controlling monarchs and peasants alike was the threat of excommunication. When implemented, excommunication threatened individuals with the loss of grace essential for salvation. While under excommunication, persons could not act as judge, juror, witness, or attorney. They could not be guardians, executors, or parties to contract. After death, they received no Christian burial.

The second weapon was the interdict, a curse aimed not at individuals but upon a nation. Its power included the suspension of all public worship, and even the withdrawal of the sacraments from the lands of disobedient rulers. Pope Innocent III successfully applied or threatened the interdict eighty-five times against uncooperative princes. Wielding these spiritual weapons, Innocent and his successors during the thirteenth century led Christianity to its peak of political and cultural influence. The dreams—and delusions—of the papacy in this period appear preeminently in the crusades.

The period between 1300 and 1500 marked a turning point in Western history. It witnessed what has been called "the decline of the Middle Ages" because the idea of Christendom came under attack. During this period we see not only the further decline of the empire, but the dramatic loss of papal prestige. The fourteenth century is perhaps too early to speak of nations in the modern sense of the term, but more and more, people were getting used to the idea that they were English or French whenever their allegiance came into question, and more importantly, they found it possible to think of their "state" functioning without direct papal guidance. Europe was slowly moving away from its feudal past, and land was less important than cash. In their need to finance costly military campaigns, secular rulers in England (Edward I) and in France (Philip the Fair) simultaneously hit upon a controversial solution: tax the clergy within their realms. The pope fought back; in 1296 Boniface VIII (1230–1303) issued a document threatening excommunication for any lay ruler who taxed the clergy. Edward and Philip, believing themselves above church law, responded by threatening to seize clerical properties, thereby depriving the papal treasury of a major source of revenue. In 1302 Boniface issued *Unam sanctum*, the most extreme assertion of papal power in church history. "It is altogether necessary," he declared, "for every human being to be subject to the Roman pontiff." Allegorizing the passage in Luke 22:35–38, he announced that in the church there are two swords, the spiritual and the temporal. Both are in the power of the church, the temporal authority subject to the spiritual.

Philip burned the papal decree and began immediate proceedings to have Boniface deposed, sending a lawyer armed with authority to bring the pope to France for trial before a special church council. Boniface, now eighty-six, was arrested and died within weeks, shamed and reviled. An

unpopular pope, he was the target of widespread criticism. Shortly thereafter Dante, author of *The Divine Comedy* (written between 1308 and 1320),
reserved a place in hell for him.

This episode came to symbolize the descent of papal power. When
Boniface's successor in Rome died after a brief, ineffectual reign, Philip's
daring coup bore fruit. In 1305 the College of Cardinals elected a French-
man as Pope Clement V. Clement never set foot in Rome, preferring to stay
close to home. Clement's election marked the start of a seventy-two-year
period in church history called "the Babylonian captivity" of the papacy.
Following Clement, six successive popes, all of French origin, chose to
reside in the small town of Avignon rather than in Rome. One pope supported France in its war with England, and other nations chose sides and
entered the fight.

By 1360 turmoil in Italy made it clear that the Avignon papacy could
not continue indefinitely. In 1377 the aged Pope Gregory XI returned to
Rome, to be succeeded a year later by Urban VI, an Italian. All the cardinals were present. The next months, following unpopular decisions by
Urban, the cardinals suddenly declared that the people of Rome had forced
the election of an apostate and declared the proceedings invalid. A month
later, Urban responded by creating a new College of Cardinals, electing the
French Clement VIII in his place. Clement moved to Avignon, and now
there were two popes, one in Avignon and one in Rome, marking a chapter
in papal history called the Great Schism. Various nations and groups supported one or the other, and the popes became involved in armed conflict
with each other. In an effort to stop the scandal, an attempt was made to
depose both and set a new one on the throne in Rome. The result was that
for a few years there were three popes.

Finally, in 1414, the Holy Roman Emperor Sigismund assembled at
the German city of Constance the most impressive church gathering of this
era. For the first time voting took place on a purely national basis, each
nation receiving one vote. The structure of the Council of Constance was
highly significant, indicating that the church was accepting a new align-
ment of power. In 1417 the Council of Florence persuaded one incumbent
pope to step aside and deposed the others, effectively ending the schism.

The conciliar movement aimed at limiting the power of the papacy.
Constance decreed that general councils were superior to popes and that
councils should meet regularly. Political corruption and immorality in the
Vatican continued, however, reaching unbelievable depths under Roderigo

Borgia, who ruled as Alexander VI (1492–1503). The challenge of the Protestant Reformation was at hand.

The Crusades

In the seventh century, Damascus, Jerusalem, and other centers of Christianity fell to Islam. By the eighth century, one-half of all Christians lived under Islamic rule. For centuries pilgrims had traveled unopposed from Europe to the Holy Land, the birthplace of Christ, but during the eleventh century, Christian pilgrims encountered difficulties in their travels. The problem was exacerbated by the presence of Seljuk Turks, new and fanatical converts to Islam in the eastern Mediterranean. After seizing Jerusalem from their fellow Muslims, the Seljuks then swept north into Asia Minor. At the battle of Manzikert (1071) they captured the Eastern emperor and scattered his army. Within a few years Asia Minor, the chief source of Byzantine revenue and troops, was lost, and tales of alleged Turkish mistreatment of Christian pilgrims began circulating throughout Europe.

The rise of the Seljuks proved a traumatic shock for Christendom. At Manzikert the Turkish warriors inflicted on Byzantium a defeat from which it never fully recovered. In the wake of their victory, the Turks settled Asia Minor and thereby opened up a corridor for the later Ottoman invasion of Europe. The threat to the Eastern Empire in turn galvanized the Latin West into mounting the great counteroffensive of the Crusades.

In 1095, after the Eastern emperor sent an urgent appeal for help, Pope Urban II proclaimed the First Crusade to regain the Holy Land. Preaching at the Council of Clermont in southeastern France, the pope urged Christians to take up a cause that promised both spiritual and material gain. All who died in this holy war, fighting for God, would have their sins forgiven and go immediately to heaven. As Urban ended his impassioned appeal, the crowd responded with the memorable words, "*Deus Vult*" ("God wills it"). *Deus Vult* became the crusader battle cry against the Muslim enemy.

From the end of the eleventh century to the end of the thirteenth, Christian Europe, led by the popes, launched seven major crusades against Islam. The First Crusade was the most successful. With some five thousand knights and infantry, mostly from France, Germany, and Italy, the crusader army overcame the resistance of the Turks, who were no longer united. Its greatest achievement was the capture of Jerusalem in 1099, four years after the pope had called for the crusade. It was a bloody affair, ending in the slaughter not only of Muslims but of many Jews as well.

The First Crusade captured a strip of territory along the eastern coast of the Mediterranean and created the Latin Kingdom of Jerusalem, which endured until 1291, when its last remnant fell to the Muslims. In 1147, three years after Edessa fell into Muslim hands, Bernard of Clairvaux, the famous Christian reformer, called for the Second Crusade. Despite a strong response—the church mustered two hundred thousand holy crusaders— the results were dismal. Most crusaders died in the endeavor, and many Jews were slaughtered along the way. After two years, the remaining crusaders simply melted away.

In 1187 Saladin, the sultan of Egypt and Syria, brought vigorous leadership to the Muslims. Considered one of the greatest Muslim warriors of all time, Saladin was also a great diplomat. When Jerusalem fell to his forces, Christians responded with a Third Crusade. Its leader was one of the most famous medieval kings, Richard the Lion-Hearted of England. To keep the Muslims united, Saladin proclaimed *jihad*, or holy war, against the Christians. However, his chivalry and commonsense approach to diplomacy was evident when he proposed that Richard should marry his sister and thus receive Palestine as a wedding present. Denying his proposal, Richard finally agreed to a three-year truce and free access to Jerusalem for Christian pilgrims.

The Fourth Crusade of 1202–1204 was a special disaster. Under the influence of Venetian merchants, who were mostly concerned with plunder and power, the Crusade turned aside from its supposed objective and came to Constantinople in 1204. The battle-ready crusader army, consisting of Venetian, French, and Flemish soldiers, had little trouble conquering the city. On Good Friday, the crusaders sacked the city and immediately began robbing it of its treasures. The looting, which went on for years, included such holy places as churches and monasteries. The crusaders set up a Latin kingdom (1204–1261), a disastrous rule from which the ancient city never fully recovered. The conquest widened the schism between the Greek and the Latin churches and hastened the fall of the city to the Ottoman Turks in 1453.

Other crusaders marched east during the thirteenth century, but none achieved the original goal, the return of the Holy Land to Christian control. The era of the Crusades ended in 1291 when Acre, the last crusader stronghold in Palestine, fell to the Muslim warriors. Acre's conquerors destroyed everything, and what they could not destroy they covered with earth and rock. For centuries, Acre remained forgotten. Today the fortifications remain, and buried beneath the 200-year-old Turkish settlement lie the partially excavated ruins of the ancient crusader center.

The long-range results of two centuries of crusading zeal were dismal. If the primary goals of the Crusades were to win the Holy Land, to repel the advance of Islam, and to heal the schism between the Eastern and Western churches, then the Crusades failed. Unfortunately, the crusaders and their papal sponsors ignored an essential Christian truth, namely, that the sword is never God's way to expand or even to defend the church. For the next seven centuries the word "crusade" conveyed a negative message, as Christians tried to dismiss the bloody affair as religious extremism.

The Medieval Synthesis and Sacramental Theology

The Christendom of the European Middle Ages affected the practice of the Christian faith in every way. The "medieval synthesis," as it is sometimes called, attempted to harmonize the sacred and the secular spheres of life, bringing all realms of life—political, social, religious, and economic—under the authority and protection of the church.

The central religious convictions of Christendom was that human beings needed to be saved from sin, and that this salvation was achieved by the merit of Christ communicated through God's grace. Thomas Aquinas, the leading theologian of the late Middle Ages, helped explain the process of redemption. Since no human act can achieve saving grace, Aquinas contended that Christ's sacrifice on the cross was the only act worthy of God's grace. Because of Christ's deity and sinlessness, his death was more than adequate to pay for the sins of humanity. His "overpayment" is available to human beings in a heavenly "treasury of merit."

Aquinas distinguished between two types of grace. Operative grace is the divine help in which God is the sole mover. While God moves the soul, humans are also movers, active participants in salvation. Thus grace is both "operative" (given by God alone) and "cooperative" (humans work with God), and Aquinas believed that people can merit rewards from God. In addition to Christ's grace are "works of supererogation." These works, performed by "saints," that is, by individuals who have performed acts in excess of the demands or requirements of duty, also accumulate in the treasury of merit. According to this perspective, human salvation is achieved by both grace and works, the result of operative and cooperative grace.

How do sinners receive grace? Viewing grace as a quality or substance, infused into the human soul through the sacraments, Aquinas endorsed the medieval conviction that God distributes grace through the seven sacraments, secured and dispensed by the church: baptism (initiation),[1] confirmation, Eucharist, penance (reconciliation), ordination (holy orders), marriage, and extreme unction (last rights or anointing of the sick). Without the sacraments there can be no forgiveness, and hence no ultimate union with Christ.

Believing there were no sins so grave that entering religion would not be suitable satisfaction for them, medieval Christians often entered religious vocations, aspiring to the priesthood and ultimately to the papacy. This vision of salvation and the meritorious life extolled the virtues of the monastic and celibate life as a higher calling, further separating the spiritual from the sacred. Hence, those who joined the monastic life were following a higher calling than those engaged in a secular life. In their confession of sin, reception of the sacraments, and knowledge of the Bible, lay Christians were dependent on those who were more spiritual, whose calling enabled them to perform meritorious works.

Cathedrals, Worship, and the Christian Life

During the twelfth and thirteenth centuries, the papacy led an admirable attempt to constitute a perfect society on earth. The great Gothic cathedrals of this time—Notre Dame, erected between 1163 and 1235 on a small island in Paris; the cathedral of Chartres, equaling the elevation of a skyscraper of thirty stories; Strasbourg Cathedral, rising forty stories— were designed to create the illusion of soaring. The use of flying buttresses eliminated the massive walls of earlier churches and made possible slender pillars that reached up into infinity. Even the sculptured forms of saints or angels standing in the niches were elongated, their necks, arms, and legs soaring heavenward. Notre Dame, Chartres, and Strasbourg were examples of a veritable fever of church construction then infecting Europe. Between

---

1. The terms in parentheses indicate modern terminology used by the Catholic Church.

1170 and 1270, more than five hundred great churches were built in Gothic style in France alone.

Western churches built along Gothic lines displayed cruciform architecture, meaning that the church was shaped like a cross. The nave (the main part of the sanctuary) usually faced east, the end containing an altar and often an elaborate, decorated window, through which light would shine in the early part of the day. The west end, facing the main entrance, sometimes contained a baptismal font, a large decorated bowl with water blessed for baptism. The north and south transepts, representing the "arms" of the cross, contained rooms or chapels for smaller gatherings. In later designs, the crossing was generally under a tower or dome.

For eight centuries Gothic cathedrals throughout Europe have inspired worshipers and awed tourists. Gothic architecture was the architect's version of the medieval synthesis, joining human reason and divine revelation. The medieval masters of this style tried to portray in stone and glass humanity's central religious quest: the human aspiration upward and the divine descent to humanity. Such language is, of course, figurative, for God is no more above than below in any spatial sense. But humans have always expressed their spiritual journey in terms of ascent, and God's truth in terms of descent. Various architectural elements contribute to this grand vision: pillars, arches, and steeples point skyward; colorful windows refract God's light earthward.

Windows in the Gothic cathedrals could be large and plentiful because the outside pillars and buttresses eliminated the need for thick walls. Between the shafts of stone, architects set windows of brilliant glass, using crimson, blue, purple, and ruby to tell the story of redemption from creation to consummation. The famous rose windows and other forms of stained-glass windows created a "bible for the illiterate." Every scene of Christ's life was depicted in glorious color, together with rich allusions to other biblical scenes. The windows of cathedrals were, in this respect, not unlike the illuminated biblical manuscripts of the medieval period. The effect was breathtaking. As the setting sun cast its rays upon the colored glass, even a cobbler could sense kinship with Moses, Isaiah, Jesus, Paul, Augustine, and Benedict. The Middle Ages were not all dark, as the hundreds of Gothic cathedrals so readily testify.

Worship within these cathedrals corresponded to the magnificent architectural structure, emphasizing liturgy as a public sacrifice performed by professionals on behalf of the people. Incense, the music of plainsongs sung by a great choir, teams of richly robed priests chanting the mysteries of the Latin Mass, the Eucharist—all the senses were involved in worship. The altar contained the body of Christ. At a climactic moment, participants went forward to kneel before the altar, on which the body of Christ was offered afresh. The sacred Mass,[2] the climactic moment of worship, enacted the doctrine of "transubstantiation," where the bread and wine were changed into the actual body and blood of Christ. (As Thomas Aquinas explained it, the material "accidents" of bread and wine remain after the consecration, but the "substance" is the body of Christ.) Only the priest might drink the cup, lest Christ's blood be spilled, but by receiving the host (the consecrated bread), participants would taste God's body and become sanctified once again.

Sermons in medieval church worship often focused on the seven deadly sins: lust, gluttony, greed, sloth, anger, envy, and pride. The priest would exhort parishioners to practice the seven cardinal virtues: chastity, abstinence, liberality, diligence, patience, kindness, and humility. Using a philosophical approach, Aquinas developed a list that distinguished between the natural virtues, borrowing four from the Greek philosophers—wisdom, courage, self-control, and justice—and the supernatural virtues, borrowing three from the New Testament—faith, hope and love. Priests emphasized the seven works of mercy: feed the hungry, provide drink to the thirsty, clothe the naked, visit the sick, house the homeless, ransom captives, and bury the dead.

Scholasticism: Philosophy and Theology, Faith and Reason

During the twelfth century, in a span of some eighty years, four great universities were founded in Europe: Bologna in 1119, Paris in 1150, Oxford in 1167, and Cambridge in 1200. The thirteenth century, however, has been called the most Christian in history, for it expanded that foundation. With the building of great cathedrals came a new emphasis of education. Since cathedrals (churches of the bishops) were located in cities, their schools to train parish priests were in time opened to all. The great cathedrals gave birth to medieval universities, for the supreme task of the university was to understand and explain God's revealed truth. During this period, worship

---

2. The term "Mass" is derived from the Latin word *missa*, meaning "dismissal," a word used in the concluding words of the Mass in Latin, "*Ite, missa est*": "Go, the dismissal is made."

came to be understood as more than an act, and liturgy as more than ritual; together they were a way of life, requiring the totality of one's being, body and soul, heart and mind.

Scholars speak of this period in the history of Christian thought as "scholasticism," because a distinctive method of scholarship arose and because a unique theology emerged. The aim of scholarship was twofold: to reconcile Christian doctrine and human reason (theology and philosophy) and to arrange Christian teaching into an orderly system. The purpose was not to search for new truth, since the chief doctrines of the faith were regarded as fixed, but rather to demonstrate the reasonableness of the doctrines and to explain their implications.

Technically not a scholastic, Anselm of Canterbury (1033–1109) is regarded as the "father of scholasticism." A thinker and logician of unparalleled power and originality, Anselm replaced the static mentality of previous generations with a rousing search for new avenues and possibilities for understanding and living. His questing spirit is apparent in his theological program "faith seeking understanding." Anselm applied the quest to know and to understand in arguments for the existence of God and the necessity of the incarnation. His ontological argument, based upon the conception provided by faith that God "is that than which nothing greater can be conceived," may not qualify as a proof for God, but it continues to fascinate scholars and students alike. His *Why God Became Man*, based on the "satisfaction" theory of human redemption, profoundly influenced all ensuing theories of atonement.

The curriculum of the cathedral school began with grammar, rhetoric, logic, arithmetic, geometry, music, and astronomy—the seven liberal arts—and then moved on to the advanced study of law or theology, the professional schools that prepared leaders for church and state. The first part of the liberal arts was the *trivium* (grammar, logic, and rhetoric), followed by the *quadrivium* (arithmetic, geometry, music, and astronomy). To this should be added philosophy, regarded as the entry point into theology. The few texts available came from a handful of scholars of the early Middle Ages, such as Cassiodorous, a sixth-century Roman whose *Handbook of Sacred and Secular Learning* defined the liberal arts and interpreted the Bible. Another was his contemporary Boethius, whose *Consolation of Philosophy* attempted to reconcile the misfortunes of life with the concept of a benevolent, omnipotent God. These scholars, together with Augustine,

Pope Gregory the Great, and a few other church fathers, became authorities, whose words the medieval students rarely dared contradict.

A new day appeared, however, with the coming of the universities and the magnetism of popular teachers whose skill and enthusiasm for learning attracted students. The earliest of these so-called Schoolmen were Peter Abelard (1079–1142), who established himself in Paris, and Peter Lombard (1100–1160), whose books of *Sentences* became the standard textbook for Catholic theology and the basis of commentary by subsequent masters. In his *Thus and Not Thus*, Abelard brought dialectical reasoning to theology as he worked through 158 apparent contradictions in Christian philosophy and theology. Abelard's four books of *Sentences* provided doctrinal statements and scriptural proofs organized according to such dogmatic categories as the Trinity, creation, sin, Incarnation, moral virtue, the sacraments, and "last things" (death, judgment, heaven, and hell). Scholasticism developed in this setting and came to stand for painstaking questioning, examining, and arranging details into a system of logic. In addition to lectures, the method of teaching was the disputation. Two or more masters and occasionally students debated text readings, employing a question-and-answer approach developed by Abelard. The scholastic disputation stirred heated clashes and bitter debates. Wars of logic ran for years between masters, with adherents cheering their hero with stomping and whistling. Something important was happening: students were learning to think, and passionately so. Unquestioning acceptance of traditional authorities was no longer assured, and even the conclusions of Christian doctrine were being investigated.

The event that marked the flowering of the universities was the grouping of students and masters into guilds. As artisans had done before them, scholars banded together for mutual interest and protection, and called themselves a *universitas*, the medieval name for a corporate group. Initially, universities were not huge buildings on sprawling campuses but rather utilized existing buildings. Students moved about from one "faculty" or "master" to another in the various monastic and cathedral schools. The growth of colleges with distinct student bodies and faculties came with the establishment of student residence halls as growth in student numbers dictated. There were no "sciences" in the contemporary sense, hence no need for laboratories. Reading texts, lecturing based on texts, and notetaking made up the essential pedagogy. Students paid masters directly after a lecture and on the basis of its quality.

It is important to be aware of the entirely Christian character of the medieval university: everything was in the service of the church and depended on the support of the church. The study of law was canon law (the law administered in all ecclesiastical courts, which defined the rights, duties, and powers of the laity and clergy within the church) and the study of theology was Catholic theology. Theology was "the queen of the sciences," not only because its knowledge undergirded the most important professions, but also because it provided the fullest expression of the medieval conception of reality.

The development of a professional clergy, as in the Franciscans and Dominicans, as well as the development of a professional diplomatic corps, demanded higher levels of education. In the thirteenth and fourteenth centuries, monks and mendicants represented the most learned people. This did not include ordinary clergy, however, who remained woefully undereducated until the sixteenth century.

The greatest thinker of the period was Thomas Aquinas (1225–1274), a Dominican friar of noble birth who spent his professional life as professor of theology at the University of Paris. He influenced philosophical theology more than any other individual between Augustine in the fifth century and the Reformers in the sixteenth century. Already considered preeminent among Schoolmen by the time of his death, in time he would be promoted as the "Angelic Doctor" and official theologian of Catholicism.

During his short life he produced a staggering volume of thought, including commentaries on the philosophical writings of Aristotle, commentaries on scripture, liturgical works, philosophical treatises, and some eighty-five sermons. His greatest works, however, are the two *Summas* (systematic encyclopedias), the *Summa Contra Gentiles* and the *Summa Theologica*. Following the basic structure of Lombard's *Sentences*, the four parts of the *Summa Theologica* proceed inexorably through every question that faith poses to the human intellect, including those posed by philosophy. Influenced by Aristotle, Aquinas boldly developed five rational proofs for the existence of God, based on arguments from motion, causality, contingency, degrees of perfection, and design. Since Immanuel Kant's refutation of them in the eighteenth century, most thinkers have recognized them to be invalid as proofs. At most, they establish the probability that God exists rather than actually demonstrating the necessity of God's existence. Thomas regarded God's existence as the last or highest proof of philosophy and as the first truth of theology. His system provides the best example of the medieval synthesis, a scholastic method that views reason and revelation as correlative, not antithetical. Distinguishing theology from philosophy, Aquinas exalted reason while also exposing its fallibility. His life work was to insist that "all truth is God's truth," meaning that good thinking never leads the learner away but always toward God's truth.

The debate over truth did not cease with the Middle Ages. The struggle came to a head as Martin Luther and the Reformers grew increasingly dissatisfied with the medieval epistemological tradition. Emphasizing the noetic (sinful) effects of sin on reason and the human will, Luther denounced Thomistic rationalism, calling unregenerate reason "the Devil's whore." For the Reformers, scripture, not reason or reasonable belief, was the primary source of Christian thought.

Monks and Mystics

Because the monastic movement often challenged the church, it served as a source of renewal. Following a period of striking ecclesiastical degeneration in the ninth and tenth centuries, the founding of a monastery at Cluny in 910 ushered in administrative and spiritual reforms that began to be felt over the next century and a half, even to the highest reaches of the Vatican. Over time, however, wealth and power had a corrupting effect on the rigor of monastic life. The entry of the nobility into the monastery and their inevitable ascent to power led, in turn, to the election of abbots of Cluny as bishops, and even as popes. By the year 1100, more than one thousand Benedictine monasteries belonged to the Cluniac order. Over time, the Benedictine motto—work and prayer—lost one of its central aspects, manual labor, as monks increasingly focused on prayer and intellectual labor. The library and scriptorium became sites for study, teaching, and the copying of manuscripts. Out of such labor arose the distinctive monastic culture that has been called "the love of learning."

The influence of Cluny remained strong until the early twelfth century, and even at that date produced a final remarkable leader in Peter the Venerable (1094–1156). Peter became abbot in 1122 and defended Cluny's commitment to scholarship against another famous monastic reformer, Bernard of Clairvaux (1090–1153). Bernard began as a monk of a second great reforming monastery in France, the Abbey of Citeaux, founded in 1098. Its monks, known as Cistercians, sought a more rigorous observance of rules than was practiced in communities associated with Cluny. Within a century, some five hundred monasteries became associated with Citeaux. The central feature of Cistercian monks was the embrace of manual labor as an ideal, returning to the balance between work and prayer that the Benedictine Rule had first envisaged.

Bernard became the most famous—and sometimes the most contentious—of the reformers in the Benedictine tradition. In 1115 he left Citeaux to found a monastery at Clairvaux. Bernard was a man of great ability and strong opinion who actively exerted power on a number of fronts. Kings, bishops, and even popes looked to him for guidance. At the synod of Troyes in 1128, he wrote the rules and helped approve the new order of Knights Templar. He later intervened in a disputed papal election and for a time was the most influential churchmen of his day. He was a preacher of stunning ability, evident in his "Homilies on the Song of Songs," a masterpiece of mystical theology. Bernard took his role as reformer seriously, sharply criticizing the Cluniac monks and attacking as heretic the brilliant theologian Abelard in 1140. Many earlier mystics turned to the divinity of Christ; Bernard turned to the human Jesus. His contemplation of Jesus' life led him to poetry, and today millions of Christians still sing hymns attributed to Bernard: "O Sacred Head Now Wounded," "Jesus, Thou Joy of Loving Hearts," and "Jesus, the Very Thought of Thee."

Even though the Fourth Lateran Council (1215) prohibited the establishment of new religious orders, Pope Innocent III had already approved two significant innovations to monastic life. The emergence of the Dominicans and the Franciscans in the thirteenth century sparked another cycle of renewal in the life, thought, and service of the church. These orders became known as mendicant (the term comes from the Latin word for "beggars"), and the term "friar" distinguished them from monks because, unlike monks, they went forth to live and serve among the people. Just as monastic houses had once arisen to minister in the countryside, so the mendicant friars now emerged to meet the spiritual needs of townspeople.

The first of the mendicant orders to be approved was founded by Francis of Assisi (1182–1226) in 1209. Abandoning his wealth and status to serve Christ in poverty, the charismatic Francis left home in ragged clothes, wandering the countryside with followers he called his "little brothers." Preaching the joys of poverty and paying attention to outcasts, they survived by depending on alms. A noblewoman named Clare, a friend of Francis from Assisi, founded a corresponding order of women known as the Poor Clares.

Francis loved nature; legend says he preached to the birds. In his "Canticle of the Sun," still prayed by many, he praised God for "our brother the sun, our sister the moon, and our mother the earth." As his life neared its close, he even praised God for "our sister . . . death." Before his conversion, we are told, Francis abhorred lepers. One day, however, he met a leper while riding his horse near Assisi. Though the sight of the leper filled him with disgust, Francis got off his horse and kissed the leper. When the leper put out his hand, Francis gave him money. Upon mounting his horse, he looked around and could not see the leper. He realized it was the face of Jesus he had kissed. The story of Francis has provided perhaps the best-loved model of Christlikeness in the history of the church.

The early history of the Franciscans is complex, and over time it became difficult to maintain Francis's original, radical ideals. The order eventually committed itself to scholarship and gave rise to great theologians and mystical teachers such as Duns Scotus (1265–1308) and Giovanni di Fidanza, better known as St. Bonaventure (1217–1274).

The second order of mendicants, the Dominicans, was founded by the Spaniard Dominic de Guzmán (1170–1221). He studied arts and theology, and then sold his possessions during a famine to help the poor. He became enthralled with the ideal of preaching the gospel to pagans before founding an order of preachers, approved by Innocent III in 1216. The great learning and dedication of this order produced great theologians such as Thomas Aquinas and great mystics such as Meister Eckhart, John Tauler, and Henry Suso.

Because of their zeal to oppose heresy, both Dominicans and Franciscans were used by the papacy in the process of inquisition. Together, these mendicant orders not only served as instruments of papal policy, but they energized evangelization and the care of the poor. Their commitment to the intellectual life also made them leading movements in the development of medieval universities.

The fourteenth and fifteen centuries saw the flourishing of mysticism as an expression of Christian faith. We have already noted the presence of mystics among the mendicant orders. To them can be added the female mystics Catherine of Siena (1347–1380) and Birgitta of Sweden (1303–1373), whose mystical vision were surprisingly activist, calling for the unification of the papacy and the reform of the clergy. The fourteenth century experienced the Great Plague, or the Black Death, which began in 1331 and extended to 1351. It decimated Europe as it did the rest of the inhabited world. The plague was preceded by the great famine of 1315 to 1317, caused by centuries of moderate climate followed by what climatologists term "the little ice age." Between 1310 and 1330 there were severe winters and cold summers. Beginning in 1315, this climatic shift brought decreased crops and a famine that spread across Europe, leading to the death of some 10 percent of the population of Northern Europe. The starvation caused extreme social crime, including widespread theft and murder. A mere nine years later, the plague hit. The bubonic plague, spread by fleas carried by rats, killed half the population of China before spreading to the Middle East and Europe, were it yielded similar results.

During this period the papacy was also caught up in the dynastic struggles of the Holy Roman emperors as well as other kingdoms. From 1337 to 1453, England and France fought the "Hundred Years War," partly as an expression of nationalism and partly as a distorted version of holy war. Joan of Arc (1412–1431), later declared a saint by the church, played a small role in this endless war in response to visions—heavenly voices, she claimed—rallying the French while still a teenager. Captured by the British, she was burned at the stake as a heretic.

Mysticism was particularly evident in England in the fourteenth century. Among the most powerful and remarkably beautiful of the mystical works of this period is *The Cloud of Unknowing*, an anonymous guide to the contemplative life written for monastic readers. The book recognizes that between humans and God there is an impenetrable cloud, so that the point is not knowing God but loving God. Of the writings of the mystics of the late Middle Ages, one still widely read is *The Imitation of Christ*. Attributed to the fifteenth-century Thomas à Kempis, the book may be based in part on earlier works. It begins: "He that followeth Me walketh not in darkness, saith the Lord. . . . Let therefore our chief endeavor be to meditate upon the life of Jesus Christ." For the author, as for Christians in general, the life of Christ exceeds all others.

Among the anchorites (those who lived as hermits within the context of the cathedrals) are two English figures, Richard Rolle (1300–1349), known for his beautiful poems on the passion of Christ, and Julian of Norwich (1342–1416), who used female attributions to the divine in her series of visions she called "Showings." Her *Revelations of Divine Love*, written around 1395 and widely acknowledge as one of the classics of the spiritual life, is the first book in the English language known to have been written by a woman. The century that saw the Black Death ravage Europe also witnessed a rebirth of classical learning.

Heretics and Inquisition

Modern Christians believe deeply that religious faith is a matter of personal choice, but medieval Christians viewed faith as the foundation of society. Denying doctrine was tantamount to treason, and when people turned against the church, they entered the ranks of heretics. Christendom functioned as a sociopolitical body, and Christian faith was its source of life and vitality. Thus, heresy in Christendom was no more acceptable than cancer in the body.

So what is heresy? For medieval Catholics, heresy was the denial by a baptized person of any revealed truth of the Christian faith. Among these truths were the unity of the church and the authority of the pope as head of the church. Therefore, disobedience to established authority was considered heresy. In dealing with heretics, the church had two primary objectives: converting the heretic and preserving Christian society. How far would the church go to protect society?

Heresy drove the medieval church to dangerous extremes, employing violence to safeguard society. Creating the Inquisition, both as an instrument of torture and of execution, the church accepted a line of action all but impossible to reconcile with the peaceable kingdom toward which it aspired. Historian Bruce Shelley, commenting on the irony, notes that "in driving out one devil the church opened the door for seven others." The contradiction was not widely apparent at the time. The same church that sent crusading armies against infidels could command the burning of heretics. Almost everyone agreed that a pure church was the will of God, but where can one find the one pure church? Is it in the papal palace in Rome, in crusading armies, or, as Francis of Assisi thought, in the poor and needy of the world?

One of the earliest voices against the worldliness of the medieval church was Arnold, an abbot in the town of Brescia, in northern Italy. In a series of sermons, he urged the church to surrender its property and secular power to the state and return to the poverty and simplicity of the early church. The pope, Innocent II, replied by banishing Arnold from Italy. After five years in exile, Arnold appeared in Rome, where he joined a movement to overthrow papal domination. In 1155 he was captured and executed by burning, his ashes thrown into the Tiber River.

Shortly thereafter another voice for poverty arose in France, that of Peter Waldo (1140–1218), a rich merchant of Lyons. Inspired to forsake worldly success, he sought a priest to find out how to live like Christ. The priest cited the answer Jesus gave to the rich young ruler: "If you wish to be perfect, go, sell your possessions, and give the money to the poor" (Matt. 19:21). Providing an adequate income for his wife and daughters, he gave the rest of his estate to the poor. To launch his mission, Waldo enlisted two priests to translate portions of the Bible into French. He gained a few followers and sent them out two by two, after the biblical pattern, to teach and explain the scriptures. Waldo's unauthorized preaching soon met stiff opposition, resulting in the group's excommunication in 1184 by Pope Lucius III. The Waldensians, as they came to be known, were clearly a back-to-the-Bible movement, and in that they anticipated the Reformers, though their view of salvation, a life of penance and poverty, lacked the emphasis of salvation by grace, central to the Reformation.

A third dissenting movement, and by far the most problematic for the medieval church, was a group called Cathari, meaning "pure ones." Because they were influential in the town of Albi in southern France, some people called them Albigenses. Like the Gnostics in the early church, the Cathari viewed the universe as the scene of an eternal conflict between two powers, the one good and the other evil. Matter, including the human body, is evil, and that meant that Christians should avoid practices such as marriage, sexual intercourse, eating meat, and material possessions. Christ, to the Cathari, was not a human being but a life-giving spirit, and because he was not human, salvation by death on a cross was not possible. The Cathari were heretical in ways that Arnold and Waldo were not. Whereas Arnold and Waldo refused to submit to church authorities, the Cathari rejected the authority of Christianity itself. By 1200, the Cathari were spreading at an alarming rate. The Roman church responded with crusades and the Inquisition.

Innocent III was determined to crush the Albigensian heresy. The northern French were anxious to invade southern France, then a separate country. When Innocent called for a crusade—not against the Muslims but against Christian heretics—the northern French came pillaging and murdering, uprooting the Albigenses and claiming the ravaged territories of the south. An early version of the Inquisition had appeared earlier, in 1184, when Pope Lucius required bishops to "inquire" into the beliefs of their subjects. If the inquiry resulted in the charge of heresy or of harboring a heretic, the result was immediate excommunication. In 1215 the Fourth Lateran Council provided for the state's punishment of heretics, including the confiscation of their property, excommunication for those unwilling to move against the heretic, and complete forgiveness of sins for those cooperating.

In 1220 the pope took the Inquisition from the hands of the bishops and turned it over to the newly-formed Dominican order, and nine years later the Synod of Toulouse systematized inquisitorial policies, leaving the alleged heretic with virtually no rights. The final significant step came in 1252, when Pope Innocent IV authorized torture as a means of getting information and confessions from accused heretics.

In the fourteenth century, two brave individuals—John Wycliffe, an Englishman, and John Hus, a Czech—dared challenge the church's authority. John Wycliffe (1300–1384), a professor at Oxford, attacked the idea that the church is a hierarchical organization ruled by the pope. His view was like that of Augustine, who distinguished the institutional church from the kingdom of God. The church, he argued, is not the hierarchy but all the elect, whose lives produce the fruit of their election. The lives of many bishops and priests, he noted, show that they are not among the elect. Wycliffe also protested the wealth of the church, which at that time owned about one-third of the land in England. In his day there were rival popes, each declaring the other damned. On that point, at least, Wycliffe agreed. He believed the Bible should be the authority, not the pope. Some of his followers, later called Lollards, began traveling barefoot around England preaching his ideas and helping to disseminate his translation of the Bible, written in the language of the common people.

Wycliffe aroused greatest hostility for his attack upon the traditional doctrine of transubstantiation. In 1380 he published twelve arguments demonstrating that Christ is present in the elements sacramentally but not materially. His denial of transubstantiation gave his enemies their opportunity. His support dwindled to a small minority at Oxford.

The church responded by damning Wycliffe. He was forced to leave his post at Oxford and was imprisoned for a time. Later, protected by a wealthy nobleman, he resumed his work as a parish priest, and at his death he was buried in consecrated ground. Thirty one years later, however, the Council of Constance ordered his bones dug up, burned, and scattered in the river. Threatened by any translation made by a heretic and not under church supervision, church officials attempted to find and burn all copies of Wycliffe's English Bible.

The long-range significance of Wycliffe's teaching lies in his emphasis on the spiritual freedom of the righteous person. Every person, whether priest or lay, holds an equal place in the eyes of God. The mediating priesthood and the sacrificial masses of the medieval church are no longer essential. The personal relation between an individual and God is central. Thus Wycliffe anticipated Luther's doctrine of justification by faith alone.

From this doctrine of the invisible church of the elect, Wycliffe drew practical conclusions. The true church is a unity that knows nothing of papal primacies and hierarchies, or of holy orders, monks, and friars. Nor can salvation be conditioned by masses, indulgences,[3] penance, or other such rituals. Opposed to pardons, absolutions, the worship of images, the adoration of the saints and the treasury of their merits, and the distinction between venial and mortal sins, he retained belief in purgatory and extreme unction. Images, he said, if they increase devotion, need not be removed, and prayers for the dead were not necessarily wrong. Confession he held to be useful, provided it was voluntary. The standard Wycliffe used to judge the institutional church was the teachings of scripture, and he asserted the right of every individual to examine the Bible directly.

Wycliffe's influence spread to the Continent, where John Hus (1369–1415) took up the cause. Like Wycliffe, Hus preached against the worldliness of the rival popes and many priests, argued that indulgences bring no forgiveness of sin, and wrote that the Bible should be the authority in the church. He adopted Wycliffe's view of the church as an elect company, with Christ, not the pope, its true head. Hus was excommunicated and forced to leave his teaching position at the University of Prague, though he continued writing and preaching. In 1415 he was ordered to appear before the Council of Constance, a council summoned to bring reform to the church. He agreed to renounce any teachings that could be shown to be false, using

---

3. In the teaching of the Roman Catholic Church, indulgences are means to reduce punishment for sins. Indulgences were introduced by the early church and granted to Christians awaiting martyrdom. They draw on the treasury of merit accumulated by Christ and the saints and are granted for specific works or deeds performed by the devout. By the late Middle Ages, the abuses of indulgences, mainly through commercialization, had become a serious problem within the church, the target of attacks by Martin Luther and all Protestant theologians. Eventually the Catholic Church curbed the excesses, but indulgences continue to play a role in modern Catholic religious life.

the Bible as authority for such proof. That council had already ordered the burning of Wycliffe's bones, and Hus acknowledged that he approved many of Wycliffe's teachings. The council condemned him and a month later stripped him of his priestly robes and shaved his head, covering it with a paper crown on which were pictures of demons. As he was led in chains to be burned at the stake, he was taken past a bonfire of his books.

Many were horrified by what the council had done, and Bohemian nationalism lent support to Hus's followers. Hundreds of noblemen assembled to announce their agreement with his doctrines. The pope sent various crusades to attack these rebellious Bohemians, and repeatedly the crusaders were defeated. At the time of the Reformation, some of the Hussites allied with the Lutherans and others with the Calvinists. Known as Moravians, from their roots in Moravia, these pre-Reformation Protestants continue today and are widely admired for their evangelistic mission work, their deeds of service, and their witness on behalf of the cause of nonviolence and peace.

Renaissance

The traditional date for the fall of the (Western) Roman Empire is September 4, 476. That event left Europe fractured and subject to rule by a line of German kings who called their domain the Holy Roman Empire. By the twelfth century, a loose collection of republics began taking shape in the Italian peninsula, which together aimed to recover the glory of ancient Rome. Their efforts would revitalize Europe and provide a blueprint for the modern Western world. The thirteenth and fourteenth centuries witnessed the flowering of the period known as the Renaissance, the rebirth of classical ideals, from some of the greatest minds of all times. It produced some of the finest works of art, architecture, and engineering the world has ever known. No other period of Western civilization can boast of producing so much genius. And nowhere was this genius more evident than in the Italian city of Florence.

The foundation of the Renaissance was the city. In the twelfth and thirteenth centuries, Italy witnessed the rebirth of the city, born from the system of feudalism. Within these newly liberated cities merchants, rather than the traditional aristocracy, emerged as leaders of this vibrant urban life in Italy. Lucrative possibilities existed in banking, insurance, trade, and most other activities that would come to be associated with a modern economy. This

PHASE 7: RENAISSANCE (1095–1500)

new style of existence was far removed from the life of the itinerant merchants of the early Middle Ages, traveling peddlers who simply toted their goods from fair to fair. Making new demands upon those who practiced it, this style of life required education—an education directed toward secular ends, not toward the service of the church, to which almost all academic pursuit had been dedicated for a thousand years. But the real driving force behind the growth of secular learning was the demand for trained lawyers created by the sheer complexity of the new society. The study of the law, in turn, revived enthusiasm for Latin and Greek and the authors of classical times. The result was a phenomenon that came to be known as humanism.

Florence reached its peak between the eleventh and fifteenth centuries, when it became wealthy because of textile manufacture, trade, and banking. After several experiments with representative government, Florence was ruled by an oligarchy of wealthy aristocrats, among whom the Medici family became dominant in the fifteen century. Under the patronage of these wealthy families, the arts and literature flourished as nowhere else in Europe. Lorenzo de' Medici, who ruled Florence in the late fifteenth century, was perhaps the greatest patron of the arts in the history of the West.

Florence was the city of such writers as Dante, Petrarch, and Boccaccio and of artists and engineers such as Alberti, Botticelli, Brunelleschi, Cellini, Leonardo da Vinci, and Michelangelo. Because of its dominance in literature, the Florentine language became the literary language of Italy. Humanism brought new philosophical ideas and a full appreciation of classicism. In Florence, Machiavelli inaugurated the new political science, Guicciardini introduced modern historical prose, and Galileo created and developed experimental science.

The modern mind has not yet come to grips with the setting of its own birth and the nature of its parent. Was the Renaissance a period or a movement, an evolution or a revolution, an economic phenomenon or spontaneous intellectual combustion? Only one thing is certain: Italy was the seedbed of the Renaissance and Florence its finest flower. Florence's artistic and literary movements inaugurated the Renaissance, deeply challenging the certainties of the medieval worldview and forever altering the way the Western world thought and expressed itself.

About the year 1450, Johannes Gutenberg invented the printing press, and this helped produce a cultural revolution. Now the works of scholars could be disseminated and ancient manuscripts copied and preserved relatively free from error. The Latin Vulgate had been the only scripture most had known, but the new interest in ancient manuscripts focused attention on the study of the Bible in its original languages of Greek and Hebrew. By 1380, John Wycliffe led a team of scholars at Oxford in the translation of the Bible into English, inspiring Martin Luther (1483–1546) in Germany and William Tyndale (1494–1536) in England, and it was only a matter of time before laypeople would begin reading the scriptures in their vernacular language.

Study Questions

1. Whom do you consider the chief protagonist in the seventh phase of the church's history (twelfth through fifteenth centuries CE)? Support your answer.

2. Do you agree with the author's choice that the flowering of the Renaissance in Florence, Italy is this epoch's turning point? Why or why not? Is there another event you consider more noteworthy? If so, what is it? Support your choice.

3. In this epoch, does "the church" live up to its nature and destiny as God's new creation? Why or why not?

4. What values and dangers do you see in having a pope who is the visible head and spokesperson for Christians?

5. What light does this chapter shed on church-state relations?

6. What lessons can we learn from the Crusades?

7. Assess the merits of the perspective known as the "medieval synthesis." How did this approach influence the late medieval understanding of sin, salvation, and the sacraments?

8. Discuss the merit of parochial versus public education today. Would you encourage or discourage your children from attending Christian (or Catholic) colleges and universities? Why or why not?

9. What "proofs" did Thomas Aquinas provide for the existence of God? Which do you find most persuasive? Which do you find least persuasive?

10. Have you ever thought of joining a monastic community? Why or why not?

11. How did the Renaissance prepare the way for the Reformation?

12. How did the Renaissance prepare the way for modernity?

Part 3

Reformation

(1500–present)

Chapter 8

Phase 8: Reformation (1500–1700)

Catholics, Protestants, and Radicals

Significant Events: Two events vie for significance during the Protestant Reformation: (1) Calvin's ministry in Geneva (including his preaching and teaching activity and the publication of his *Institutes of the Christian Religion*) and (2) the Council of Trent (including the Roman Church's official response to Protestantism, attempts at self-reformation, and the resultant missionary movement that expanded Catholicism globally).

Turning Points: Three events qualify as turning points for this era: (1) Luther's attempts to reform the Roman Church, including the posting of his Ninety-Five Theses, his defense at the imperial Diet of Worms, and his writings, which helped elucidate the three Protestant principles; (2) the Schleitheim Confession, which clarified the meaning of Christian discipleship and led to the denominational theory; and (3) the English Act of Supremacy (1534), which helped establish regional forms of Christianity. In my estimation, Luther's life and legacy hold priority, for they set the tone for what followed.

Among the many important ecclesiastical developments and events during the sixteenth and seventeenth centuries, the following helped shape the church's conception of faith, vocation, and governance:

1. Martin Luther and the dawn of Protestantism

2. Ulrich Zwingli, John Calvin, John Knox, and Reformed Christianity

3. The Anabaptist tradition (Radical Reformers)

4. Anglicanism and the English Reformation

5. Puritans and Quakers in England and in America

6. The Catholic Reformation

During the Reformation of the sixteenth century, Protestant thinkers began questioning doctrines and practices established during the medieval period, including ecclesiastical hierarchicalism, the authority of the pope, the estrangement between laity and clergy, sacramentalism, monasticism, the veneration of relics and saints, the emphasis on good works as meritorious for salvation, and the sale of indulgences. In so doing, most Protestants were not rejecting church authority, but rather subordinating it to biblical constraints. While retaining the ancient creeds and the theological formulations of the great ecumenical councils of the fourth and fifth centuries, mainline Protestants rejected those doctrines, practices, and ceremonies for which no clear warrant existed in the Bible, or which seemed to contradict its letter and intent.

The spirit of reform erupted with surprising intensity in the sixteenth century, giving birth to Protestantism and challenging papal leadership of Western Christendom. Four major traditions marked early Protestantism: Lutheran, Anabaptist, Reformed, and Anglican Christianity. Shortly thereafter, Roman Catholic Christianity regrouped and, led by the Jesuits, recovered its moral zeal. Bloody struggles between Catholics and Protestants followed, and Europe was ravaged by war before it became obvious that Western Christendom was permanently divided.

Martin Luther and the Dawn of Protestantism

What is Protestantism? According to church sociologist Ernst Troelsch, Protestantism is a variation of Catholicism, asking four traditional Catholic questions and arriving at different answers. The four questions that Protestantism answered in a new way are: (1) How is a person saved? (2) Where does religious authority lie? (3) What is the church? and (4) What is the essence of Christian living? During the sixteenth century, Protestant Reformers agreed on the essentials, but fresh answers emerged in Martin Luther's conflict with Rome.

The Protestant Reformation brought profound changes to European culture, for the Reformers repudiated the synthesis mentality that had dominated Christian thought for centuries. Many secular historians have argued that political, economic, and social issues inspired the major transformations of the sixteenth century. While these forces influenced the development and course of the Reformation, spiritual and moral issues were primary. Above all else, the Reformers sought to correct the doctrine and life of the church. Their movement represented "a revolt of conscience."

Two major worldviews molded medieval intellectual and religious culture: the Greek and the biblical traditions. The Reformers sought to repudiate medieval thought, with its reliance upon reason. In their opinion, medieval thinkers had made a conscious and thoroughgoing attempt to fuse radically different traditions into one theological system. The Reformers' attack upon extravagances of the papal court, the sale of indulgences and church offices, and excessive church taxation were part of a larger campaign to return the church to its biblical foundation. Their cry became *ad fontes*, "back to the sources," meaning that they wished to return to the scriptures of the Old and New Testaments.

The son of a peasant miner, Martin Luther (1483–1546) had every intention of becoming a lawyer until one day in 1505 he was caught in a thunderstorm. Struck by a bolt of lightning, he prayed to the patroness of miners, "St. Anne, save me, and I'll become a monk." He kept his vow and two weeks later entered an Augustinian monastery. Obsessed with his own sin, he tried austere acts of penance such as prolonged fasting, sleeping outdoors in freezing weather, and self-flagellation. The purity and wrath of God, however, proved to be too great, and no amount of penance soothed his spirit.

The troubled monk was assigned to the chair of biblical studies at the recently established Wittenberg University, where he found a different view of God. In 1515, while pondering Paul's epistle to the Romans, Luther came upon the statement that "the just shall live by his faith" (1:17). Here was the key to his dilemma. The answer lay in Christ's identity with sinful humanity. Luther understood clearly now the gospel message: salvation is only by faith in Christ. As a gift of God's grace, it cannot be earned, but merely affirmed by an act of faith. Luther had come by his famous doctrine of justification by faith alone. He saw how sharply it clashed with the Roman Church's doctrine of justification by faith and good works. The implications of Luther's discovery were enormous. If salvation comes through faith in

Christ alone, the intercession of priests, masses, and prayers to the saints was unnecessary. The mediation of the institutional church, through hierarchical, sacramental, and monastic means, was superfluous.

Luther, like other Reformers, had no desire to start a new religion, denomination, or sect, but rather to reform the church of its excess. He had no idea where his spiritual discovery was leading, but he knew it was important. It took a flagrant abuse of church finances, the sale of indulgences, to propel him into confrontation with papal authority. Luther's displeasure increased noticeably during 1517, when the Dominican John Tetzel traveled throughout Germany on behalf of a papal fundraising campaign to complete the construction of St. Peter's basilica in Rome. In exchange for a contribution, Tetzel boasted, he would provide donors with an indulgence that would even apply beyond the grave and free souls from purgatory. "As soon as the coin in the coffer rings," went his jingle, "the soul from purgatory springs."

The Reformation is often said to have begun on October 31, 1517, when, protesting the sale of indulgences, Luther nailed his Ninety-Five Theses to the bulletin board on the door of the church at Wittenberg. While this statement did not present his theology, it represented a proposal for theological debate. Copies of Luther's theses were published and republished all over Europe, sparking a theological revolution. Luther came to regard the printing press as one of the great gifts of God.

Within a short time, the German Dominicans denounced Luther to Rome as preaching "dangerous doctrines." The Vatican issued a series of counter-theses, arguing that anyone who criticized the sale of indulgences was guilty of heresy. Luther decided to put his case before the German people. Utilizing the printing press, his reply came through a vast literary production. In one year alone (1520) he published five major works, relying on biblical arguments for support. His *Treatise on Good Works* demonstrated how faith in Christ was the only good work that God expected from repentant sinners. In *The Papacy of Rome* he attacked the pope directly, calling him Antichrist because he kept people from understanding and heeding the message of the gospel. His *Address to the Christian Nobility of the German Nation* called on the princes of northern Europe to throw off the tyranny—economic and political as well as spiritual—that bound them to Rome. His *Babylonian Captivity of the Church* examined the sevenfold system of sacraments, claiming to find only baptism and the Lord's Supper (and perhaps confession) as authorized by Christ in the New Testament. In contrast to the sharp polemics of these works, Luther published *The Freedom of a Christian*, a conciliatory effort explaining how saving grace results in doing good works.

Among the ideas in these writings, three gained emphasis: (1) the supremacy of scripture as the only source and rule for Christian faith and practice (*sola scriptura*), (2) justification by grace received by faith alone (*sola gratia/sola fide*), and (3) the priesthood of believers (all church members are called to be "priests" to one another, the keys of the kingdom having been granted to the whole community [cf. Matt 18:18; 16:19]). Known as the "three principles of Protestantism," these ideals countered essential aspects of medieval Catholicism: (1) "scripture alone" opposed Roman emphasis on the twofold authority of scripture and tradition, which made the decrees of popes and councils the only legitimate interpreters of the Bible; (2) "grace alone" opposed the Roman theory that faith and good works cooperated as sources of justification; (3) "the priesthood of believers" opposed the theory of the church as a vast hierarchy, which made ordained priests the necessary mediators between God and humanity.

In June 1520, Pope Leo X issued a decree condemning Luther and giving him sixty days to turn from his heretical course. Luther received his copy in October. At the end of his sixty-day period of grace, he led a throng of students outside Wittenberg and burned copies of medieval church documents, adding for good measure a copy of the decree condemning him. That was his answer. In 1521 the pope declared him a heretic, making complete his excommunication. The problem now fell into the hands of Charles V, a young man of twenty-one who, in addition to serving as king of Spain, had recently been elected Holy Roman Emperor. He summoned Luther to the imperial Diet (assembly) meeting at the German city of Worms to recant. Before the assembly Luther again insisted that only biblical authority would sway him: "I will not recant, for to go against conscience is neither honest nor safe. Here I stand, I cannot do otherwise." With these words, Protestantism was born. Protestants would obey the Bible before all other authorities. Europe—and the church—would never be the same.

Charles V gave Luther twenty-one days before the sentence fell. It never came. Luther was saved from arrest and death by the prince of Saxony, Duke Frederick the Wise, whose domains included Wittenberg. The duke gave Luther sanctuary at Wartburg Castle, where he remained for nearly a year, disguised as a minor nobleman. During this time, he translated the New Testament into German, an important step toward reshaping public and private worship in Germany. (In 1534 Luther completed his translation of the entire Bible, on which he worked with the help of colleagues for over a decade.) Meanwhile the revolt against Rome spread and new reformers appeared on the scene. Princes, dukes, and electors defied the condemnation of Luther by giving support to the new movement. In 1522 Luther returned to Wittenberg to put into effect the spiritual reform that became the model for much of Germany. He called for the abolition of the office of bishop, arguing that the churches needed pastors, not dignitaries. Advocating for the abandonment of celibacy for monks and nuns, in 1525 Luther married Katherine von Bora, herself a former nun.

The last twenty years of his life were not as dramatic as the years between 1517 and 1525, which had made him both the most revered and the most hated person in Europe. Among his favorite writings he singled out the Small Catechism of 1529, which through simple questions and answers explained the Ten Commandments, the Apostles' Creed, and the Lord's Prayer. In that same year, Luther engaged in a momentous debate with Ulrich Zwingli, a distinguished preacher from the Swiss city of Zurich. The two reformers found that they could agree on most points of doctrine and practice, but not on the meaning of the Lord's Supper. Luther held that Christ was truly present in the Supper, Zwingli that he was present only symbolically. Inability to resolve that troubling issue indicated more clearly than any previous event that the reform movement would lead to Protestant churches rather than to a reform of the one Western church.

By 1530, when a summit conference of Reformation leaders convened in Augsburg to draw up a common statement of faith, leadership of the movement had begun to pass from Luther. The Reformer was still an outlaw and unable to attend. The task of presenting Lutheranism fell to Philip Melanchthon, a young professor of Greek at Wittenberg and Luther's closest colleague. The Augsburg Confession, signed by several important princes in attendance, became the doctrinal standard for the Lutheran churches that were emerging in Germany, Scandinavia, and Eastern Europe. After 1530 Emperor Charles V made clear his intention to crush the growing heresy. In defense, the Lutheran princes banded together. The combatants reached a compromise in the Peace of Augsburg (1555), which allowed each prince to decide the religion of his subjects and ordered all Catholic bishops to give up their property if they turned Lutheran. The effects of these provisions were profound. Lutheranism became a state religion in large portions of the empire. Religious opinions became the private property of the princes, and individuals had to believe whatever form of Christianity their prince wanted them to believe.

Luther's greatest contribution, however, was not political but religious. He took four Christian concerns and offered radically new answers. To the question, How is a person saved? Luther replied, "not by works but by faith alone." To the question, Where does religious authority lie? he answered, "not in the institutional Catholic church but in the Word of God found in the Bible." To the question, What is the church? he responded, "the whole community of Christian believers, since all are priests before God." And to the question, What is the essence of Christian living? he replied, "serving God in any useful calling, whether ordained or lay." To this day, any classical description of Protestantism must echo those responses.[1]

Zwingli, Calvin, Knox, and Reformed Christianity

If one thinks of the Protestant Reformers along a spectrum running from conservative to truly radical, we would place Luther along the conservative end. Despite his bold new ideas, he still affirmed many elements of Catholic worship. If we continue moving left on the spectrum, we come next to a group we call Reformed Christians. They wanted even greater change than Luther, and their ideas had major implications for politics. To the far left are the Anabaptists (Radical Reformers), for their notions of society were the most far-reaching and extreme.

Two years after Luther posted his theses on the parish door, Ulrich Zwingli (1484–1531) became pastor of the Great Minster Church in Zurich. Unlike the fiery Luther, Zwingli came to the fore as a pastor. Because his primary concern was with worship and devotional practice, he became an early exponent of the "Reformed" branch of Protestantism. Like Luther, Zwingli had a Renaissance education, and he read ancient church theology in Latin and Greek. Under the influence of the famous humanist scholar Erasmus (1466–1536), the Catholic linguist who compiled and edited the Greek New Testament, Zwingli had come to revere the language and message of the New Testament. A patriot, Zwingli resented the power of Catholic bishops in Switzerland. They were often corrupt and more interested in secular than religious power.

1. Shelley, *Church History*, 257.

Zwingli became critical of Catholic veneration of saints, the ritual of the Mass, and all the rules about feasting and fasting. He wanted to reform Christian practice so that it was closer to the instructions provided in the New Testament, at least as he read them. Zwingli's understanding of the Lord's Supper is important. Luther, you might recall, held that Christ was truly present in the Supper, whereas Zwingli held that he was present only symbolically. This helps us see that the starting point of the Reformed break with Catholicism was a critique of idolatry, not a critique of religious law, as it was with Luther. Moreover, Reformed Protestants generally had more confidence that God used grace to perfect Christians over time, to enable them to better follow the commandments. From this perspective, Zwingli found Luther's explanation of justification too individualist. He was worried about how it would work in practice, in a Christian community.

In 1523, Zurich politicians decided to reform the churches in their territory, with Zwingli's help. He started with worship, not a university curriculum, as did Luther. Zwingli urged the officials to moderation, but they wanted radical change. They wanted to destroy icons and all suggestion of idolatry. By 1525 the Swiss Reformation turned violent when Zwingli participated in a civil war that pitted Protestants against Catholics. In 1531, Zwingli died on the battlefield, and the Reformed torch passed to John Calvin (1509–1564), the second-generation Reformer who consolidated Protestant gains and became the Reformation's most important scholar. Like Luther, he attempted to reform doctrine and church organization, and like Zwingli, he was concerned with reforming worship and devotional practice. But unlike both, he also attempted to bring the socio-political order into harmony with the teachings of scripture.

Born in Noyon (Picardy), France, he studied law to please his father. However, his real passion was for ancient languages and literature. After his father died, he trained to be a priest, but he became disillusioned with the French clergy, seeing them as immoral and ignorant. Like Luther, he experienced a dramatic conversion, although he was not driven by guilt or fear as his German counterpart. He began to preach to congregations in the area, and started his career as a prolific writer expounding Protestant ideals. When severe persecution broke out against Protestant Reformers, Calvin found refuge in the Swiss city of Basel, and there, at the age of twenty-seven, he completed the first edition of his most influential work, the *Institutes of the Christian Religion*. By the time the final edition was published in 1559, this work had grown from a short exposition of Christian doctrine to the most significant theological work of the Reformation. The preface of the first edition, a letter to Francis I of France protesting his persecution of the Protestants, is a masterpiece of apologetic literature. No one had spoken so effectively on their behalf, and with this letter Calvin assumed a position of leadership in the Protestant cause. After its publication, Calvin sought haven in Strasbourg, but warfare forced him to travel by way of Geneva.

The Geneva to which Calvin came was a vigorous, liberty-loving city of some ten thousand inhabitants. Under William Farel's leadership, the small independent republic had recently become nominally Protestant. Its churches had been seized for Protestantism and its four monasteries and a nunnery closed. The Council in charge of political affairs had taken drastic measures to regulate private morals and to compel attendance at sermons. Despite these measures, Geneva's leaders were primarily motivated by political rather than religious consideration. In the city, which was a magnet for exiles and expatriates, the political climate was unpredictable. Because these were perilous times, Calvin wished to travel through Geneva incognito.

When Farel discovered that Calvin was in town, he went to meet him. Farel was then in the midst of a vigorous but unorganized attempt to establish the new Genevan Protestant church. The chaos of the situation required the touch of a master organizer, and Farel was quick to detect in Calvin the helper he needed. Calvin was reluctant to give up the prospect of a quiet life of study at Strasbourg, for he was by nature retiring and studious. But Farel pressed him into service with an argument that was almost an imprecation: "I denounce unto you, in the name of Almighty God, that if, under the pretext of prosecuting your studies, you refuse to labor with us in this work of the Lord, the Lord will curse you, as seeking yourself rather than Christ." Upon hearing these words, Calvin gave up his intended journey and enlisted in the service of Geneva.

In Geneva, Calvin established a system of civic and ecclesiastical governance that rejected papal authority and created a central hub from which Reformation theology could be propagated. Working with unusual dedication throughout his career, he neglected neither the priestly nor the prophetic duties of his office. Theodore Beza, his early biographer, estimates that Calvin preached 286 times a year, while also lecturing 180 times. His growing reputation brought people from far and near to Geneva in search of his advice, and he maintained a voluminous correspondence, of which four thousand letters remain. Any matter arising in one of the Reformed churches, of which there were a great many by this time, was almost certainly brought to his attention for settlement.

The Protestant Reformation, based upon concepts such as the priesthood of all believers, the importance of the individual conscience, and the supremacy of scripture, made widespread literacy important. For a long time Calvin wished to set up a college—a municipal school system for all children—with the academy as the center of instruction for the very best students. Such a school had been founded in the fifteenth century, but no longer suited the requirements of the day. The establishment in 1559 of his academy, with Beza as rector of what soon became a full university, was Calvin's crowning achievement in the building of a Christian state. It provided free instruction for all grades from primary work through high school. Though the need of preparing men for the ministry was an important reason for the establishment of the university, Calvin was also motivated by a profound desire to train an educated Protestant laity. Broadly educated himself, he attracted learned scholars to the school and helped elevate its reputation and extend its influence.

The endeavor flourished. The academy, which attracted students from all over Europe, served as a model for other academies around the world and eventually became the University of Geneva. Lest we think that Calvin was simply founding a university, we must keep in mind that he considered the crown of education to be theology, for which all arts and sciences were a preparation. Students were trained, not for degrees or lucrative employment, but to serve God as preachers or as godly civil servants.

When one examines the life of John Calvin, and the many demands upon his life as a cleric, one wonders how he found the time and energy for education, religious or secular. Yet it was such a priority that in his latter years he is known to have taught ten hours a day, six days a week. Such an emphasis on education, however, is not surprising. The humanism of the Renaissance stimulated unprecedented academic ferment and a concern for academic freedom. Earnest debates took place in the universities about the nature of the church and the source and extent of the authority of the papacy, of church councils, and of princes. The invention of the printing press, while making the Bible increasingly available to the general public, allowed quick broadcasting of ideas. Popular discontent at moral corruption in the church, coupled with the spread of nationalistic fervor, led support for a reformation as never before.

Calvin's starting point was the sovereignty of God. The fundamental principle informing every chapter of the *Institutes* is his view of God as majestic and sovereign over all creation. Calvin's main thesis was that human duty is not to know God, because God is transcendent. Instead, our duty is to worship and obey. Only worship can bridge the gap between humanity and divinity.

Calvin used the term "election" to explain how God's sovereignty operates in salvation. His stress on the sovereignty of God led him to the extraordinary (and controversial) doctrine of double predestination. He taught that before the beginning of time, God ordained some to hell and elected others for heaven. Predestination can be found in scripture (see, for example, Rom. 8:29–31, Eph. 1:4–5, John 5:21; 6:44; and 15:16), though it is important to emphasize that the Bible is characterized by tension between sovereignty and human responsibility. While the roots of predestination go back to Augustine, no theologian carried the logical consequences of the doctrine to such an extreme as Calvin. Like Augustine, Calvin believed in the "depravity of man." Calvin did not deny human freedom, for in his view humans are free, but only to sin. Ultimately, whatever good resides in us has God as its source.

While the doctrine of predestination is easily dismissed by modern Christians and non-Christians alike, it is important to understand that Calvin's idea of predestination came out of his observation of the human condition. Calvin looked around and saw that some people heard God's word and responded, while others just didn't listen. He needed an explanation for why some people reject the gospel and seem immune to God's grace, when God is all-powerful and just. Calvin was not an ivory-tower theologian, but a practical theologian with a logical mind. To him, predestination made sense. The doctrine was not intended to be shared with unbelievers, for its ultimate purpose was to assure the believer of God's steadfast love. "If God is for us," Paul asks rhetorically, "who is against us?" (Rom. 8:31).

At the end of the sixteenth and the beginning of the seventeenth centuries, Jacob Arminius (1560–1609), a Dutch theologian, proposed an alternative to the view of predestination shared by Augustine, Luther, and Calvin. Arminius believed that God's foreknowledge preceded God's predestination, and that therefore God's election is not absolute, but conditioned. God chooses individuals based on foreknowing whether they would freely accept or reject Christ and his work of salvation. Arminius sought a middle ground between Calvin's belief in absolute predestination and Pelagius's teaching on human autonomy. Unlike Pelagius, Arminius believed that original sin cripples the human will. Without God's preparatory grace humans are dead in sin. Unlike universalists, who argue that Christ's death paid the penalty for everyone's sin, Arminians argue that Christ's salvation is available only to those who choose to accept it. Salvation, therefore, is a cooperative effort between humans and God, much as Thomas Aquinas taught in his medieval synthesis.

Arminius's theology strongly swayed Protestant thought, particularly evangelicalism. John Wesley popularized Arminian ideas in England's Evangelical Awakening of the eighteenth century and made them central to Methodist theology. Many American denominations, such as Baptists, independents, and holiness groups, are committed to Arminian views.

Despite theological controversy, Reformed theology had a powerful political effect across Europe. Luther tended to consider the state supreme, and German princes often determined where and how the gospel would be preached. But Calvin taught that no state, religious or secular, had any claim to absolute power. Calvin's Geneva encouraged the growth of representative assemblies, and stressed their right to resist the tyranny of monarchs. From Geneva, many students returned to their own countries to establish Calvinist principles. In sixteenth-century Europe, Calvinist resistance to the exercise of arbitrary power by monarchs was a key factor in the development of modern constitutional governments.

In France, Calvinism remained a minority, but thanks to influential converts among the nobility, the movement gained strategic importance. Known as Huguenots, French Calvinists threatened to seize leadership of the country when thousands were massacred on St. Bartholomew's Day in 1572. In the Netherlands, Calvinism offered a rallying point for opposition to the oppressive rule of Catholic Spain. In Scotland, under the influence of John Knox (c. 1513–1572), Calvinists created something unique. When civil war broke out in 1559, Knox rushed home from Geneva to point his country in the direction of Calvinism. By the summer of 1560, Calvinists were in control of Edinburgh. Knox drafted the articles of religion that parliament accepted for the country, thereby abolishing Roman Catholicism. Today, Scotland remains the most devoutly Calvinist country in the world.

The Anabaptist Tradition (Radical Reformers)

The Protestant Reformation resulted in the division of Christendom, but not in its abandonment. The idea of Christendom survived the sixteenth century Reformation practically unscathed. The Protestant Reformers held to the idea as firmly as the Catholics. What they sought was a reformed Christendom, not the possibility of opting out. One group, later called Anabaptists or Radical Reformers, disagreed.

This movement started out as the "left flank" of the Swiss Reformer Ulrich Zwingli. Disagreeing with Luther, who allowed in worship and in practice whatever the Bible did not prohibit, Zwingli established the principle that whatever the Bible did not commend should be discarded. For this reason, the Reformation in Zurich striped away traditional symbols of the Roman church such as candles, statues, music, and pictures. Later, in England, people called this behavior Puritanism. In one matter, however, Zwingli, was inconsistent, for he commended the ancient Christian practice of baptizing infants, even though there is no clear example in scripture. Zwingli thought that baptizing infants was crucial for holding a community together, the basis of good citizenship. He said that infant baptism was a Christian version of the Jewish ritual of circumcision, a sign of the people's covenant with God. Not all of Zwingli's followers agreed.

Conrad Grebel and Felix Manz, both well-educated men of standing in Zurich, supported Zwingli's initial reforms. But in their study of the Bible they came to see obvious differences in the apostolic churches and those of their own day. In 1525, the city council of Zurich arranged a public debate on the question of baptism, and after hearing arguments on both sides, the council sided with Zwingli and his followers. As a result, the council required all parents to baptize their children. Failure to do so would result in banishment. A few days later, a group of individuals met at the Manz house to decide how to respond. George Blaurock, a former priest, went to Conrad Grebel and asked to be baptized as an adult, upon confession of personal faith in Jesus Christ. Grebel baptized him on the spot and Blaurock proceeded to baptize the others. Thus, Anabaptism (rebaptism) was born.

Shortly after, the small company of believers relocated to the nearby village of Zollikon, where they established the first "free church," free from state jurisdiction. In 1526 the Zurich council decided that Anabaptists were threatening the very fabric of society, and it decreed that anyone practicing rebaptism would be put to death by drowning. During the Reformation years, between four and five thousand Anabaptists were executed by fire, water, and sword. In 1527, Felix Manz became the first Anabaptist martyr. That same year, an early conference of Anabaptists took place at Schleitheim, marking the first synod of the Protestant Reformation. The group adopted the Schleitheim Confession, a highly significant document.

In 1529, the imperial Diet of Speyer proclaimed Anabaptism a heresy, and every court in Christendom was obliged to condemn the heretics to death. Many fled to Germany and Austria, where they continued to experience persecution. Others found refuge in Moravia, where they founded a Christian commune called the *Bruderhof*. Consolidated under the leadership of Jakob Hutter, these groups came to be known as Hutterites.

In the mid 1530s, a fanatical Anabaptist community developed in the city of Münster, near the Netherlands. They were followers of a strange figure called Jan Matthijs, who declared that Christ was about to return to earth, and that he would establish an earthly kingdom in Münster. Scholars call this view chiliasm, meaning belief in a thousand-year earthly kingdom of Christ. In 1534, crowds believing that the Last Days were approaching seized control of the town. Matthijs was killed in battle, only to be replaced by even more extreme leaders. In 1534 John of Leiden, a former innkeeper, seized power and ruled as a despot. Claiming new revelations from God, he introduced the Old Testament practice of polygamy and claimed that he was the divinely anointed king of the world, a successor to King David of Israel. His rule lasted less than a year, and despite widespread hunger, due to the local bishop's decision to starve the radicals into surrender, morale remained high. In the summer of 1535, two traitors led the bishop's forces into the town, which they conquered quickly. In the end, John and two of his lieutenants were publicly executed. Today, visitors to Münster can look up at the bell tower of St. Lambert's Cathedral and see high up, above the clock, three iron cages hanging from chains. The cages are empty now, but in 1535 they contained three mutilated corpses, a gruesome reminder of what could happen to those who challenged ecclesiastical power.

In the aftermath of the suppression of Münster, the dispirited Anabaptists gained courage through the ministry of Menno Simons (1496–1561), a former priest who traveled widely to visit scattered Anabaptist groups of northern Europe. Committed to pacifism, in time his name came to stand for the movement's repudiation of violence. Although he did not found the movement, many descendants of the Anabaptists are called Mennonites. Americans see them driving their horses and buggies across idyllic country roads, refusing to own automobiles, use electricity, or wear buttons and zippers. Actually, only one section of the Mennonites, the Old Order Amish, holds firmly to the old ways. Most Mennonites look like other Americans and consume their share of energy like the rest of us.

What unites this group of reformers is not a style of dress or a mode of transportation, but a shared set of belief and values, such as the four major principles adopted at Schleitheim:

- *Discipleship.* To be a Christian one must have a relationship with Jesus Christ. Such faith transcends doctrines and leads to a transformed style of life. For the Anabaptists, discipleship refuses participation in worldly power, including bearing arms, holding political office, and taking oaths. In the sixteenth century, such abandonment of citizenship constituted treason.

- *Love.* The principle of love, logically developed from discipleship, requires pacifism. Anabaptists would not go to war, defend themselves against attacks, or participate in any coercion by the state.

- *Congregationalism.* Decision-making rests with the entire membership, not with bishops, priests, or other church officials. In Anabaptist assemblies, all members are baptized as adults, upon profession of faith in Christ. In deciding matters of doctrine, the authority of scripture is primary, its interpretation given by the consensus of local members. In matters of church discipline, the believers also act corporately.

- *Separation of church and state.* The church, said the Anabaptists, is distinct from society, even if society claims to be Christian. Christ's true followers are a pilgrim people, perpetual aliens in a sinful world.

Many of these beliefs are now accepted by other Christians. The distant relatives of the Anabaptists today include Quakers, Baptists, and, to some extent, Congregationalists. Anabaptists wanted radical social change. Their goal was to restore apostolic Christianity. Unlike Lutherans, who followed the notion of the "territorial church," for they considered the population of a given territory members of their church, Anabaptists followed the notion of the "gathered church," where individuals have the freedom to join the congregation of their choice. Such freedom begins with conversion, and for Anabaptists, it is this experience of spiritual regeneration that makes one fit for baptism.

The true church, the radicals insisted, is always a community of saints, dedicated disciples in a wicked world. Like the missionary monks of the Middle Ages, Anabaptists wished to shape society by their example of radical discipleship.

Anglicanism and the English Reformation

If the Lutheran reformation began in a monastic cell, the Calvinist reformation at a scholar's desk, and the Anabaptist reformation at a prayer meeting, then the English reformation began in the bedroom, specifically with the problem of succession to the royal throne.

In a sense, England had two reformations, a constitutional one under King Henry VIII (1509–1547) and a theological one under the Puritans a century later. Under Henry, nothing changed doctrinally. England simply rejected the authority of Rome. In this respect, England established what later generations called civil religion.

Henry's problem was that he had no son born of his queen, Catherine of Aragon. Catherine, daughter of Ferdinand and Isabella of Spain, had delivered five children, but the only survivor beyond infancy was the princess Mary. In 1527 Henry asked Pope Clement VII to declare his marriage to Catherine invalid. The pope might have entertained the idea, had not Catherine been the aunt of Charles V, Holy Roman Emperor and king of Spain. At the moment the pope could ill afford to offend the emperor, so he stalled. Henry decided to take matters into his own hands. He adopted the suggestion of one of his advisers that he present his case to scholarly professors for their opinion. The response was mixed, but it gave Henry cause for action. In 1533 he secretly married Anne Boleyn, a lady-in-waiting of the court, and the marriage produced a girl, Elizabeth. When the pope countered Henry's move by excommunicating him, Henry decided to overthrow papal authority in England. Antipapal sympathies in England were running high, and so Henry moved quickly on a series of fronts.

Henry's new archbishop of Canterbury, Thomas Cranmer, ratified Henry's divorce and remarriage, and in 1534, Henry's "Reformation Parliament" passed an Act of Supremacy, which formalized England's break with Rome. By making Henry the only supreme head of the Anglican Church (the Church of England), England's church pushed the Reformation beyond the intent of the first Reformers, who hoped to reform Western Christendom but not to establish separate or regional forms of the Christian faith. The Act of Supremacy forever changed the face of Christianity in the West.

In establishing the Church of England, however, Henry intended no break with Catholic dogma. He considered himself, in fact, a guardian of the old faith. His goal was an English Catholic Church, instead of a Roman Catholic one. The Statute of Six Articles in 1539 upheld such Catholic elements as clerical celibacy, the private Mass, and confessions to a priest. Only two serious changes marked religious life in England: the suppression of monasteries and the order of the publication of an English Bible for use in the churches. The pioneering effort in the translation of the English Bible was that of William Tyndale, completed by Miles Coverdale. Henry authorized that a version of this Bible, called the "Great Bible," be distributed throughout the realm. This Bible became a model for the King James Bible of 1611.

After Henry's death in 1547, his only son, ten-year-old Edward VI, followed his father to the throne. Edward's mother was Jane Seymour, whom Henry had married after he had Anne Boleyn executed on charges of adultery. During Edward's brief reign, England witnessed significant changes, including priests allowed to marry and the old Latin service of worship replaced by the Book of Common Prayer, in English. In 1553 Archbishop Cranmer produced the Forty-Two Articles, which defined the faith of the Church of England along Protestant lines.

The swing toward Protestantism came to a sudden halt when Edward died in 1553 and Mary, the daughter of Catherine, ascended the throne. Devoutly Catholic, Mary tried to lead England back to Rome. In four short years she sent nearly three hundred Protestants, including Archbishop Cranmer, to the stake. Later, John Foxe collected reports of these martyrdoms in his *Book of Martyrs* (1571), which incited the English people to a longstanding horror of Catholicism. With the accession to the throne of Elizabeth I in 1558, the Anglican Church assumed its distinctive character, neither Roman nor Reformed. In accepting the Bible as the final authority, and in recognizing baptism and the Eucharist as sacraments, Elizabeth's Thirty-Nine Articles (1563) were essentially Protestant, but the liturgy retained Catholic elements and bishops in apostolic succession governed the Church. In time Anglican theologians spoke of this compromise as a *via media*, a Middle Way between Protestantism and Catholicism.

Some of the exiles forced out of England during Mary's reign were not so sure. They had read their Bibles and developed their own ideas about a true reformation in England. When they returned from the Continent to Elizabeth's England, they felt dispossessed. We know these Reformers as Puritans.

Puritans and Quakers in England and in America

Puritanism, England's second reformation, first appeared during the reign of Elizabeth. It had a new style of preaching, a message aimed not at the head but at the heart. In its quest to reshape England, the Puritan movement passed through three periods: First, under Queen Elizabeth (1558–1603), it tried to purify the Church of England along the lines of Calvin's Geneva. Second, under James I and Charles I (1603–1642), it resisted the claims of the monarchy and suffered under royal pressures designed to force conformity to a high-church style Christianity. Third, during England's Civil War and Oliver Cromwell's rule (1653–1658), Puritans had a chance to shape the national church in England but failed due to internal dissension.

Thanks to their study of the Bible, Puritans came to think of themselves as God's New Israel. The key to their understanding of the Bible and of themselves rested in their comprehension of the fundamental biblical concept called "covenant." The Puritans, like the ancient Hebrews, believed that spiritual contracts exist between God and humans. The most fundamental was the covenant of grace. By grace believers become God's people. Their personal allegiance to God makes them slaves to no earthly authority.

In 1603 Queen Elizabeth's lengthy reign came to a close when she died without an heir. James VI, son of Mary Queen of Scots, became James I of England, uniting for the first time the two kingdoms. James agreed to have a new translation of the scriptures made in 1611, but on nothing else of significance would he yield to the Puritans. The ceremonies, the Prayer Book, and the bishops of the Church of England would remain. And if the Puritans did not like it, they would submit to the king or be driven from the land. James made it plain that he meant to rule as an absolute monarch. In 1611 he dissolved Parliament and for the next ten years he ruled without it. Some in the Puritan movement became impatient for change. By 1608 two groups moved to Holland for safety and freedom of religion. After ten years in Holland, one congregation, led by John Robinson, returned to England, where they joined others in the thought of travel to the new continent of America. They had heard of the English colony planted in Virginia, and in

September 1620 some one hundred passengers set sail from Plymouth in a ship called the *Mayflower*.

In 1625, when Charles I succeeded James to the English throne, he was determined to put into practice his father's theories about the divine right of kings. He found a willing collaborator in Archbishop William Laud, who believed that God had ordained bishops to govern his church. With the king's support, Laud reintroduced stained glass windows, crosses, even crucifixes, and insisted that worship be conducted according to the Prayer Book and no other. Laud's authoritarian policies drove some Puritans toward separatism and others across the Atlantic to America.

In 1630, more than four hundred immigrants gathered at Southampton, preparing to sail to the New World. John Cotton, a minister who would later join them across the sea, preached a farewell sermon. Based on 2 Samuel 7:10, Cotton's sermon declared that like the ancient Israelites, these immigrants were God's chosen people, headed for a new Promised Land. In this land they would be afflicted no longer, as before.

The group left under the leadership of John Winthrop, with hopes of creating a society that reinforced a biblical view of the state. In an address on board the *Arabella*, given within sight of land in Boston Harbor, John Winthrop laid out the principles upon which this new society would be based. It was clear that they wished to escape the harassment of the government in England and of the English Church, but also that they wished to establish their own version of a state church, unified yet intolerant toward dissent. The address included one of the most quoted statements in American history: "For we must consider that we shall be as a city upon a hill, the eyes of all people are upon us." Winthrop believed that if this colony succeeded, all England would follow.

John Davenport, a minister in Massachusetts Bay Colony during the 1630s and 1640s, declared that "church and state were co-ordinate powers in the same place, reaching forth to help each other, for the welfare of both." In other words, the state backed the church's spiritual decrees, while the church backed the state's civil laws. For two generations the members of the Bay Colony ruled by a policy of religious conformity, even as the same policy proved futile in England. Individuals could face severe punishment on numerous grounds, including for failure to attend church services, for denying Christ's resurrection, or for showing irreverence for the Bible.

Not surprisingly, New England Puritans spawned their own dissenters, men and women who appealed to the truth they knew from scripture.

Anne Hutchinson was one, Roger Williams another. For daring to contradict the pastor, Anne Hutchinson was cast into the wilderness, with her newborn infant. Dissenting Quakers were dragged through the streets, put in stocks, and even hanged, before the English government put a stop to it. Roger Williams, a young pastor in Boston who disagreed with Governor Winthrop on several issues, including the concept of forced worship, was expelled and went south to the present state of Rhode Island, where he established Providence Plantation, a colony based upon the principles of religious liberty and the separation of church and state.

In England, civil war broke out when Charles tried to force his brand of Anglicanism upon the Presbyterian Scots. They rose in opposition, their primary allegiance being to the church rather than to the state. When Royalist members of Parliament left London to join the forces defending the king, the majority Parliamentary Party was free at last to institute the reform of the church that the Puritans had wanted. Scores of Puritan theologians met at Westminster to create a new form of worship and a new form of government for the Church of England. The Westminster Assembly, meeting between 1643 and 1649, produced the Westminster Confession of Faith to replace the Thirty-Nine Articles, as well as a Larger and Shorter Catechism for use in the churches. These writings alone made the assembly one of the most significant gatherings of Christian history. Many Presbyterians and Congregationalists use these documents to this day.

The seemingly endless debate on dogma, and the intolerance of nonconformist Christians that arose in England and on the Continent in the sixteenth and seventeenth centuries, led many Christians to seek refuge in inner piety. One such figure was George Fox (1624–1691), born of humble origin in a small English village. At the age of nineteen, disgusted by the licentiousness around him, he began a life of wandering, seeking divine illumination. His study of the Christian scriptures and his attendance of varied religious meetings led him to the conviction that all the religious sects were in error, and that public worship was an abomination.

Church buildings, clergy, hymns, sermons, sacraments, creeds, liturgies—all seemed to him hindrances to life in the Spirit. Against all of these, Fox placed the "inner light," a pathway common to all human beings, no matter their race, faith, or creed. True Christianity was not a matter of conforming to a set of doctrines or performing rituals led by a professional priest. Rather a true believer was one who was being illuminated by an inner light.

In religious gatherings across England, Fox declared that he had been ordered by the Spirit to announce his spiritual version of Christianity. For disturbing the proceedings he was repeatedly beaten, thrown out of meetings, and cast into jail. His followers grew rapidly, calling themselves "Friends," but others began calling them Quakers, for their religious enthusiasm. Espousing their belief in equality, they spoke out against war, violence, slavery, paying tithes, and swearing by oath. When he was not in prison, Fox traveled throughout England and abroad, visiting Scotland, Ireland, and the European Continent, as well as the Caribbean and North America. In all these places he gained converts, and by the time of his death, his followers were counted by the tens of thousands.

The most famous of his followers was William Penn, after whom the state of Pennsylvania is named. In 1681 Penn received a charter to found a colony in North America in which there would be complete religious freedom. By then various other British colonies were in existence in the New World, but with the exception of Rhode Island, all were marked by religious intolerance. Despite his land grant, Penn was convinced that the Indians, and not the crown, were the legitimate owners of the land. And he hoped to establish such cordial relations with them that the settlers would have no need to defend themselves. The capital of this "holy experiment" would be called Philadelphia—the city of "fraternal love." Under the leadership of Penn, the first governor of the colony, relations with the Indians were excellent, and for a long time his dream of a peaceful settlement was a reality. In England it was not until the "Glorious Revolution" that accompanied the accession of William and Mary (1689) that full religious tolerance for the Quakers and all other dissenting groups was made into law.

The religious diversity of the American colonies called for a new understanding of the church, based on the denominational theory. While the word "denomination" to describe a religious group came into vogue abut 1740, during the evangelical revival led by John Wesley and George Whitefield, the concept arose earlier, under Puritan leadership. Denominationalism, as originally conceived, is the opposite of sectarianism. While a sect claims the authority of Christ for itself alone, considering itself the only true body of Christ, the word "denomination" implies that the Christian group called or denominated by a particular name is but one member of a larger group, the church, to which all denominations belong.

This denominational view of the church found only limited acceptance in England, even after the Act of Toleration in 1689 recognized the rights of

Presbyterians, Congregationalists, Baptists, and Quakers to worship freely. In the English colonies of America, however, the denominational theory gained increasing acceptance. The promise of religious freedom provided a powerful incentive to accept the hazards of life in the New World. There, dissenters need not hide or go underground; they became pioneers—moving across rivers, through the wilderness, and over the mountains. Sanctuary was always possible in open space.

Quakers came to Pennsylvania, Catholics to Maryland, and Dutch Reformed to New York. Later came Swedish Lutherans, French Huguenots, English Baptists, and Scottish Presbyterians. Ultimately, the concept of America emerged from cultural and religious pluralism as Catholic immigrants and refugees joined Jews from Europe; Muslims from Africa and the Middle East; Hindus from India; and Buddhists, Confucians, and Taoists from the Far East.

The Catholic Reformation

It took the Church of Rome some time to respond fully to the Protestant challenge. At first the defiance was local and personal, but when Catholicism finally realized the seriousness of the revolt, it responded comprehensively. Some historians have interpreted the response as a counterattack against Protestantism, while others have described it as a genuine revival of Catholic piety. The truth is the movement was both a Counter-Reformation and a Catholic Reformation.

The mystical experience was a large part of Catholicism's recovery. The sixteenth century produced a remarkable variety of Catholic saints, including the English humanist Thomas More, the missionary Francis of Sales, the Spanish mystics Teresa of Avila and John of the Cross, and the most influential of all, the Spanish soldier Ignatius Loyola.

Throughout the 1520s and 1530s the pope and Emperor Charles V disagreed over the calling of a general council. Luther had called for a council of the church as early as 1518. The idea gained the support of the German princes and the emperor, but the popes feared such an assembly. They remembered the councils at Constance and Basel, and they feared losing ground yet again. No serious reform came until the papacy of Paul III (1534–1549). He started with the College of Cardinals, appointing those who favored reform. He then appointed members to a reform commission, and their report called for the need to give greater attention to spiritual matters. By 1545 reform was on the rise. The pope's new rigor was apparent in his use of the Inquisition and in his creation of the Index of Prohibited Books. The Index listed all the books of the Reformers, as well as Protestant Bibles. In Spain, where the Inquisition was particularly severe, merely to possess one of the banned books was punishable by death.

In this setting the pope approved Ignatius Loyola's new Society of Jesus. Loyola (1491–1556), a Spanish nobleman who became a monk after having been injured fighting against the French, had come up with a plan for spiritual discipline called *Spiritual Exercises*. A distillation of his own religious experiences during and following his conversion, the *Exercises* prescribe a path to spiritual perfection, four "weeks" of meditation, beginning with sin, death, judgment, and hell, and then moving on to Christ's life, death, and resurrection. Ignatius had become such a fervent Christian that the Spanish Inquisition imprisoned and examined him about his teaching. Perturbed, he left for Paris, where he spent seven years at the university, gathering around him the first of his permanent companions, including the young Spaniard Francis Xavier.

In 1540 Pope Paul III approved the Society of Jesus (the Jesuits, as they came to be called) as a new religious order. To the earlier vows of poverty, chastity, and obedience to superiors, the Jesuits added a fourth vow, expressing special loyalty to the pope. The aim of the order was to restore the Roman Catholic Church to the position of spiritual power and influence it had held during the late medieval period. In the process, the Jesuits became the greatest single force in Catholicism's campaign to reverse the Protestant gains. In addition, the first generation under Loyola's zealous leadership sent missionaries overseas to convert the heathen.

In the history of Christianity, the years between 1500 and 1650 might be called "the age of global expansion," since between those years Roman Catholic monks and friars carried the gospel to Spanish colonies throughout Latin America and Portuguese ports along the coasts of Africa and Asia.

India and the Far East

In 1540, Francis Xavier (1506–1552) received a commission from the pope and the king of Portugal that extended to the whole of the Far East. He arrived in India in 1542, in Malacca on the Malay Peninsula in 1545, and in 1549 he sailed for Japan, where he was welcomed by feudal barons eager for trade with the outside world. Buddhism was out of favor, and no national religion presented stiff opposition to the gospel. The Jesuit work met with remarkable success. Before the end of the century missionaries could count three hundred thousand converts, hundreds of churches, and two Christian colleges. The Jesuits dominated the Christian mission in Japan until the end of the sixteenth century, when new rulers launched a policy of persecution of Christians.

After two years of preaching in Japan, Xavier decided it was time to enter China. The ruling Ming dynasty had no interest in contacts with the outside world. Confucianism was dominant in the empire; governing the family and ethics by its ideals. Xavier returned to India to secure the necessary authority, but on the passage east he found it difficult to get beyond Singapore. Hoping to smuggle himself into Canton, he took a ship as far as an island off the coast of south China. There he fell ill and died, bringing to an end one of the most imaginative careers in missionary annals.

The doorway to China that Xavier failed to find opened to his spiritual successor, Matteo Ricci (1552–1610). Ricci settled in Macao, a small island off the coast of China that had recently become a Portuguese colony. Matteo had studied mathematics, astronomy, and cosmology in Rome before heading east, and this training proved invaluable in China. In Macao he learned the Chinese language and customs, and in 1583 he secured permission to visit Chaoch'ing, the provincial capital. With their traditional respect for the scholar, the Chinese responded well to a person who dressed in the garb of a Mandarin, spoke their language, and was able to open to them new fields of learning. Step by step he moved toward Peking, the capital of the empire, securing permission to enter in 1600. Ricci brought two clocks to gain imperial favor. The emperor was quite pleased with the gifts and allowed Ricci to remain in the capital for ten years as an astronomer and mathematician. Under Ricci's guidance, the Jesuit mission in Peking flourished. A number of notable families and scholars converted to Christianity, and by the time of Ricci's death in 1610, the church numbered two thousand. His successor, Adam Schall von Bell (1591–1666), carried the scholarly work to an even higher level. In 1650 Schall built a public church in Peking and gained religious freedom for Christianity throughout the empire. At Schall's death there were almost 20,000 Christians in China.

The Chinese mission met with misfortune, not from the Chinese, but from Dominican and Franciscan missionaries who argued that Jesuit adaptation to Chinese ways had gone too far. In 1631, when Franciscans and Dominicans arrived in Peking, they were shocked at what they found. The word used to translate the Christian word "Mass" in the Jesuit catechism was the Chinese character for the ceremony of ancestor worship. They reported their experience to Rome and the quarrel over "the rites" began. One pope approved, another disapproved, until after a century the mission in China fell into serious decline.

Latin America

When Columbus "discovered" America in 1492, Spain was entering the age of its greatest power as well as constructing its image as the standard-bearer of Catholicism. The Spain that conquered the Americas was by far the most powerful state in sixteenth-century Europe. Its power was used both for the extension of the greatest empire the world had seen since the fall of Rome and for the advancement of Catholic Christianity. It had at its disposal not only great lawyers, philosophers, and theologians, but an army of missionaries—Dominican, Franciscan, and later Jesuit—unrivalled in all of Europe. In 1493, when Pope Alexander VI granted to the kings of Spain and Portugal the "*patronato*," he made it clear that he was granting both sovereignty and total responsibility for evangelization of all the new lands their subjects would uncover. Thus Dominicans, Franciscans, Augustinians, or Jesuits sailed on nearly every ship, as eager to convert the heathen as any captain to find a new port for trade.

To avoid rivalry between Portugal and Spain, the pope drew a line on the map from the North Pole to the South. All lands to the west of the line, he said, belonged to Spain; all to the east belonged to Portugal. That boundary helps explain why Brazil is Portuguese-speaking today and the rest of Latin America is Spanish.

While the motivation of the papal decree established the character of the invasion as one of evangelization, the motivation and behavior of the conquerors was quite different. Here was a gang of adventurers, mostly men quite insignificant at home, risking their lives in pursuit of gold. In the Antilles, where they first landed, there was little gold. The growing population of settlers felt they needed native laborers to achieve success. But since the Spanish king had forbidden the enslavement of pagan subjects, the natives were conscripted into an *encomienda*, granted to a Conquistador, where the natives were compelled to work in his mines or in the fields, while the women were seized as concubines. However, far from becoming an efficient labor force, the natives simply withered under their brutal treatment, extreme social disorientation, and a wave of European-imported diseases. Gradually the natives would be replaced by the importation of black slaves from Africa.

In religious terms, the greatest long-term Catholic global success would be in Central and South America, where the conquered peoples all accepted forms of Catholicism, heavily mixed with local beliefs. In formal terms, the conversion of the Indians was steady and impressive. By the 1570s the continent had an extensive network of bishoprics, stretching from Mexico City to Lima, Peru. Natives were baptized in vast numbers, on occasion running to thousands in a single day. When the various orders of friars began work in the Americas, it was to convert to Christianity the Indian societies.

Some religious orders, especially the Dominicans and Jesuits, struggled courageously to prevent natives from being exploited by greedy European colonists. The greatest protector and advocate for the Indians was Bartolomé de Las Casas (1484–1566), who risked his life and reputation criticizing Spanish imperialism. On account of his uninhibited denunciation of colonial brutality and because of his positive influence on royal policy, Las Casas became very unpopular. He remains, however, one of the supreme religious figures of the sixteenth century and perhaps the most important missionary intellectual of the post-medieval period.

Because religious control in remote areas was not under diocesan control, these areas came under the influence of the Jesuits. As in India, China, and Japan, in South America Jesuit missionaries tried to transform Christianity into a form that would be comprehensible and relevant to the natives. The enlightened Jesuit position was that as long as converts accepted Catholic Christianity, it could be of a Chinese, Indian, Japanese, or Native American variety, just as Europe had its French and Spanish forms of the common truth. By the eighteenth century, their missions in Paraguay alone included over one hundred thousand people, where they created social conditions that were practically ideal.

By 1824, the arrival of independence across Latin America affected the Catholic Church in many ways. While few of the new political leaders were consciously anti-Catholic, the Inquisition was abolished, and in most places Protestants were allowed freedom of worship. Many countries built Catholicism into their constitutions, but in some cases this was merely window dressing.

The Council of Trent

No Catholic response to Protestantism proved more decisive than the Council of Trent, the most important council between Nicaea (325) and Vatican II (1962–1965). Under the influence of the Jesuits, Trent developed into a powerful weapon of the Counter Reformation. The council met in three main sessions: 1545–1547, 1551–1552, and 1562–1563. Throughout the sessions the Italians were strongly represented, while other areas, notably France, were underrepresented. During the second series of sessions, a number of Protestants were present, but their voice was negligible. From start to finish the council reflected Rome's militant stance.

Everything the Protestant Reformation represented was rejected at Trent. The Reformers emphasized that justification is imputed to the believer by faith alone. The council held that justification is both external to the believer as well as internal, infused into the believer through the sacraments. The Reformers stressed salvation by grace alone; the council emphasized grace and human cooperation with God. The Protestants taught the religious authority of scripture alone; the council insisted on the popes and bishops as the essential interpreters of the Bible.

Thus the Council of Trent guaranteed that modern Roman Catholicism would be governed by divine and human collaboration. The pope remained; the seven sacraments remained; the sacrifice of the Mass remained; saints, confessions, and indulgences remained. The one thing that did not endure, however, was the unity of the church. The Protestant Reformation and the Catholic Counter Reformation shattered the religious unity of Western Christendom.

Study Questions

1. Whom do you consider the chief protagonist in the Reformation phase of the church's history (sixteenth and seventeenth centuries CE)? Support your answer.

2. Do you agree with the author's choice that Luther's life and legacy represent this epoch's turning point? Why or why not? Is there another event you consider more noteworthy? If so, what is it? Support your choice.

3. In this epoch, does "the church" live up to its nature and destiny as God's new creation? Why or why not?

4. Many Americans believe that God rewards humans according to whether they are bad or good. How would Luther respond? According to Romans 1:17, a favorite text of Luther, what does the "justice" or "righteousness" of God mean?

5. Explain the views of Calvin and Arminius on predestination. Do you consider this doctrine essential for Christians? Why or why not?

6. In your estimation, what contributions did the Radical Reformers make to Christianity?

7. How is the Anglican Church (or the Episcopal Church in the United States) a *via media* (middle way) between Catholicism and Protestantism?

8. Assess the contributions of the Puritans to religion in American society. Discuss the merits of their attempt to establish the kingdom of God on earth.

9. What impact did the Quakers have on American society? In your estimation, are Quakers truly Christian?

10. In your estimation, what are the principal contributions of the Jesuit movement?

11. Discuss the struggles that occurred among mission-minded Roman Catholics as they strove to reach foreign cultures with the gospel.

12. In your estimation, what are the key contributions of the Protestant Reformation?

Chapter 9

Phase 9: Enlightenment (1700–Present)

Liberalism, Fundamentalism, and Ecumenism

Significant Event: The modern period saw the separation of church and state and the end of Western Christendom. Now, for the first time in recent history, we distinguish between significant events in society and in the church. 1. The significant event in society is the French Revolution, for it brought with it the universal declaration of human rights and an anticlerical effort that marked the end of European Christendom. 2. Two events vie for significance in the church: (a) the formation of the World Council of Churches (an expression of global ecumenism), and (b) Vatican II (an expression aimed at modernizing the Catholic Church and the reconciliation of all Christians).

Turning Point: 1. My choice for turning point in society is the emphasis on reason characterized by René Descartes's "methodical doubt," an approach that represents the birth of modern philosophy. This stance, inherited from Renaissance humanists, led to the birth of modern science and the technological revolution that created the modern world. 2. My choice for the turning point in the church is the formation of religious societies, voluntary parachurch organizations that mobilized the great global missionary and social efforts of the nineteenth and twentieth centuries.

Among the many important ecclesiastical developments and events during the sixteenth and seventeenth centuries, the following helped shape the church's conception of faith, vocation, and governance:

1. Modernism and secularism

2. Scientific and philosophical advances

3. Nationalism

4. Pietism, evangelicalism, and the Great Awakening

5. Protestant missions

6. Protestant liberalism and fundamentalism

7. The ecumenical movement and Roman Catholic response

The Reformers, rejecting the medieval synthesis, built a way of life on the foundation of faith and revelation. The Enlightenment, by contrast, rejected supernatural religion, building a way of life on the foundation of science and human reason. Questioning authorities external to the thinker, secular thinkers used science and human reason to replace the Christian faith as the cornerstone of Western culture. Christians struggled between faith and reason, entertaining new beliefs while questioning their own. Many were seriously divided over ways to face the problems and opportunities caused by political, technological, and scientific advances. Some compartmentalized their lives, erecting walls of separation between faith and reason. Others met the crisis through conversion and spiritual experience. Still others turned to doctrine for support, constructing fundamentalist responses to the challenges of secularism, scientism, atheism, modernism, and materialism. The twentieth century brought additional ideological challenges: Communism, Nazism, and Americanism. How would Christians respond? In Europe, the church declined; in America, it expanded and contracted; and in the Global South, charismatic Christianity emerged with explosive force.

Modernism and Secularism

The Middle Ages and the Reformation were centuries of faith in the sense that reason served faith and the mind obeyed authority. To Catholics it was church authority, to Protestants biblical authority, but in either case, faith came first, not reason. The Enlightenment changed that orientation; reason replaced faith, and concerns for this life replace preparation for the next. Science, prosperity, and reason were the best guides to happiness, not emotions, myths, or superstition. The spirit of this age was nothing less than an intellectual revolution, a new way of looking at God, the world, and oneself.

The Enlightenment gave birth to modernism and its twin, secularism. If hatred of religious bigotry, coupled with a devotion to religious pluralism, has a familiar ring, it is because the modern ethos is not outdated. It lives today in the values of the Western world.

The seeds of the Enlightenment lie in the Renaissance, a movement that also gave impetus to the Reformation. Renaissance means "rebirth," and refers to the recovery of the values of classical Greek and Roman civilization expressed in literature, politics, and the arts. In one sense, the Reformation was not possible without the influence of Renaissance humanism, which sought human flourishing.

Perhaps the best example of the rebirth of the classical spirit was Erasmus of Rotterdam (1467–1536). In a series of satires highlighted by *Praise of Folly*, he ridiculed monasticism, excesses in the church (such as indulgences, veneration of relics, and masses for the dead) and the rigors of scholasticism by the use of irony, wit, and common sense. His stress on Bible reading and study made him an early reformer, but in 1524 a conflict erupted between Luther and Erasmus. Luther believed that apart from grace, the human will was in bondage to sin, whereas Erasmus supported free will, and with it human moral responsibility. The differences between the Reformation and the Renaissance lie there, in their view of human nature. The Reformers preached original sin and looked upon the world as fallen from its created goodness; Renaissance thinkers had a positive estimate of human nature and the universe itself. This confidence in human ability flowered during the Enlightenment.

Another root of the Enlightenment emerged from the century of religious conflicts between 1550 and 1650, including the English Civil War, the persecution of the French Huguenots, the Spanish Inquisition, and the Thirty Years' War (1618–1648), the deadliest religious war and one of the most destructive conflicts in human history. Religious prejudice seemed like a far greater danger than atheism. Thus, a thirst for tolerance and truths common to all people spread.

Scientific and Philosophical Advance

Modern Physics and Cosmology

The contributions of modern scientists have led to a series of shifts in worldview known successively as Copernican, Newtonian, and Einsteinium.

Curiously, each view contradicted the previous understanding of the cosmos. While initially resisted as heretical, each eventually became acceptable, replacing the previous mindset. Like the biological narrative of life on earth, the story of the cosmic universe continues to be revised, its portrait redrawn.

Modern science arose in the sixteenth and seventeenth centuries, filling humans with visions of an age of peace and harmony. The pioneers of modern science created new ways to think about the universe. Nicolaus Copernicus (1473–1543) insisted that the sun, not the earth, was the center of our universe. Johannes Kepler (1571–1630) concluded that the sun emitted a magnetic force that moved the planets in their courses. Galileo Galilei (1564–1642) made a telescope to observe the moons of Jupiter, adding further support to the Copernican theory of the universe. Isaac Newton (1642–1727), the most illustrious scientist of the Enlightenment, was able to unite all the laws of motion in his monumental work, *Mathematical Principles of Natural Philosophy* (1687). The universe, he argued is one great machine operating according to unalterable laws, harmonized in a master principle of the universe, the law of gravitation.

Though a devout Christian, Newton's concept challenged the medieval notion of unseen spirits—angels and demons. His theory considered such beliefs as superstitious, replacing them with a universe operated by physical laws, explained by mathematics. The sudden access to the mysteries of the universe seemed to magnify the role of human reason while minimizing the role of divine revelation. If the universe is a smooth-running machine with all its parts coordinated by one grand design, this frees humans to find meaning and happiness on their own.

This, then, is the fundamental idea of the Enlightenment, that humans are able to find truth by using the scientific method—an experimental approach that combines reason with the senses—rather than rely upon ancient values and beliefs, rooted in superstition and ignorance. The theological implications of such humanistic optimism are significant. In this environment, God seemed less necessary to sustain the world. In the new model, the sun displaced the earth as the center. Some believed that humanity had been displaced as the crowning apex of creation in the center of God's world. Others felt that God had been displaced as well.

The nineteenth century witnessed profound developments in the field of biology. While traditional cooperation between Christian faith and scientific endeavor survived longer than popular stereotypes suggest, still the trend was toward a conception of the world in which traditional beliefs concerning God's power and creative wisdom were superfluous. Charles Darwin's *Origin of Species* (1859) was actually more ambiguous on these matters than later commentary admits, since Darwin retained the possibility of some kind of divine origin of life. Moreover, some of Darwin's early followers thought that his description of "natural selection" was compatible with God's purposeful design of the world. Yet Darwin's theory soon became a symbol of science proceeding on its own without reference to a Creator.

In the twentieth century, the acceptance of new theories of relativity and quantum mechanics greatly changed scientists' conception of the structure of the universe. Scientists such as Albert Einstein (1879–1955) and Werner Heisenberg (1901–1976) questioned the Newtonian worldview. Einstein's theories of general and special relativity led to new views of gravity and profoundly affected our understanding of the concepts of space and time, and Heisenberg proposed, as a principle of nature, that uncertainty characterizes human understanding of the subatomic realm of reality. As a result, physicists abandoned the earlier ideal of predictability in scientific experiments, adopting a new approach, the method of "wave" or "quantum" mechanics, which yields only probabilities regarding individual events.

Modern Philosophy

Modern philosophers are primarily concerned with epistemology, that is, with the concept of knowledge, not simply with factual knowledge (what can be known), but with the process of knowing (how one acquires certainty). Until the 1600s, philosophy had been concerned primarily with the nature of God and with existence itself. However, that concern changed dramatically in the seventeenth century. During the modern period, philosophers and intellectuals in general became obsessed with epistemology.

At this time, the concern of philosophers was directed toward finding a new source of certainty. Protestant and Renaissance rejection of church authority, humanistic optimism in society, and the birth of modern science, all shook the foundations of medieval faith. As a consequence, seventeenth-century epistemologies explored two basic alternatives: rationalism (that certainty arises primarily from human reason), and empiricism, (that certainty arises principally from human sense experience).

The figure who perhaps best exemplifies modern rationalism is René Descartes (1596–1650. Descartes, above all, sought to know what is certain. He lived in a rapidly changing world in which long-held foundational principles were being challenged, including religious and scientific teachings. Skepticism flourished. Descartes, however, was not a skeptic. He was a devout Catholic who contended that human beings are capable of attaining certainty in knowledge, but that before people can obtain certainty, they must first become aware of how dubious or uncertain most of their accepted beliefs are. Descartes began his *Meditations on First Philosophy* with what he called "methodical doubt," and on the basis of this methodology he concluded that there was only one thing that he could not somehow doubt, and that was his thinking self. This discovery of an innate idea, clear and distinct to reason, he summarized with the Latin phrase, "*Cogito ergo sum*," which means "I think, therefore, I exist."

The important result of Descartes's approach is that knowledge in every case begins with knowledge of one's existence. Self becomes the starting point for knowledge, not God, and its justification is reason. Thus, human autonomy replaced divine sovereignty as the foundation of modern thought.

In time, as confidence in reason soared, many intellectuals began dismissing appeals to scripture as superstitious nonsense. A group of French thinkers and writers known as the *philosophes* brought the Enlightenment to its climax. These were not philosophers in the academic sense but rather men of letters, observers of society who analyzed its evils and advocated reform. They aimed to spread knowledge and emancipate the human spirit. These were not atheists, as we might call them today, for most believed in a supreme being but denied that he interfered in the affairs of the world. They were deists, believers in what has been called the watchmaker God: God created the world as a watchmaker makes a watch, and then wound it up and let it run. Since God was a perfect watchmaker, there was no need to interfere with the watch. Hence the deists rejected miracles and special revelations or anything that seemed to be an interference of God with the world.

The most influential propagandist for deism was Voltaire (1694–1778), who personified the skepticism of the French Enlightenment. He achieved his greatest fame as a relentless critic of the established churches, Protestant and Catholic alike, sickened by the intolerance and petty squabbles that seemed to characterize organized religion. Voltaire, Jean-Jacques Rousseau

(1712–1778), Denis Diderot (1713–1784), and other brilliant thinkers, championed tolerance, denounced superstition, and expounded the merits of deism. They held Jesus in high regard, urging contemporary Christians to emulate the morality of the ancient master and to discard the theological trappings.

While metaphysical and ethical questions formulated during the Christian centuries may have continued to preoccupy European intellectuals, the great philosophical influences of the nineteenth century—like Immanuel Kant (1724–1804) and Georg Friedrich Hegel (1770–1831) in Germany or John Stuart Mill (1806–1873) in Britain—labored to replace traditional dependence upon revelation and religious tradition with what they held were more secure foundations of the good, the true, and the beautiful. Kant's argument in his 1793 work *Religion within the Limits of Reason Alone* became an intellectual charter for many great minds of the nineteenth century: "True religion," he argued, "is to consist not in the knowing or considering of what God does or has done for our salvation but in what we must do to become worthy of it."

By the middle of the nineteenth century, even the instinctive deference to scripture as a divinely guided book was fading. A growing array of influential voices began to discard traditional attitudes toward the Bible. Known as higher critics, they became concerned with the meaning of the biblical text. To achieve this end, they studied the background, authorship, and the historical setting of the text, applying the same methodology to the Bible as they did to other ancient books. In 1835 David Strauss published his *Life of Jesus*, which depicted the Christ of the New Testament as a product of projection back in time from the early Christian community. Ernest Renan's *Life of Jesus* in 1863 presented Jesus as a simple Galilean preacher who would have been astonished at what later generations said about his supposedly supernatural origins and powers. By the end of the nineteenth century, formal academic study of the Old Testament had been influenced by views assuming that these writings were the products of evolving Semitic experience rather than of revelations from God. Perhaps the scholar most responsible for popularizing this view was Julius Wellhausen, whose 1878 text, *Prolegomena to the History of Ancient Israel*, became one of the seminal works in biblical analysis.

During the nineteenth century, a new sense of the human self as heroic captured the imagination of influential Europeans. This exalted view of human potential often goes under the name "Romanticism," though it extends well beyond the boundaries of literary or cultural movements. This sense of human transcendence flourished in such English Romantic poets as Wordsworth, Coleridge, Shelley, and Byron. It inspired Goethe, drove the musical compositions of Beethoven and Wagner, and undergirded the spectacular rise of the novel as the dominant form of European literature. However, the Romantic sensibility could also lead its advocates to despair, as in the case of Germany's Heinrich Heine.

Perhaps the best spokesman for a Romantic view of Christianity was the German theologian Friedrich Schleiermacher (1768–1834). Called "the father of modern theology," he not only summarized the theological insights of progressive Protestantism for his time but he set the course for subsequent Christian thought. He attempted to rehabilitate religion among intellectuals, insisting that the great debates over proofs of God and the abstract doctrinal descriptions of faith were, at best, a secondary expression of religion. The theological task, he argued, could not be separated from the great movements and concerns in society. He believed that theology no longer had the luxury of being isolationist. From now on, theology had to come to grips with society, culture, and technology, and with the growing authority of science. In particular, theology had to embrace the scientific method, with its stress on experience, observation, and experimentation.

Schleiermacher's greatest contribution was his attempt to move Christianity into the realm of the heart. To be human, he argued, is to be religious, for at the heart of human experience lies what Schleiermacher called "God-consciousness," the awareness of humanity's absolute dependence upon God. After Schleiermacher, the idea became commonplace that religions are differing expressions of a common inner religious experience shared by all people. In 1834 Schleiermacher popularized his ideas in a series of lectures entitled *Religious Speeches to Its Cultured Despisers*. The uniqueness of Christ, he argued, is not in some doctrine about Jesus or in his miraculous nature. The real miracle is Jesus himself. In him we find a person who demonstrated the sense of God-consciousness to a supreme degree. The church is the living witness to the fact that down through the centuries individuals have come to a vital God consciousness through their contact with the life of Jesus. Religious practice, focused on God-awareness, can lead to the true reunion of humanity. Schleiermacher was the "father of modern theology" primarily because he shifted the basis of the Christian faith from the Bible to "religious experience."

Another Christian thinker who emphasized experience is Søren Kierkegaard (1813–1855), the noted Danish Christian existentialist. Though existentialists emphasize individual existence, their views represent not a philosophy or a system but a way of life. Reacting against the dehumanizing tendencies of modern society, precipitated by the industrial revolution, existentialists concentrate on subjective, inward human attitudes, particularly on fear and dread, anxiety and guilt. They are more concerned with what people do than with what people think, though thought is not abandoned. Existence and one's thoughts about existence interact and feed on each other.

For Kierkegaard, truth is not something cold and objective, a system of ideas to be grasped intellectually, but rather is internal, personal, and emotional. Truth is whatever an individual believes intensely. Such truth is active, not passive, and is paradoxical by nature, for it is characterized by objective uncertainty. Active truth entails "a leap of faith," for it requires trust and commitment before it can be known. To be valid, religious truth must penetrate one's personal existence, for if it does not become one's own, it is meaningless. Truth must be lived, passionately.

Overall, developments in European economic, social, national, intellectual, and cultural life spelled the end of Western Christendom. Christianity had not been banished from Europe, but over the course of the nineteenth century it came to be marginalized. As the religious influence of the various churches waned, the ranks of the faithful dramatically thinned. During this period, perhaps the most powerful critique of traditional Christianity is associated with the German philosopher Friedrich Nietzsche (1844–1900), who argued that human civilization had reached the stage at which it could dispense with the notion of God. His famous statement, "God is dead! And we have killed him!" expressed the general cultural atmosphere that finds no place for God. Out of Nietzsche's declaration came the "Death of God" movement in the 1960s. One of its exponents, William Hamilton, said of the movement: "We are not talking about the absence of the experience of God, but about the experience of the absence of God. . . . This is not an experience that is peculiar to a neurotic few, nor is it private or inward. Death of God is a public event in our history." Contrasting this view with the "Romantic" view of religion, one wonders who was right, Nietzsche, Schleiermacher, or neither.

Over time, a group of thinkers developed an approach that combined elements of Reformed orthodoxy with elements of Protestant liberalism, resulting in a new form of synthesis called Neo-orthodoxy. The First World War witnessed a growing disillusionment with the liberal theology that had come to be associated with Schleiermacher. A movement developed that argued that Schleiermacher had effectively reduced Christianity from a God-centered to a human-centered affair. Liberal theology seemed to be about human values, but the war, they found, brought into question the human capacity for goodness. In time, the movement came to be associated with the position of the Swiss theologian Karl Barth (1886–1968), especially the manner in which he applied the theological concerns of Reformed orthodoxy. Barth gave these ideas systematic exposition in his *Church Dogmatics* (1936–1969), one of the most significant theological achievements of the twentieth century.

The primary theme that resonates throughout the *Dogmatics* is the need to take seriously the self-revelation of God in Christ through scripture. Like the Reformers, Barth drew attention to the transcendence or "otherness" of God, the discontinuity between God and humanity, the centrality of scripture, and the importance of preaching. Barth saw theology as a discipline that keeps the proclamation of the church faithful to its foundation in Jesus Christ.

Neo-orthodoxy has been criticized on a number of fronts, particularly for its emphasis upon the otherness of God, which leads to God being viewed as distant and potentially irrelevant. Some have accused Barth's approach as fideistic ("fideism," or "blind faith," is a belief system that so emphasizes faith as to drive an irreparable wedge between faith and reason). Furthermore, Neo-orthodoxy is obliged to dismiss other religions as distortions and perversions of God's truth. Conservatives fault Barth for his unorthodox perspectives on predestination and the atonement.

Building on the contributions of Augustine and Calvin, Barth used a unique christological approach to arrive at a startling conclusion. For Barth, predestination refers not to the election of select humans for preferential treatment but rather to God's election of Jesus Christ to serve as mediator between humanity and deity. Barth's starting point is with God's free and sovereign decision to enter into fellowship with all humanity. By electing Christ for the redemption of humanity, it is Christ who is rejected, not humanity. The cross, representing God's judgment upon sin, is God's "No" to humanity. However, this "No" does not result in the exclusion and rejection of humanity, for God's "No" to sin is borne by Christ, who died for all. In Christ, then, we find God's judgment *and* God's redemption, God's "No" to sin and God's "Yes" to grace. Because Christ is the sole elected individual, his mediatorial role leads to God's final word to humanity, which remains "Yes." Barth's doctrine of predestination, pointing to universal restoration and the salvation of all humanity, eliminates condemnation of humanity. The only one who is predestined to condemnation is Jesus Christ, who from all eternity willed to represent humanity. Barth's perspective, though hopeful, is rejected by many evangelical and fundamentalist Christians, who consider that his methodology and conclusions compromise the traditional Christian doctrines of human nature, sin, and grace.

If philosophy, theology, and mythology can be said to respond to the views of the day, a philosophical movement developed in the late twentieth century that embraces the optimism of the rationalists, the skepticism of the empiricists, the pessimism of Nietzsche, and the indeterminacy of Einsteinian physics. It is called postmodernism, a way of thinking that builds on the assumption that what we call reality is constructed by the mind, and that human understanding is interpretation rather than acquisition of accurate, objective information. From this it follows that knowledge is relative, subjective, and fallible rather than certain and absolute, and that truth is inherently ambiguous.

While some observers decry this movement as iconoclastic and relativistic, that is, as deconstructive of certainty, truth, and assurance, postmodernism has an upside, for in arguing that humans can never arrive at a wholly accurate version of truth, it opens the door to faith and to polyvalent approaches to questions of truth and meaning. Fundamental to postmodern thought is the conviction that sense data cannot force humans to adopt a particular worldview, whether philosophical, scientific, or religious. Thus, humans have a choice in what they affirm—as well as immense responsibility.

Nationalism

In a thought-provoking study entitled *The Secularization of the European Mind*, Owen Chadwick once suggested that the years between 1650 and 1750 were "the seminal years of modern intellectual history." But it would take another century and a half before the results of these ideas affected broader European society. The reason, Chadwick explains, is that secularization is not the same as Enlightenment. Enlightenment was of the few, secularization is of the many.

Over the course of the nineteenth century, a new post-Christian Europe began everywhere to emerge. Beginning in the 1760s, country after country felt the unrest. The American Revolution in the 1770s inspired a group of radicals in Europe. The desire for basic human rights, springing from both Enlightenment and biblical sources, was expressed in Jefferson's famous statement in the Declaration of Independence that humans "are endowed by their Creator with certain unalienable rights; that among these are life, liberty and the pursuit of happiness." Human rights were firmly protected by the Bill of Rights, appended to the Constitution in 1791.[1] The First Amendment, with its famous disestablishment clause, affirmed the free exercise of religion while making clear that Congress could not establish a state church. Of course, keeping religion and state separate would be easier in theory than in practice.

The storming of the Bastille by a surly mob on July 14, 1789 ushered in a new age, "the age of progress." The Bastille was a symbol of the Old Regime: the absolute rule of monarchs and the traditional feudal society consisting of the Catholic Church, wealthy aristocrats, and powerless commoners. The winds of the new age were forecast in the motto of the French Revolution: "Liberty, Equality, and Fraternity."

The popular uprising in Paris set off riots throughout the countryside in which peasants destroyed records of their servitude and created panic among aristocrats. By the end of August 1789, most of the French aristocracy's traditional feudal privileges had been wiped out and a bold "Declaration of the Rights of Man and of the Citizen" had passed into law. The Declaration codified most of the demands of the Enlightenment: it declared that the natural rights of human beings were sacred and inalienable; it established rights for people to express their views freely; it prohibited arbitrary arrest and protected the rights of the accused. It also declared that France belonged to its citizens, not to its monarchs. The European world as it once had been was passing away.

France formed a republic, and became an effective revolutionary regime that passed through a period of violence and confusion before ending

---

1. As is well known, these documents envisioned civil rights as belonging primarily to white, land-owning males. The fight for universal rights for women and people of color, while still ongoing, is closer to reality than ever before, thanks to the heroic efforts of people like Elizabeth Freeman, Lucretia Mott, Elizabeth Cady Stanton, William Lloyd Garrison, Lucy Stone, Frederick Douglass, Susan B. Anthony, Harriet Tubman, Eugene Debs, Jane Addams, W. E. B. Du Bois, Ralph Abernathy, Rosa Parks, Jesse Jackson, Al Sharpton, and Martin Luther King, Jr.

with a *coup d'état* and General Napoleon Bonaparte's accession to power. In the interim, hundreds of political suspects were executed. The execution of King Louis XVI and his queen, Marie Antoinette in 1793 shocked Europeans almost as much as the Puritans' execution of England's Charles I had done a century and a half earlier. In the early 1790s the revolutionary National Assembly attempted to reform the church along the lines of Enlightenment ideals. The representatives made priests employees of the federal government and resolved to reduce and even to eliminate any papal influence in local church matters.

In 1970 revolutionaries forced clergy to take an oath of loyalty to the new regime. Many priests refused to do so and fled. The government banned all religious vestments and locked up hundreds of priests, monks, and nuns on suspicion of treason. The resentment against clerical wealth and power unleashed a storm of anticlerical sentiment. Eventually, the revolution began to take on a religious character all its own. A new calendar removed all traces of Christianity. Parish churches were converted to Temples of Reason. When Napoleon seized the reins of power, he had the good sense to introduce a less radical stance toward religion in general, highlighted by an agreement with the pope, the Concordat of 1801, which restored the Church of Rome to a special place in France, though it had lost forever its position of power.

The dechristianization effort of the French Revolution represented the end—or at least the beginning of the end—of European Christendom as the dominant expression of Christianity in the world. The anticlerical bent of the French Revolution influenced other nationalistic movements in Europe. Negotiations neutralizing the authority of the churches contributed to Bismark's strategy in unifying a German nation in 1871. The parallel movement that led to the unification of an Italian state about the same time moved more aggressively against traditional religion by forcefully divesting the pope of the Papal States in Italy. For centuries Italy had been split into Italian states in addition to the papal territories running across the peninsula. In the middle of the nineteenth century a movement for Italian unity arose in Sardinia calling for the overthrow of all alien powers in Italy and the unity of the entire peninsula in a modern Italian nation. This revolutionary spirit could not tolerate the continuation of the Papal States, a medieval state in the heart of Italy. The national unity movement, headed by King Victor Emmanuel II of Sardinia (1849–1878), gathered momentum that could not be stopped. Between 1859 and 1860, large portions of the Papal States fell to the nationalists. In 1861 Victor Emmanuel was proclaimed king of Italy. The new government offered the pope an annual subsidy, but Pope Pius IX responded with threats of excommunications. He forbade Italy's Catholics to participate in political elections. The result was an increasingly anticlerical course in the Italian government. This unpleasant condition reached no solution until Benito Mussolini concluded the Lateran Treaty in 1929. In the treaty, the pope renounced all claims to the former Papal States and received full sovereignty in the small Vatican State.

Pietism, Evangelicalism, and the Great Awakening

On the heels of the vigorous, creative movement called the Reformation came a cautious period called confessionalism or "Protestant Scholasticism." In the sixteenth century, Luther had proclaimed the doctrine of justifying faith, whereby believers surrendered their heart to the mercy of God. In the seventeenth century, however, his dedicated followers turned faith into a mental exercise. The Christian life became less a personal relation to Christ and more a matter of outward conformity. Faithful attendance at public worship and reception of the sacraments offered by ordained orthodox clergy were the essential marks of a good Christian.

Pietism on the Continent and evangelicalism in the English-speaking world arose as a reaction to this institutionalizing of the Reformation. These movements represented a shift in religious orientation, from the head to the heart, from doctrinal orthodoxy to the centrality of personal faith. Pietists abandoned hopes of universal Christendoms, state christendoms, and Puritan commonwealths. They believed that Christianity started with the individual and with the regeneration of the heart. Thus, for the first time in Christian history, the idea of conversions of baptized Christians came to prominence. For that reason, pietists sought to shift the center of the Christian life from the state churches, into which a person was born and bred, to intimate fellowships of those who freely chose to worship in a spiritual manner.

Pietism can be traced historically to currents within German Lutheranism in the seventeenth century. Influences from beyond German-speaking lands were encouraging a more vital Christian faith and practice. A resurgence of godly living and wholesome theology in Holland spilled over into Germany. Devotional works by English Puritans like Richard Baxter (1615–1691) and John Bunyan (1628–1688) were being translated into German. But in many places these signs of spiritual life were obscured by the formalism and insincerity of church leaders. In this context, three early leaders worked for spiritual reform: Philip Jacob Spener (1635–1705), often called the father of pietism, August Hermann Francke (1663–1727), and Count Nikolaus von Zinzendorf (1700–1760), best known for his work with the Moravians. Under Zinzendorf, the Moravians carried the pietistic concern for personal spirituality almost literally around the world, with important missions in India, the West Indies, North America, and elsewhere. In 1753, the English preacher John Wesley encountered a company of Moravians during his voyage to the New World colony of Georgia. What he saw of their behavior and what he learned of their faith contributed directly to his own evangelical awakening.

Pietism made an enormous contribution to Christianity. It shifted emphasis from theological controversy to the care of souls. It made preaching and pastoral visitation central to Protestant ministry. It enriched Christian music, and it underscored the importance of the laity for a vital church. Perhaps its greatest legacy was its emphasis on small groups and the devotional reading of the Bible. Supporting all these emphases was the pietist's dominant theme: regeneration, by which they meant not doctrinal renewal but experiential renewal. The intensely personal way that pietists described regeneration often turned Christianity into a drama of the human soul, the scene of a desperate struggle between good and evil. In this sense, pietism was the foundation of all modern revivals.

The Catholic Church of the seventeenth century did not lack spiritual heroes. It produced an attractive exemplar of the Christian faith, the French mathematician and philosopher Blaise Pascal (1623–1662), who demonstrated in his life and thought how to connect head and heart, intellect with conviction. He wasn't all head, as some of his rational contemporaries, or all heart, as some of his spiritual contemporaries, but somehow fully both. A child prodigy, Pascal gained the admiration of mathematicians and scientists in Paris for his invention of the calculating machine and for his discoveries of the basic principles of atmospheric and hydraulic pressures. Committed to the scientific method, his writings on geometry and probability theory strongly influenced the development of economics and social science. A person of vast intellectual ability, he became an avid student of the Bible, finding in it principles for inner spiritual transformation.

Due to his premature death at the age of thirty-nine, he was unable to complete a projected book on the evidence for Christianity. After his death, friends found portions of his writing on faith and reason, which they published under the title *Pensées* (Reflections). At the time of his death, a servant noticed a curious bulge in the great scientist's jacket. Opening the lining, he found a folded parchment written in Pascal's hand. The words spoke of a religious conversion he had experienced on the night of November 23, 1654: "Fire! God of Abraham, God of Isaac, God of Jacob, not of the philosophers and the scholars. Certainty, certainty, feeling, joy, peace. God of Jesus Christ. . . . May I never be separated from Him." The words were the record of Pascal's mystical experience in the presence of God.

Fully immersed in the "age of reason," Pascal knew he could not ignore the domain of the heart: "the heart has reasons that reason cannot know." According to this conception, faith and reason belong to different orders, but they need not be opposed to one another. In his view, Christian faith is not a leap *within* the order of the intellect—a leap that violates the essence of that order—but a leap *from* the order of the intellect to the order of the heart. Pascal understood the human condition so deeply yet so clearly that Christians in our own time still gain perspective from him for their own spiritual pilgrimage.

In England, the dramatic spiritual renewal associated with pietism came to be known as the Evangelical Awakening. Evangelicalism came to be associated with the spirituality of brothers John and Charles Wesley, founders of a movement known as Methodism, and in the American colonies the movement led to the Great Awakening, associated with the revivalist preachers George Whitefield (1714–1770) and Jonathan Edwards (1703–1758).

In the early decades of the eighteenth century, England was a most unlikely place for a nationwide revival of vital faith. Among the rich and the educated, the Enlightenment had shoved religion from the center of life to its periphery. In the established Anglican Church and in the nonconformist denominations such as the Baptists and Congregationalists, the zeal of the Puritans seemed to be a thing of the past. The order of the day was moderation in all things.

The fifteenth of nineteen children, John Wesley (1703–1791) was reared in a god-fearing home, the son of an ordained Anglican pastor. While at Oxford University, he and Charles became leaders of a band of students who wished to take their religion seriously. Alarmed at the spread of deism at the university, they drew up a plan of study and a rule of life that stressed prayer, Bible reading, and frequent attendance at Holy

Communion. The small group attracted attention and some derision from the lax undergraduates, who called them the Bible Moths, Methodists, and other names. The Methodist label stuck.

John and Charles received an invitation to visit the newly chartered American colony of Georgia, but other than their encounter with the Moravians, the entire episode proved to be a failure, and the brothers soon returned to England. On his way home John wrote in his journal, "I went to America to convert the Indians, but, oh, who shall convert me?" Two years later, on the evening of May 24, 1738, he attended a Moravian prayer meeting in Aldersgate Street that forever changed his life. While listening to the reading of Luther's preface to the epistle to the Romans, he felt his heart "strangely warmed," and that became the moment of his conversion. Finding the assurance of salvation he had lacked, he embraced a new sense of purpose that would sustain him for a half century of evangelistic ministry. He had discovered his life's message, but he needed a method.

George Whitefield, nine years younger than John, had gone to Georgia in 1738 but returned to England in the fall of that year to be ordained. Not satisfied with the opportunities given him in church pulpits and eager to reach the masses of people, he began in 1739 to preach in the open fields to coal miners who seldom cared to enter a church. His voice was clear and strong, and he discovered that his fervent preaching moved the hardened and weary men to tears. When the miners pled for divine mercy in great numbers, Whitefield urged Wesley to follow his lead. The results were amazing. On one occasion, John preached to over three thousand people in the open air, and conversions took place readily. The Methodist revival had begun. Encouraged by the initial response, John preached in jails, in inns, on vessels, wherever people gathered; "I look upon all the world as my parish," he wrote. He traveled across England, mostly on horseback, logging some 250,000 miles in his lifetime, the equivalent of ten times around the world.

As the work grew, John decided to employ laymen from the religious societies as preachers and personal assistants. He carefully avoided calling them ministers and he refused them any authority to administer the sacraments. Throughout his life he resisted all pressures from his followers and all charges from Anglican clergy that suggested separation from the Anglican Church. "I live and die," he said, "a member of the Church of England." In America, however, the needs of the Methodists led him to significant steps toward separation. The American societies needed ordained leader, but when Wesley's appeals to the Bishop of London proved fruitless, he took matters into his own hands. He appointed two of his lay preachers for the American ministry and commissioned Thomas Coke as superintendent of the American Methodists. The Methodist Church in America became a new, distinct denomination in 1784, and after John's death, the English Methodists followed their American brethren into separation from the Anglican Church.

For his part, John's brother, Charles (1707–1788), who itinerated almost as actively for many years, became well known as a hymn-writer, composing over six thousand hymns to spread the good news of God's grace. To this day, when English-speaking Christians gather to worship, they often sing his hymns. Perhaps his best loved was "Jesus Lover of my Soul." It was sung in societies all over Britain and America.

In 1739 George Whitefield brought his powerful voice and magnetic style to the American colonies, preaching his way through Georgia, the Carolinas, Virginia, Maryland, Pennsylvania, and New York. By 1740, at the invitation of Boston ministers, he moved northward, preaching in Boston and at Northampton, where Jonathan Edwards was leading revivals, and through the towns of Connecticut, attracting massive crowds wherever he appeared. The regional revivals united into the first national Great Awakening. From 1740 to 1742 the Awakening had swept 25,000 to 50,000 members into New England churches alone, resulting in the formation of thousands of new congregations.

To be sure, the Wesleys did not act alone. They were only the most visible English leaders in the more general movement of pietistic renewal that, from the late seventeenth century, would eventually encompass Europe and North America. The impact of Methodism carried far beyond the Methodist Church. It renewed the religious life of England and her colonies, elevated the life of the poor, and stimulated missions overseas and the social concern of evangelicals in the nineteenth and twentieth centuries. In both style and message, the adjustments made by the John and Charles Wesley and their fellow Anglican George Whitefield proved to be the single most important factor in transforming the religion of the Reformation into modern Protestant evangelicalism.

After World War II, evangelical Christianity returned to public prominence in America with the evangelistic ministry of Billy Graham (1918–2018). Beginning with a 1949 campaign in Los Angeles, Graham soon conducted preaching campaigns (called crusades) in major cities around the United States and around the world. Graham became a household name by preaching to thousands in every major stadium in the United States, by a regularly scheduled radio broadcast, and by telecasts on national networks. In his global travels, he saw firsthand the need for cross-cultural Christian fellowship and ecumenical cooperation, tactics that sometimes put him at odds with observers that were more conservative. But whatever his sins of omission or commission, over the course of the twentieth century, no one except the popes of the Roman Catholic Church symbolized the universality of Christianity for more people than Billy Graham.

Protestant Missions

At the beginning of the nineteenth century, Protestant Christianity scarcely existed outside Europe and America. The story is quite different today. Christianity is now a global religion, spread across the globe. The nineteenth century proved to be the great era of Christian mission. For sheer magnitude, the extension of Christianity in that century is without parallel in human history. How do we explain this sudden explosion of Protestant energy aimed at converting the world to Christ?

The original impetus came from the pietists, particularly the Moravians. During the first century after they were reconstituted under the leadership of Count von Zinzendorf in the early 1720s, approximately two thousand (one-fourth of them women) volunteered for cross-cultural missionary service. The immediate answer, however, is found in the host of non-denominational societies established by evangelicals in England to minister to social ills and to spread the gospel overseas. These societies were not churches in the traditional sense of sacraments, creeds, and ordained ministers. They were groups of individual Christians volunteering together for some specific objective: the distribution of Bibles, for example, the needs of prisoners, or the relief of the poor. Such societies may be seen as forerunners of today's parachurch organizations, faith-based entities that work outside and across denominations to engage in social welfare and evangelism.[2]

In England, the informal headquarters for evangelical causes was a hamlet near London called Clapham. The community was the country

2. Some well-known examples include the American Bible Society, the Billy Graham Evangelistic Association, Bread for the World, Christian Children's Fund, InterVarsity Christian Fellowship, World Vision, and Wycliffe Bible Translators.

residence of a group of wealthy and ardent evangelicals who were committed to practice "saintliness in daily life." They often met for Bible study, conversation, and prayer in the home of a wealthy banker, Henry Thornton. The unquestioned leader of the group was William Wilberforce (1759–1833), an influential politician who became the voice of the abolition movement in Parliament. Under his leadership, the group discussed the wrongs and injustices of their country and the strategy they would need to implement to establish justice. The group formed or inspired numerous societies to address a host of evangelical causes: The Church Missionary Society, the British and Foreign Bible Society, The Society for Bettering the Condition of the Poor, The Society for the Reformation of Prison Discipline, and many more. The greatest concern centered on the campaign to abolish slavery, starting with the abolition of the slave trade. The abolitionists achieved their initial victory in 1807, when Parliament halted the legal traffic in human lives. Wilberforce continued the battle for complete emancipation until age and poor health forced him from Parliament. He enlisted the help of younger evangelicals, who continued the cause. The Clapham society remains the shining example of how a few individuals can change their world.

In 1779, an English cobbler named William Carey (1761–1834) was converted to faith in Christ. After gaining some preaching experience he became pastor of a Baptist chapel, supporting his family by teaching and shoemaking. His passion was the conversion of unbelievers in India. In 1792 he published *An Enquiry into the Obligation of Christians to Use Means for the Conversion of the Heathen*. He ended his appeal with practical proposals for the preaching of the gospel throughout the world. As a result, in 1792 he and twelve colleagues formed the Baptist Missionary Society, and within a year Carey and his family were on their way to India. In 1799 two fellow Baptists joined Carey and the three colleagues worked to organize a growing network of mission stations near Calcutta. Like earlier Jesuit missionaries to the Far East, Carey and his companions plunged into the intricacies of Hindu thought, regarding knowledge of local culture and beliefs an essential part of their task. By 1825 Carey had supervised six complete translations of the Bible, as well as published grammars, dictionaries, and translations of Eastern books.

Carey represents the first of many Protestant missionary pioneers to venture into the unknown, some named—like Robert Morrison, John Williams, Adoniram Judson, Alexander Duff, Allen Gardiner, Hudson Taylor, Robert MoVat, David Livingstone, Mary Slessor, Lottie Moon, and Albert

Schweitzer—and many long forgotten because they died in a matter of months in some malaria-infested tropical climate or at the hands of some savage tribe.

In the United States the first foreign missionary society was the American Board of Commissioners for Foreign Missions (1810), formed by the Congregationalist Church on the initiative of a group of students at the newly created Andover Theological Seminary. In a few years Baptists, Presbyterians, and other major denominations followed the Congregationalists in creating missionary agencies. By the end of the nineteenth century, almost every Christian body, from the Orthodox Church of Russia to the Salvation Army, and almost every country, from the Lutheran Church of Finland to the Waldensian Church of Italy, had its share in the missionary enterprise overseas.

A wide variety of humanitarian ministries accompanied the widespread preaching of the gospel. Mission agencies established schools, hospitals, and centers for training nurses and doctors. They reduced many languages and dialects to writing and translated the Bible and other writings into these languages. They also introduced public health measures and better agricultural techniques. In some cases, these activities were closely related to the goal of conversion, but many emerged from the recognition of social and physical needs that no Christian could ignore.

Protestant Liberalism and Fundamentalism

The climax of a century of progressive European theology was reached in a series of lectures titled *What is Christianity?* (1900). In these lectures, the learned scholar Adolf von Harnack (1851–1930) argued that the simple gospel preached by Jesus had been largely lost when it was translated into a Hellenistic idiom. Harnack felt that the original teaching of Jesus could be summarized as the fatherhood of God, the brotherhood of man, and the infinite value of the human soul. Such views are labeled "liberal" by conservative Christians, for they appear to betray the core biblical values upon which Protestantism was founded.

Modernism—or liberalism, as it is sometimes called in church circles—is an attempt to adjust religious ideas to the needs of contemporary society. Harry Emerson Fosdick, minister at the influential Riverside Church in New York City, put it well when he said the central aim of liberal theology was to make it possible for a person "to be both an intelligent modern and a serious Christian." Protestant liberalism engages a problem as old as Christianity itself, attempting to make faith meaningful in a changing world without distorting or destroying the gospel. The apostle Paul tried and succeeded. The early Gnostics tried and failed. The jury is still out on liberalism. No one expressed the irony of liberalism better than H. Richard Niebuhr did when he discerned in liberalism "a God without wrath bringing people without sin into a kingdom without judgment through the ministrations of a Christ without a cross."

Definitions of religious liberalism are as varied as those of political liberalism. Some scholars question whether religious liberals have a common theology. They prefer an outlook or an approach rather than a distinct theological agenda. Thus, Henry Sloane Coffin at New York's Union Seminary once said that liberalism is an approach that reveres truth supremely and therefore craves freedom to discuss, to publish, and to pursue what it believes to be true.

Liberals believe that Christian theology must come to terms with modern science. Refusing to accept religious beliefs exclusively on authority, they insist that faith has to pass the tests of reason and experience. Christians, they argue, should keep their minds open to truth from any source. New facts may well change traditional beliefs that rest exclusively on custom and time, but unexamined faith is not worth having. The liberal goals are truth, coherence, harmony, and unity.

Liberals see the divisions of Protestant denominations as weakening Christianity. Hence, they stress the underlying unity of the various groups, and work to achieve denominational unification. For liberals, advances in the study of philology, archaeology, anthropology, and history lead to reinterpretations of the Bible. Modern biblical scholarship argues that the books of Moses, for example, were not written by Moses, or the Gospels by eyewitnesses. Because the Bible is said to reflect the social, cultural, and political events of its human authors, it is not considered an inerrant source of timeless truth. Liberals insist that the Bible of the scholars is more exciting and more relevant than that of the conservatives, because it is more human. A historical product, the Bible shows men and women's struggles to comprehend God, as well as God's attempts to reach them. Examining the biblical genres of history, poetry, myth, wisdom, and law, liberal scholars find in the Bible a complex interplay between the divine and the human, illustrative of the growth in religious consciousness from the early Hebrews to the first Christians.

Liberalism and its polar opposite, fundamentalism, were already well-defined movements as early as 1900. By the 1930s, liberals occupied nearly one-third of the pulpits in American Protestantism and controlled at least half of the seminaries. Fundamentalists arose to stem the tide. Even before Nazism, Marxism, and the two World Wars dealt a major blow to belief in progress and the perfectibility of humankind, fundamentalist Christians accused liberals of having destroyed Christianity in their quest for modernity and prepared to engage them in battle to preserve what they regarded as the essence of the faith. Fundamentalism, a name derived from a series of pamphlets published between 1910 and 1914, was a movement cutting across denominational lines and growing out of evangelical Protestantism. What was new was not so much its content as its temper: a militant response to threats to its version of the gospel and a willingness to attack all competitors. Fundamentalists insisted that liberalism, by undercutting the authority of the Bible, denied the most important Christian doctrines. Thus, fundamentalists advocated constant study of the Bible, for no part was irrelevant.

World War I delayed the outbreak of the "modernist-fundamentalist" controversy in the Protestant denominations. However, shortly after the American soldiers returned from Europe, fundamentalist Christians launched their own war of words over the values and dangers of liberal theology in the church. One of the principal battlegrounds occurred in 1925 in Dayton, Tennessee, when William Jennings Bryan and Clarence Darrow nearly came to blows in a packed courtroom. The setting was the trial of John Scopes, who had violated Tennessee's law against the teaching of evolution in the public schools. Both lawyers saw the larger dimensions of the trial. Bryan, a three-time candidate for president of the United States and the secretary of state in the cabinet of President Woodrow Wilson, wished to preserve the authority of the Bible. Clarence Darrow, Chicago's brilliant lawyer, argued that nothing else than intellectual freedom was on trial. When all was over, Scopes was found guilty and fined a token sum. Bryan won in Dayton, but Darrow in the rest of the country. Five days after the trial Bryan passed away in his sleep; the evangelical crusade against the findings of modern science died with him.

The Ecumenical Movement and Roman Catholic Response

The 1910 World Missionary Conference meeting in Edinburgh, Scotland, marks the beginning of the twentieth-century ecumenical movement.[3] For ten days, over one thousand distinguished British, American, and European delegates from around the globe led the discussions on such diverse topics as the church in the mission field, the place of education in national Christian life, the message of Christian missions in relation to non-Christian faiths, and the promotion of Christian unity. In discussing missions, the delegates discovered a great sense of unity and purpose.

The conference also represents the high tide of Western missionary expansion, which had gathered strength throughout the nineteenth century. In that century, the proportion of the world's population associated with Christian churches increased more rapidly than at any time since the fourth century. Where less than a quarter of the world could be identified as Christian in 1800, almost 35 percent could be so numbered at the time of the Edinburgh conference.

While the delegates at Edinburgh had lived through an unprecedented expansion of the church, much of it the direct result of missionary effort, the conference also marked the end of an epoch, perhaps the final moment when worldwide Christianity would be represented overwhelmingly by delegates from Britain and North America. Two World Wars, the Russian Revolution, consumerism, secularism, and religious indifference would soon tarnish the appeal of Western Christianity. The wave of the future was toward a Christianity indigenized in countless regional cultures around the world, defined as much outside of Europe and North America as previously defined by the West. The twentieth century witnessed the transition from missionary expansion to local appropriation of Christianity.

The conference ended with the shared conviction that the momentum established should continue. Discussions did continue, eventually leading to the establishment of the International Missionary Conference and less directly to the Universal Christian Conference on Life and Work (1925) and the World Conference on Faith and order (1927). In 1948 these two

---

3. "Ecumenical" means worldwide or universal. Applied to Christian churches, it implies organized efforts favoring unity, whether organizationally, through mergers of denominations or federation of churches, or theoretically, for the sake of more effective service to the world. The spirit of unity is called "ecumenicity" and the organizational effort the "ecumenical movement."

organizations merged to create the World Council of Churches, the world organization that best represents global ecumenism.

The first assembly of the World Council of Churches convened in Amsterdam in 1948, bringing together 351 delegates representing 147 denominations from 44 countries. The principal nonparticipants were the Roman Catholics, many conservative evangelicals, and the Russian Orthodox. During those early years of the World Council, the General Secretary was Willem Adolph Visser't Hooft. One of Visser't Hooft's projects after World War II was the creation of an Ecumenical Institute in Switzerland for the training of leaders in the church unity movement. Thanks to Visser't Hooft's diplomatic skills, each assembly of the World Council became a mosaic of cultures, continents, and concerns. Every gathering had theological conservatives from Eastern Orthodox countries; secular theologians from Europe and North America; evangelicals from Europe, Africa, and Asia; confessional Christians from Northern Europe; and liberal theologians from South America.

The World Council does not claim to be a church. According to its constitution, it cannot legislate for its member churches. Its aim is understanding and cooperation among its members and Christian unity wherever possible. Later assemblies followed the assembly in Amsterdam, including at Evanston, Illinois (1954); New Delhi, India (1961); Uppsala, Sweden (1968); and Nairobi, Kenya (1975). At New Delhi, the Russian Orthodox Church joined the Council. Over time, doctrinal emphasis declined and social concerns increased.

In the United States, the National Council of Churches best marks American ecumenism. The movement began in 1908, when thirty-one American denominations joined the Federal Council of Churches. In 1950, the Federal Council was absorbed into the National Council of Churches of Christ. While the council desires to represent all American denominations, the members range from centrist to progressive. Conservatives generally view the organization with suspicion, considering its pronouncements on social, economic, and political questions to be motivated by liberal theology.

Roman Catholic Response: Vatican II

The Roman Catholic Church, the oldest organization in the world, is also the largest, growing from around 665 million in 1970 to 1.16 billion in 2011. By comparison, the scale for Protestants is 258 million in 1970 to

514 million in 2011; for Orthodox from 144 million in 1970 to 271 million in 2011, and for Independent Christians from 86 million in 1970 to 378 million in 2011.

The First Vatican Council, convened in 1870, marked the Vatican's reply to its loss of sovereignty in Italy. That council represented the culmination of a movement called "ultramontanism," which stood for devotion to the Roman Church. Following the French Revolution and the turmoil of the Napoleonic years, a peculiar loyalty to the papacy had developed in Italy. Some Catholics extolled the papacy as the only source of civil order and public morality. In 1854, Pope Pius IX (1846–1878) had declared as dogma the traditional belief that Mary had been conceived without original sin. The subject of the decision was not new, but rather the manner in which it was proclaimed. This was not a decision by a council, but a declaration *ex cathedra*, meaning the pope spoke for the church "from the chair" and with the authority of St. Peter.

Questions arose, asking whether the pope alone, without council, could decide dogma. The question of papal infallibility became the focus of Vatican I. The initial vote: 451 delegates in favor, 88 opposed, and 62 accepting with reservations, affirmed the results. Vatican I asserted two fundamental truths for Catholicism: the primacy of the pope and the infallibility of the pope. Immediately after the vote on infallibility, the council had to disband, due to the outbreak of the Franco-Prussian War and the occupation of Rome by Italian nationalists. Surrounded by the hostile forces of liberalism, socialism, and nationalism, the Roman Church chose to withdraw for safety behind the walls of an exalted and infallible papacy.

The Second Vatican Council, known as Vatican II, created an entirely different image of the Church, and accomplished a great deal more. It met in four sessions, from 1962 to 1965, and produced significant results, the most important for Catholicism since the sixteenth-century Council of Trent. From its inception, when 2,540 delegates arrived in Rome, it was apparent Vatican II would be a council unlike any other. There were 230 delegates from the United States, a country that had been mission territory until 1908. The American group was second only to the Italian, which had 430 members. There were 230 Africans and more than 300 from Asia.

Vatican II was the first council not called to combat heresy, pronounce new dogmas, or marshal the church against hostile forces. When Pope John XXIII (1958–1963) announced his intention to convene a general council, he said its purpose would be *aggiornamento*, an Italian term for "bringing up to date." It suggests not only outward adaptation to contemporary society but also inward change of thought. John apparently planned for the council to turn from the legal patterns of the past to the pastoral concerns of the present. The pope's opening speech showed that Vatican II was called not against but rather for something. The days of the state church, he recognized, were over. In the age coming to birth, he said, the church must not seek to maintain its authority by threats, excommunication, and other weapons of repression. He spoke of the church as a "Pilgrim People," and together with other pilgrims, caring for the weak and disadvantaged. Its means should be persuasion, and its method "the medicine of mercy." The church's modernization, he hoped, would bring nearer the time of the reunion of Christians, when Christ's prayer "that they may be one" should be fulfilled.

The Council's three practical concerns, (1) to reform and revitalize the church, (2) to enhance lay participation in the life of the church, and (3) to take steps toward the reconciliation of all Christians, launched a tidal wave of change. The decade after the close of the council proved to be turbulent for the Catholic Church as average Catholics tried to adjust. Many sweeping changes were made, some of the most significant in the Church's history, including:

- Affirmed collegiality, whereby all bishops share authority with the pope.
- Created an order of deacons that included married men.
- Recognized non-Catholic Christians as true Christians.
- Allowed the vernacular in many parts of the mass.
- Encouraged the use of modern techniques to study the Bible.
- Allowed worship in non-Catholic churches.
- Created ecumenical dialogue with other Christians and also with non-Christians.
- Officially declared that Jews were no longer to be held responsible for the death of Jesus.

In the wake of the Vatican II, Roman Catholicism could not remain the same. The council stimulated a profusion of Catholic special-interest groups—charismatic, socially active, modernist, biblical, conservative, ecumenical, and more. Amid all the upheaval, the Catholic Church experienced a major exodus of priests, brothers, and nuns. From 1962 to 1974 the total number of seminarians in the United States alone decreased by 31 percent, and between 1966 and 1972 nearly eight thousand American priests left public ministry.

As the 1970s closed, the Church of Rome had ventured some distance from the secure walls of her medieval fortress. Upon the election of Pope Francis in 2013, most Catholics view the future with hope, for in electing the first pope from the Americas and the first Jesuit, the Church was signaling its willingness to chart a new course. Choosing his papal name in honor of Saint Francis of Assisi, Francis is noted for his humility, his concern for the poor, and his commitment to interfaith dialogue.

Like their Protestant "separated brethren," Catholics find their journey through the twentieth and into the twenty-first centuries a perilous and often uncertain pilgrimage. The distance between Protestants, Catholics, and Orthodox Christians has narrowed, as has the distance between Christians and non-Christians in general. The ecumenical dream, based on Christ's prayer for unity, is more alive today than ever.

Study Questions

1. Whom do you consider the chief protagonist in the Enlightenment (Modern) phase of the church's history (eighteenth through twentieth centuries CE)? Support your answer.

2. Do you agree with the author's choice that the emergence of religious societies represents this epoch's turning point? Why or why not? Is there another event you consider more noteworthy? If so, what is it? Support your choice.

3. In this epoch, does "the church" live up to its nature and destiny as God's new creation? Why or why not?

4. How did new trends in science and the elevation of reason impact Christian life and thought in the eighteenth and nineteenth centuries?

5. What factors worked together to bring about the demise of European Christendom?

6. What can Christians learn from the Methodist revivalists?

7. The evangelicals and pietists of the eighteenth century sparked the first significant push toward cross-cultural missions among Protestants.

What characteristics of their faith make this era the beginning of Protestant missions?

8. Do you believe that Christians should actively share their faith with non-Christians? If so, what are the most effective ways to evangelize non-Christians?

9. How did Vatican II change the direction of Catholicism?

10. What can Protestants learn from Catholic Christians? What can Catholics learn from Protestant Christians?

11. What are some of the ways that the church needs to respond to the increasing secularization of the West?

Epilogue: Awakening

The Global South, Pentecostalism, and the Emerging Church

The data is clear: religious affiliation is plummeting across the breadth of Christian denominations. Yet interest in spirituality is on the rise, and pundits are calling for a new Awakening in America.

Historians of American religion generally recognize three significant awakenings in the United States: the First Great Awakening (1730–1760) marked the end of European styles of church organization and created an experiential, democratic community of faith called evangelicalism. The denominations embracing revivalism most heartily—particularly the Baptists and Methodists—grew to become the largest Protestant churches, with adherents numbering two-thirds of all Protestants.

The Second Great Awakening (1800–1830) ended Calvinist theological dominance and initiated new understandings of free will that resulted in a voluntary system for church membership and benevolence work. Historians have described this awakening as an Americanization of religion. It gave rise to new denominations like the Disciples of Christ, Unitarians, Universalists, and Christianity-based sects like the Shakers and Mormons. It also created voluntary societies for distributing Bibles and tracts, founded Sunday schools, and saw large numbers of African-Americans become Christians and create their own pattern of worship. For the first time, churches sought to enlist women in missionary and benevolent organizations. Persons influenced by the revival sought to apply Jesus' teachings by creating public schools, founding colleges, building penitentiaries, humanizing the treatment of the insane, and addressing the consumption of alcoholic beverages.

In a series of prayer meetings beginning in 1837, Phoebe Palmer, a Methodist laywoman in New York City, sought to revitalize churches by advocating that members should go beyond conversion to a second act of grace, or sanctification. This "holiness" movement, combined with revivals in the late 1850s, resulted in the creation of new denominations such as the Free Methodists, the Church of the Nazarene, and the Church of God (Anderson, Indiana). To these belongs The Salvation Army, which brought a distinctive holiness emphasis to the urban poor. Founded in England in 1865 by William and Catherine Booth, this movement thrived in America under the leadership of Booth's daughter, Evangeline Booth (1865–1950).

The Third Great Awakening (1890–1920) gave rise to the Social Gospel movement, with its progressive politics; the Pentecostal movement, with an emphasis on miraculous transformation; and nonconformist movements like the Jehovah's Witnesses, the Seventh-Day Adventists, and Christian Science. The Jehovah's Witnesses, founded by Charles Taze Russell (1852–1916), focus on concepts like the Second Coming of Christ, the end of the world, and the establishment of God's millennial kingdom on earth. The Seventh-Day Adventists, initially inspired by the predictions of William Miller (1782–1849)—who erroneously announced that Christ would return to earth in 1843, later revised to October 22, 1844—are guided by the visions of Ellen White (1827–1915), who combined millennial expectation with an emphasis upon the seventh-day, or Saturday, as the correct Sabbath for Christians. Christian Science, founded by Mary Baker Eddy (1829–1910), while reflecting neither the teachings of Christianity nor the principles of science, built upon the prestige of Christianity and science to advance an alternative view of healing that emphasizes the power of religion in health and wellbeing.

During each Awakening, old patterns of religious life gave way to new ones, spawning new organizational forms that focused on revitalizing social, economic, and political life. Some writers say America is experiencing a Fourth Great Awakening, using terms such as postmodern, emerging (or emergent), and convergence to define it. Whether the "age of belief" has ended, as the Harvard theologian Harvey Cox suggests, or the new has begun, as William McLoughlin proposed in his influential book *Revivals,*

Awakenings, and Reform (1978), our focus in this epilogue will be on three phenomena that connect the church's recent past with its immediate future:

1. The rise of the Global South

2. Pentecostalism in America

3. The emerging church

More people have become Christian in the last one hundred and fifty years than at any other time. When focusing upon the evangelistic embrace of faith, it is arguable that more has happened in the last one hundred years than in the church's previous history. The great missionary push of the late 1800s and early 1900s has contributed to this explosive growth—largely south of the Equator. This new growth seems to have its own distinctive character and Spirit-given initiative. Ironically, one-time strongholds of Christian mission in Europe and North America are seeing dormancy and decline. History will record if the new centers of Christianity in the Global South will maintain a traditional Christian character, and to what extent they will influence Western Christianity. Time will also tell the extent to which the West will experience its own renewal. Without the Spirit's stirring, however, the label post-Christian will become more fitting with time.

The Rise of the Global South

In the year 2002, two scholars pronounced the demise of Western Christendom. In the words of Andrew Walls, perhaps the leading missiologist today, "Christendom is dead, and Christianity is alive and well without it." Philip Jenkins, author of *The Next Christendom*, used different imagery to say the same thing: "The era of Western Christianity has passed within our lifetime, and the day of Southern Christianity is dawning." When Jenkins refers to "Southern Christianity," he means Africa, Asia, and Latin America. To use this term is to indicate that during the twentieth century, the center of gravity in Christianity shifted southward, from the Global West and North to the Global South, areas Westerners once thought of as the Third World.

During the twentieth century, the number of Christians in Europe and North America has declined, while those of Christians in the Southern and Eastern hemispheres has increased. In this Global South we find huge and growing Christian populations: at the dawning of the twenty-first century, 480 million in Latin America, 360 million in Africa, and 313 million in Asia, compared with 260 million in North America. The growth of Christianity in Africa has been especially dramatic. In 1900, Africa had just 10 million Christians out of a continental population of 107 million, about 9 percent. At the turn of the twenty-first century, the Christian total stood at 360 million out of a total population of 784 million, or 46 percent.

The projections for the future consolidate the trends we are witnessing: by 2025, Africa and Latin America will compete for the title of "most Christian continent." By this date, these two continents will account for half the Christians on the planet. If the trends continue as expected, by 2050 only about one-fifth of the world's Christians will be non-Hispanic Whites. "Soon," according to Jenkins, "the phrase 'a White Christian' may sound like a curious oxymoron, something like a 'Swedish Buddhist.'" If one wants to see what Christianity will look like in the near future, morally and theologically as well as demographically, one needs to examine the events taking place in Africa, Asia, and Latin America.

According to the United Nations report on population, the world's population is increasing by 1.2 percent each year, with half of that increase coming from six countries: India, China, Pakistan, Nigeria, Bangladesh, and Indonesia. Because the population of Africa, Asia, and Latin America will continue to grow, while that of Europe and most other developed areas of the world will decline, this will require mass immigration to maintain economic levels in the developed world. This shift is already occurring in Europe and North America, creating cultural tension and religious upheaval. One of the prime targets for immigration will be North America. By 2050, the population of the United States is expected to rise to 400 million, almost entirely due to immigration.

When we speak of the Christianity of the Global South, we do not have in mind simply a church that is geographically Hispanic, African, or Asian, but a church that is marked by economic poverty, political powerlessness, cultural pluralism, religious syncretism (accepts competing theologies and indigenous worldviews), and by a high concentration of youth.

The churches that have grown the fastest and made the most dramatic progress in the Global South have either been Roman Catholic (of a traditionalist and fideistic kind) or radical Protestant sects, evangelical or Pentecostal. Beginning with 1970, statistical analysis indicates the dynamism at work in these world Christian traditions: Roman Catholics have grown from around 665 million in 1970 to 1.16 billion in 2011; evangelicals from approximately 100 million worldwide in 1970 to 270 million in 2011; and Pentecostals/charismatics from approximately 70 million in 1970 to over 600 million in 2011.

Pentecostalism in America

The unmistakable character of the churches in the Global South is that they are Pentecostal-charismatic. In other words, "spiritual gifts" such as speaking in tongues, prophesying, and healings play a prominent role in public worship and private devotion.

By 1900 there were, at most, a handful of Christians who were experiencing special gifts of the Holy Spirit similar to those recorded in the New Testament (see Rom. 12:6–8; 1 Cor. 12:8–10, 28–30). By the year 2010, some 600 million Christians (more than one-fourth of the worldwide population of Christians) could be identified as Pentecostal or charismatic. (The usual difference in these terms is between Pentecostals, who are organized into denominations with distinct emphases on the gifts of the Holy Spirit,[1] and charismatics, who practice those gifts within churches that do not formally endorse this understanding of the Holy Spirit's work.)

The beginnings of modern-day Pentecostalism is usually associated with a revival that took place in 1906 at the Apostolic Faith Gospel Mission on Azusa Street in Los Angeles, California. The small group was led by William Joseph Seymour (1870–1922), a self-educated African-American preacher originally from Louisiana. In that year, Seymour conducted a lengthy series of nightly meeting at the mission. Soon visitors from around the world came to Azusa Street, returning to their homes with the message that the living presence of the Holy Spirit could be experienced as a reality in this and any age. Beyond the Western world, missionary churches and indigenous Christian movements began witnessing Pentecostal-type events.

Pentecostal and charismatic experiences have been central in the rapid expansion of Christianity outside the West, with rapidly growing churches in Brazil, Nigeria, Korea, Russia, China, and many other nations. In these situations, Pentecostal and charismatic forms of Christian faith flourish, usually by directly confronting pagan gods and animistic spirits,

---

1. The largest Pentecostal denominations in the United States are the Assemblies of God, the Church of God in Christ, the Church of God, and the Pentecostal Holiness Church.

though sometimes by accommodating with ancient practices and beliefs. Most Pentecostals hold to traditional Christian beliefs on the Trinity, human sinfulness, and the authority of the Bible. They tend to place great stress on the supernatural power of God to defeat disease and to provide other miraculous interventions in ordinary life.

In the United Stated, scholars observe three phases or waves of Pentecostal development during the twentieth century. The first wave refers to the outpouring of the Spirit at Azusa and the emergence of the major Pentecostal denominations that followed. The second wave occurred during the 1960s and early 1970s, when charismatic life spilled into mainline Protestant denominations and Catholicism. The third wave saw the embrace of "signs and wonders" by evangelical Christians. It began in the 1980s at Fuller Seminary in California, around the teaching and ministry of John Wimber. This phase produced the Vineyard network of churches and saw many evangelicals participate in the charismatic experience.

The Emerging Church

The simple imagery Paul used in speaking of spiritual gifts introduces four decisive aspects of biblical thinking on the church and its members:

- All members are indispensable.
- All members are different.
- All members are equal.
- All members are responsible.

The bottom line is this: every Christian ought to consider his or her spiritual gifts as a ministry of service to others. A church based on these principles will surely last.

Will the church of the future be charismatic? The answer remains uncertain, for the term "charismatic" is ambiguous and fluid. What is certain is that if the church as we know it will survive, it must involve both head and heart. While a core of beliefs must remain, five qualities (their first letter spelling the acrostic PIETY) define its impetus:

- Practical
- Inclusive
- Experiential

- Transformative
- Youth-centered

Despite its vital past, the greatest days of the church may still lie in the future. In that emerging church, worship will be lively, authentic, high tech, and free. The leadership will include women equally with men and will be racially representative. It will be ecumenical and non-sectarian. In other words, church worship and the Christian life will be hopeful, dynamic, and spontaneous, for that is the essence of newness, the church's resplendent quality.

Bibliography

Anderson, Bernhard W. *Understanding the Old Testament*. 5th ed. Upper Saddle River, NJ: Pearson Prentice Hall, 2007.

Cahill, Thomas. *Desire of the Everlasting Hills*. New York: Anchor, 2001.

Cross, F. L., and E. A. Livingstone. *The Oxford Dictionary of the Christian Church*. 3rd ed. Oxford: Oxford University Press, 1997.

Dowley, Tim, et al. *Eerdman's Handbook to the History of Christianity*. Grand Rapids, MI: Eerdmans, 1977.

Drane, John. *Introducing the New Testament*. Revised and Updated. Minneapolis: Fortress, 2001.

Gonzalez, Justo L. *The Story of Christianity*. 2 vols. San Francisco: Harper & Row, 1984.

Hastings, Adrian. *A World History of Christianity*. Grand Rapids, MI: Eerdmans, 1999.

Hoffecker, W. Andrew, and Gary Scott Smith. *Building a Christian World View*. 2 vols. Phillipsburg, NJ: Presbyterian and Reformed, 1986, 1988.

Hordern, William E. *A Layman's Guide to Protestant Theology*. Rev. ed. New York: Macmillan, 1968.

Irving, Dale T., and Scott W. Sunquist. *History of the World Christian Movement*. 2 vols. Maryknoll, NY: Orbis, 2006, 2012.

Jenkins, Philip. *The Next Christendom: The Coming of Global Christianity*. Rev. ed. New York: Oxford University Press, 2007.

Johnson, Luke Timothy. *The History of Christianity: From the Disciples to the Dawn of the Reformation*. 2 vols. Chantilly, VA: The Great Courses, 2012.

Kee, Howard Clark, et. al. *Christianity: A Social and Cultural History*. 2nd ed. Upper Saddle River, NJ: Prentice Hall, 1998.

Latourette, Kenneth Scott. *A History of Christianity*. New York: Harper & Brothers, 1953.

MacCulloch, Diarmaid. *Christianity: The First Three Thousand Years*. New York: Viking, 2009.

———. *The Reformation: A History*. New York: Viking, 2003.

McGrath, Alister E. *Christian Theology: An Introduction.* 5th. ed. Malden, MA: Wiley-Blackwell, 2011.

McLaren, Brian D. *A Generous Orthodoxy.* Grand Rapids, MI: Zondervan, 2004.

———. *A New Kind of Christianity: Ten Questions That Are Transforming the Faith.* New York: HarperCollins, 2010.

McManners, John. *The Oxford Illustrated History of Christianity.* New York: Oxford University Press, 1990.

Noll, Mark A. *Turning Points: Decisive Moments in the History of Christianity.* 3rd ed. Grand Rapids, MI: Baker Academic, 2012.

Plotkin, Bill. *Nature and the Human Soul: Cultivating Wholeness and Community in a Fragmented World.* Novato, CA: New World Library, 2008.

———. *Soulcraft: Crossing into Mysteries of Nature and Psyche.* Novato, CA: New World Library, 2003.

Shelley, Bruce L., and R. L. Hatchett. *Church History in Plain Language.* 4th ed. Nashville: Thomas Nelson, 2013.

Spickard, Paul R., and Kevin M. Cragg. *A Global History of Christians.* Grand Rapids, MI: Baker Academic, 1994.

Spong, John Shelby. *Biblical Literalism: A Gentile Heresy.* New York: HarperOne, 2006.

———. *Liberating the Gospels: Reading the Bible with Jewish Eyes.* New York: HarperSanFrancisco, 1996.

———. *Rescuing the Bible from Fundamentalism.* New York: HarperSanFrancisco, 1991.

———. *Why Christianity Must Change or Die.* New York: HarperOne, 1999.

Stark, Rodney. *The Rise of Christianity.* Princeton, NJ: Princeton University Press, 1996.

Urban, Linwood. *A Short History of Christian Thought.* Rev. ed. New York: Oxford University Press, 1995.

Walker, Williston. *A History of the Christian Church.* 4th ed. New York: Scribner, 1985.

Walls, Andrew F. *The Cross-Cultural Process in Christian History.* Maryknoll, NY: Orbis, 2002.

———. *The Missionary Movement in Christian History.* Maryknoll, NY: Orbis, 1996.

Ware. Timothy. *The Orthodox Church.* Baltimore: Penguin, 1969.

Worthen, Molly. *The History of Christianity II: From the Reformation to the Modern Megachurch.* 2 vols. Chantilly, VA: The Great Courses, 2017.

Subject/Name Index

SUBJECT/NAME INDEX

Innocent III (pope), 146, 147, 148, 161,
  162, 165
Inquisition, 164, 165–66, 197, 200
Iona (monastery), 125, 133
Irenaeus (bishop), 88, 89–90
Islam, 121, 129
  rise of, 142
  spread of, 142–44
Israel, xv, 10, 17, 24
  first national epic, 6–7
  history of, 19–44
  new, 52, 62, 87
  of God, 19
  United Kingdom, 6

Jacob (patriarch), xv, 3, 6, 9, 10, 16
James the Just, 52
Jenkins, Philip, 234
Jerome (monk), 116, 127
Jerusalem, destruction of, 36, 37, 47, 62,
  75–76, 87
Jesuits (Society of Jesus), 176, 197, 199,
  200
Jesus Christ
  as historical figure, 51–53
  as Logos (Word), 3–4, 103, 107
  disciples of, 51–52, 54, 55
  resurrection of. See Easter
Joan of Arc, 163
John XXIII (pope), 228
Joseph (patriarch), 9, 10, 16–17
judge (biblical office), 32–33
Julian (emperor), 100–101
Julian of Norwich, 163–64
justice, 26, 27
justification by faith, 167, 177–78, 201
Justin Martyr, 79, 88
Justinian (emperor), 140–41

Kant, Immanuel, 159, 209
Kepler, Johannes, 206
Kierkegaard, Søren, 15–16, 96, 211
King, Jr., Martin Luther, 80, 214n1
kingdom of God, xiii–xiv, 36, 57–59,
  102
Knox, John, 186

Las Casa, Bartolomé de, 200

Latourette, Kenneth Scott, xvii, 130
lay investiture, 138
Leo the Great (pope), 117, 118, 122
liberalism, 222–25, 227
Lombard, Peter, 158
Lombards, 123, 136
Lord's Prayer, the, xiii–xiv, 54
loyalty, 27
Loyola, Ignatius, 196, 197
Luther, Martin, ix, 61, 126, 160, 170,
  175, 176–81, 205

Maccabees, 40, 42, 77
Manichaeism, 110
Manzikert, battle of, 151
Marcion(ism), 81–82, 89, 90, 116
Marcus Aurelius (emperor), 77, 79
Martel, Charles, 135
martyrdom, 77–80, 92–93
McLaughlin, William, 233
medieval synthesis, 146, 153, 160, 177,
  186, 204
Mennonites, 188–89
messianic hope, 36
Methodism, 186, 219–20, 232
Methodius (monk), 127, 135
Mill, John Stuart, 209
Miller, William, 233
Milvian Bridge, battle of, 93
missions, missionaries, 197–200,
  221–23
modalism, 103
modernism, 205, 224, 225
monasticism, 124–27
monophysitism, 108, 109
Montanism, 81
Moravians, 168, 188, 217, 219, 221
Mormons, 232
Moses, 20–26, 224
Mussolini, Benito, 216
mysticism, 163–64

Napoleon Bonaparte, 51, 215
nationalism, 213–16
Neo-orthodoxy, 212
Nero (emperor), 77
Nestorius (bishop), 107–8
New Testament, 54

SUBJECT/NAME INDEX

Sinai
  covenant at, 23–26
sins (vices), 156
  mortal and venial, 167
slavery, 66, 222
Solomon (king), 6, 16, 34, 35, 36, 39
Spener, Philip Jacob, 217
stewardship, 25–26
Strauss, David, 209

Tertullian, 77, 88, 91, 103
Theodosius (emperor), 101, 105
Thirty Years War, 205
transubstantiation, 156, 166
Trent (council), 175, 201, 228
Trinity, 91, 103, 106, 113, 237
  analogy of love, 106
Troelsch, Ernst, 176
Tyndale, William, 170, 191

Ulfilas (missionary), 133
Unam sanctum, 146, 149
university education, 146, 156–59, 184

Vandals, 119
Vatican II (council), 201, 203, 227–30
vices, 156
virtues, 156

Visigoths, 101, 123, 132
Voltaire, 208

Waldo, Waldensians, 165
Walls, Andrew, 234
Wellhausen, Julius, 209
Wesley, Charles, 218, 219, 220
Wesley, John, 186, 195, 217, 218, 219, 220
Westminster Assembly, 194
White, Ellen, 233
Whitefield, George, 195, 218, 219, 220
Wilberforce, William, 222
Williams, Roger, 194
Wimber, John, 237
Winthrop, John, 193, 194
Wisdom literature, 39, 40
World Council of Churches, 203, 227
Wycliffe, John, 146, 166–68, 170

Xavier, Francis, 197–98

Yahweh, 22, 29, 30, 31, 32
Yahwist, 6

Zealots (Jewish sect), 41, 42
Zinzendorf, Nikolaus von, 217, 221
Zwingli, Ulrich, 180, 181–82, 187

Made in the USA
Las Vegas, NV
07 January 2023

65204911R00148